Med Tech

Med Tech

The Layperson's Guide to Today's Medical Miracles

Lawrence Galton

1817

HARPER & ROW, PUBLISHERS, New York
Cambridge, Philadelphia, San Francisco, London
Mexico City, São Paulo, Singapore, Sydney

The illustrator wishes to thank Roger W. Yurt, M.D. and Robert A. Riehle, M.D., of New York Hospital/Cornell Medical Center for their generous assistance in supplying up-to-date information on modern medical equipment, and Geraldine Scalia for work in pictorial research.

FIRST EDITION

Designer: C. Linda Dingler

Illustrator: Gary Tong

Library of Congress Cataloging in Publication Data

Galton, Lawrence.
  Med tech.

  Includes indexes.
  1. Medicine, Popular—Dictionaries.   I. Title.
RC81.A2G32   1985   610   84-48098
ISBN 0-06-015372-5

85 86 87 88 89 10 9 8 7 6 5 4 3 2 1

Contents

Introduction

This book brings together—for, I believe, the first time—concise and, hopefully, clear information on the many technological innovations now changing medicine and health care. In its scores of entries, it overviews and explains the latest (often seemingly exotic) diagnostic and therapeutic techniques, and reveals how they can be used for specific health problems: the serious, even life-threatening, and the lesser but annoying.

With the technological explosion nowhere more evident than in medicine, almost all of us could use a readily available means of staying current—of understanding the background and implications of what we note in fleeting media accounts, of being brought abreast of developments we do not read or hear about but which could offer great help either personally or for family or friends.

What, for example, is interventional radiology—and what are its full implications, including making much open surgery needless?

And fetal medicine . . . arthroscopy . . . adoptive pregnancy . . . nuclear magnetic resonance . . . medical lasers . . . monoclonal antibodies . . . PET scans . . . How do they work, for what, and with what results?

Do you know someone who is about to have a CAT scan, or a brain-mapping procedure? What's involved? How, instead of a hearing aid, can a simple but ingeniously engineered new and far less expensive (yes!) device help many with mild hearing loss?

Few people may know—and many would appreciate knowing for

themselves or on behalf of others—that, for example,

- for some of those paralyzed because of spinal-cord breaks, new bioengineering techniques can bypass the breaks to make walking possible again;
- for victims of severe knee and shoulder injuries—massive tears of ligaments and tendons previously almost impossible to repair—there are now fiber implants that form a scaffold on which the tissues can repair themselves;
- a new, totally implantable control device can allow many previously incontinent adults and children to lead relatively normal lives instead of being social cripples because of dependence on clamps, catheters, diapers, and rubber underwear;
- analgesia controlled by the patient, through a bedside machine, can mean far better pain relief after surgery, and a new method of delivering drugs offers cancer patients effective, long-acting pain relief while at home;
- ear bones can be replaced now to combat a common type of hearing loss;
- a new appliance corrects many lower jaw misalignments, including those responsible for extremely protruding front teeth ("buckteeth").

These are among the many developments presented succinctly but with practical detail.

You can put this book to use in several ways.

Perhaps you've heard, and are interested in knowing more, about some particular area of medical development—say, monoclonal antibodies, the so-called new magic bullets of medicine; or fetal medicine; or new devices for the disabled. Check the alphabetically arranged table of contents for pages devoted to these subjects.

Or perhaps you have a specific health problem for which you would like to find out about any and all new developments that could be pertinent. The Index of Diseases and Disorders will point to them.

Or you may choose to read straight through to get a striking picture of how much the nature of medical practice is being changed now by technology that only a few years ago might have seemed straight out of science fiction, to be realized (if at all) only in a distant future.

My hope is that you will find in what follows much that is interesting and some things that may be immediately and practically rewarding.

Adoptive Pregnancy
In vivo fertilization for infertility

Among American women of childbearing age, 4.3 million are infertile. For some of them, chances of having families may be improved by *in vivo* fertilization, also called "adoptive pregnancy." Coming on top of *in vitro* ("test tube") fertilization, the *in vivo* technique promises to be more widely applicable.

For the *in vitro* technique, an egg is surgically removed from the mother-to-be, united with sperm in a glass dish, then reinserted into the uterus. The procedure, which has a success rate of about 25 percent (for details, see FERTILIZATION IN VITRO), cannot be used for infertile women who are unable to tolerate surgery, or unable to produce healthy ova, or without functioning ovaries. (Compare SURROGATE EMBRYO TRANSFER.)

In addition to making pregnancy possible for many such women, nonsurgical adoptive pregnancy could help those who do not wish to risk normal pregnancy with their own genetic contribution because of family histories of serious genetic diseases such as cystic fibrosis, hemophilia, or Tay-Sachs disease.

Ovum Transfer.

For adoptive pregnancy, a healthy and otherwise suitable woman donor is artifically inseminated with the prospective father's sperm. Within the first week of her pregnancy, the embryo, a microscopic cluster of about 100 cells, is flushed out of her uterus and transferred to the uterus of the woman who will carry the baby to term.

Some experts—among them, Dr. Wayne Decker, executive director of the New York Fertility Research Foundation—believe that the adoptive-pregnancy approach could have a much higher success rate than the 25 percent rate for the *in vitro* method.

Although very new for humans, ovum transfer has been used in the laboratory to produce successful pregnancies in many species of animals, ranging from rats to chimps and baboons. Recently, it has come into increasing use in commercial cattle breeding. By mid-1983, at least 60,000 cattle were reported to have been born of ovum transfer in the U.S., with no apparent increase in birth-defect frequency or other pregnancy-associated problems.

A first attempt at human ovum transfer was reported early in 1983 by Dr. John Leeton and other investigators at Monash University, Melbourne, Australia. The patient was a thirty-eight-year-old woman in whom twenty-two attempts at artificial insemination had failed. She received another woman's donated egg cell after it had been fertilized in a laboratory dish. Pregnancy followed but ended in miscarriage after ten weeks.

In mid-1983, a substantially different approach was reported by Dr. John E. Buster and a team at Harbor-UCLA Medical Center, Torrance, California.

The Current Technique.

The California approach first matches the prospective mother with potential donors in terms of blood type and physical characteristics. Donor, patient, and patient's husband are evaluated through detailed medical histories, physical examinations, laboratory tests, and psychological testing and interviews to make as certain as possible that all understand and are suitable for the treatment.

The procedure is carried out when the ovulatory cycles of donor and patient are synchronized. At the right time, as determined by hormone measurements, the donor is artificially inseminated with sperm from the prospective father. About five days later, the fertilized egg is gently lavaged (washed) out of the donor's uterus and deposited by catheter (tube) in the uterus of the patient.

In their first trial, the California physicians inseminated fourteen donors. Five fertilized ova were recovered and used for five infertile recipients. All five had undergone surgery for obstructive tubal disease, had not conceived after three and a half years or more, and had expressed strong wishes not to undergo additional surgical procedures. Of the five, two became pregnant.

The 40 percent success rate in the very first trial is highly encouraging. Since no surgery is involved, the California physicians note, ovum transfer may be performed in a physician's office and may be repeated until pregnancy is achieved.

Potential Problems.

One possible problem, a unique one, with ovum transfer is that a donor might become pregnant if lavage of the uterus fails to remove a viable fertilized egg. In such a case, the donor could be offered the opportunity of abortion shortly after failure to recover the embryo. The possibility of the problem occurring, however, is considered remote. In the five California cases, the viable fertilized ova were recovered readily with the first lavage.

Ethical concerns about adoptive pregnancy may arise. Some people are opposed to any intervention in natural reproduction.

There may be legal questions as well. Litigation could develop if a woman donates an ovum and later decides to claim the resulting baby as her own. Most states hold that "baby bartering" is illegal, and this might be interpreted to include paid ovum donors.

Some legal experts believe that the new approaches to overcoming infertility will require new laws and possibly even a legal redefinition of the family.

Ames Test
For cancer-producing agents

It is not too much of an exaggeration to say that a worldwide revolution in environmental health has been triggered by the life and death of minute bacteria living in tiny glass dishes in a Berkeley, California, laboratory.

Those special microorganisms, genetically engineered by Dr. Bruce N. Ames, professor of biochemistry at the University of California-Berkeley, form the basis of a test that has become the most widely employed screen for determining whether a chemical is likely to cause cancer.

The Ames test is currently used in more than 3,000 government, industry, and university laboratories throughout the world as an early warning system. More than 5,000 chemicals have been screened. Some common ones, such as the flame retardant tris and a large number of hair dyes, were removed from the U.S. market when suspicions first raised by the test were later confirmed in animal studies. Many other potentially hazardous chemicals have been tested by industry before marketing and have been eliminated from products before they reached consumers.

The test has suggested that a wide variety of common substances, both natural and synthetic, may be carcinogenic (cancer-causing). Among them are some substances in natural foods, chemicals produced when foods are cooked, cigarette smoke, air particulates, food additives, drugs, pesticides, diesel fuel, dyes, certain plants, and even some drinking water.

Development.

By the mid-1960s, when Ames first started to work on developing the test, more than 20,000 synthetic chemicals were already on the world market. "I got fed up," he recalls, "with reading the long list of chemicals on potato chip packages and wondering whether or not potato chips were safe. At any time, something could creep into our diet that would significantly alter our gene pool, and we would never know it."

At that time, and in the early 1970s, little screening of chemicals for potential health effects was done. Scientists suspected that some human cancers might be caused by exposure to toxic chemicals, but there was no inexpensive, quick, and effective way to sort out the ones that might be hazardous.

Chemical and drug companies as well as government agencies that regulated them had to rely on time-consuming studies that involved feeding laboratory mice or rats the suspect chemical from birth to death. This usually takes almost three years and costs, in today's money, about $400,000 per study.

In contrast, the Ames test, first discussed in a scientific paper in 1971, was cheap, easy to use, fast, and highly accurate. In about forty-eight hours, at a cost of a few hundred dollars, it could flag a potentially dangerous chemical for more exhaustive study.

The test reveals the ability of a chemical to damage the genes of bacteria. Such damage—mutations—changes the inherited characteristics coded in the genes. Bacteria provide a simple, convenient way to study how chemicals affect genes, which are made of the same DNA building blocks in both microbe and man. If a chemical can damage bacterial DNA, it can probably do the same to human genetic material.

Although it is now well established that a chemical's ability to cause mutations is closely related to its cancer-causing potential, this was controversial in the early 1970s. Ames and his colleagues were among the first to conclusively demonstrate the correlation between mutagenicity and carcinogenicity. In studies of hundreds of known cancer-causing chemicals, he and Dr. Joyce McCann showed that more than 80 percent of carcinogens tested produced mutations in bacteria. Since relatively few chemicals are mutagenic, the Ames test, though not perfect, usually can discriminate between safe chemicals and those likely to pose a cancer threat.

How the Test Is Done.

The procedure revolves around special bacteria that have been deliberately altered genetically for this job. The bacteria—of the general type known as *Salmonella typhimurium*—have undergone a mutation that has led to their loss of ability to make a particular amino acid (protein building block) called "histidine." Thus, in order to grow and multiply, they require histidine as a food supplement.

Millions of the altered salmonellas are layered on a small, covered laboratory dish that has previously been filled with a growth medium lacking histidine. Then the chemical under test is placed on the dish and the dish is incubated. After two days, the number of bacterial colonies are counted.

If the chemical being tested is mutagenic, there will be large numbers of salmonellas growing in the dish, because the chemical caused the bacteria to mutate back to a form able to make its own histidine. The more colonies, the more mutagenic is the chemical.

Actually, the histidine mutation caused by the chemical is not related to cancer development, but is simply a mutation easy to identify by sight. Other DNA damage occurs at the same time; in humans, this may have a role in causing cancer.

The test has been repeatedly refined. Additional strains of bacteria, altered for sensitivity to mutagenic chemicals, have been added. Still others added in 1975 and 1982 can detect a number of mutagens previously missed by the test, including some, like radiation, that cause DNA damage by oxidation—that is, by chemical reactions involving oxygen.

Another improvement has allowed the test to more nearly simulate what happens in the body as metabolic substances produced in the body act on chemicals. Liver enzymes added to the growth medium approximate the way chemicals that are not mutagenic themselves can be converted to mutagens when affected by the metabolic enzymes of the body.

In addition to investigating how simple chemicals and complex mixtures affect bacterial DNA, Ames and others have used the test to analyze mutagens in human blood, breast milk, urine, and feces. For example, Ames and his group have shown that cigarette smokers excrete mutagens in their urine that are not present in the urine of nonsmokers.

A Complex Picture—and a Hopeful One.

All mutagens are not equal, nor are all carcinogens. But it is virtually impossible today to determine the relative danger of the hundreds of natural and synthetic mutagens and carcinogens discovered since the Ames test was introduced. Health officials as well as the public are confused about how to set priorities for dealing with the risks.

"People have become so concerned about synthetic chemicals, but epidemiologists think that most cancers are due to cigarette smoking, dietary imbalance, and other natural causes," says Ames. "Sunshine is a carcinogen; the brown edges in cooked foods contain mutagens. It's a more complex picture than we once thought."

The picture becomes still more complex—but hopeful—with the discovery of natural substances in food and the environment that inhibit or prevent the mutagenic action of chemicals.

In addition to trying now to address the question of relative risk, Ames and his colleagues recently began measuring DNA damage in humans. Results of these studies lead him to believe that one important cause of cancer and aging is DNA damage produced by oxidative reactions in the body. These reactions, which include the process of fat becoming rancid, occur when certain oxygen-containing compounds react with body constituents.

Investigating substances that prevent these interactions, Ames and co-workers have begun with uric acid, a common body waste product that also is a scavenger of certain oxygen atoms. Ames has recently suggested a hypothesis about uric acid's role in preventing aging.

Uric acid has a curious evolutionary history. Mice have very little of it and are short-lived mammals. Their bodies change uric acid to another chemical, which is then excreted.

Man, however, has lost the ability to convert uric acid and has a life-span thirty times longer than the mouse. Large amounts of the chemical are present in human blood; in fact, we have more circulating uric acid than vitamin C, another important antioxidant, or oxygen scavenger.

Ames believes that oxidation plays an important role in both cancer and aging, and that antioxidants—such as uric acid, vitamin E, beta-carotene, selenium, vitamin C, and natural sulfur-containing compounds—will prove to be important defenses against cancer.

Amniocentesis

For prenatal diagnosis
(See also CHORIONIC-VILLI SAMPLING)

More than 100,000 American babies each year are born with some form of developmental defect. Prenatal diagnostic testing can be used when it is suspected that a fetus may have an inherited anomaly.

The Procedure.

During growth in the womb, the fetus sheds cells into the amniotic fluid in which it floats. Amniocentesis involves study of some of those cells.

The test can be performed on an outpatient basis and is usually done during the fifteenth or sixteenth week of pregnancy. After locating the exact position of the fetus, usually with the aid of ultrasound imaging (see ULTRASOUND), the physician inserts a long, hollow needle through the mother's abdomen into the womb and withdraws a sample of the amniotic fluid.

Two to four weeks are required for evaluation of the sample by a process called "karyotyping" (chromosome analysis) in which the size, shape, and number of fetal chromosomes are compared to what are known to be the norm.

What It Can Reveal.

Amniocentesis can determine the sex of the fetus, information of particular value when such male disorders as hemophilia and Duchenne's muscular dystrophy may be of concern.

The test can also help diagnose the presence of Down's syndrome (mongolism), a disorder that occurs in about one of every 600 births and is characterized by physical malformations and some degree of mental retardation (see FETAL MEDICINE).

Indeed, amniocentesis is capable of detecting a lengthening list of genetic disorders, including Fabry's disease, which can produce kidney failure and death in young adulthood; Lesch-Nyhan syndrome, with its severe mental and physical retardation; Hunter's syndrome, often fatal in the first decade; fat-metabolism disorders often lethal in early childhood; Tay-Sachs disease; maple syrup urine disease; and others.

Accuracy and Safety.

In a Northwestern University study, the test proved accurate for all but three of 700 women.

Safety, too, is high.

The National Amniocentesis Registry, a government study comparing the experiences of 1,040 women who had amniocentesis with a matched group of pregnant women not having the test, found no significant differences in rates of miscarriage, stillbirth, maternal complications, fetal injury, or other untoward effects. At the age of one year, the two sets of infants showed no significant differences.

More Than One Value.

Although by no means can amniocentesis detect all potential genetic defects, it can reveal many, offering parents of a fetus virtually certain to be born seriously handicapped the option of abortion and the opportunity to try again.

Moreover, in some cases, a fetus shown to be defective may be treated successfully in the uterus. One of the first such successes was achieved for the second child of a Boston woman whose first baby had died at three months because of methylmalonic acidemia. The genetic disorder is characterized by abnormal acid accumulation in the body, recurrent vomiting, developmental retardation, and failure to thrive. When amniocentesis revealed the same disorder in the second baby, a new treatment was tried. Vitamin B_{12}, essential for proper handling of certain materials in the body, was administered to the mother in large doses with the hope that enough could be gotten to the baby. The vitamin did indeed help. The baby was born normal and remained so. (See FETAL MEDICINE.)

Still another important value of prenatal diagnostic testing is reassurance for worried couples. The overwhelming majority of women who undergo testing for possible birth defects can be reassured that the defects are not present. The National Amniocentesis Registry study found that of the 1,040 women who had amniocentesis, 995, or 95.7 percent, learned that their babies were not at risk for a defect in question. Another study, by the National Foundation–March of Dimes, found that of 2,187 women undergoing the procedure, 2,125, or 97.2 percent, learned that the suspected defect was not present.

When Is Amniocentesis Advisable?

Several categories of pregnant women may benefit: those who already have borne a defective child; those who have a family history of a defect or whose husbands do; and those who are thirty-five or older, since the risks of bearing a defective child increase with age.

Analgesia, Patient-Controlled
Relief after surgery

For anyone undergoing surgery, a source of concern is the pain that may follow in the postoperative period. A reassuring new answer could be patient-controlled analgesia (PCA), a technique that allows patients to administer their own pain-relieving medication as they feel the need for it.

Under study for several years at the University of Kentucky in Lexington, PCA has been found to provide pain relief superior to standard injections of analgesics and also to reduce considerably the amount of medication needed.

Push-Button Machine.

PCA employs a telephone-size dispensing machine. Because patients usually require fluids by vein for two or three days after major surgery, the machine is hooked up to the intravenous tubing used for the fluid administration. By pushing a button at the end of a control cord leading to the machine, patients can deliver an analgesic agent directly into their bloodstreams, providing almost immediate relief, much faster than is possible with conventional injections. Moreover, frequent small doses can be administered to assure continuous relief. A timer in the machine prevents overdosage.

PCA has been found to overcome several drawbacks of scheduled analgesic injections: the need for a nurse's attention; pain produced by the injections themselves; twenty- to forty-five-minute delays before relief starts; and sleepiness caused by large injected doses. These are not rare problems. During the last ten years, according to a report in the *Journal of the American Medical Association,* various studies have uncovered a 30 to 40 percent incidence of "grossly inadequate" analgesia or "distressing" pain in postsurgical patients receiving scheduled intramuscular doses of narcotics. Other research has shown that almost half of patients are "groggy" or "sleepy" with such regimens.

PCA Study Findings.

The University of Kentucky investigations have turned up these findings:

- There are surprisingly striking differences among patients in requirements for narcotics. The actual amount of drug needed in the bloodstream to produce a comfortable state can vary as much as thirty fold from one patient to another.
- Patients using PCA give themselves more medication immediately after surgery than patients on an intramuscular regimen receive. The peak amount of medication administered intramuscularly occurs about twenty-four hours after surgery—perhaps, as a University of Kentucky investigator puts it, because "it takes about that long for patients to be awake enough to complain vigorously." Apparently, however, patients are awake enough in the first hours after surgery to press the PCA button, and this contributes to their overall higher satisfaction with PCA.
- Even as PCA patients maintain themselves in a state of pain relief without grogginess, they use significantly less drug overall than those receiving intramuscular injections, only one-fourth as much by the fourth day.
- PCA patients have less difficulty breathing, less difficulty because of pain while coughing (essential for clearing the lungs), and are generally more active—all desirable.

Addiction?

One possible drawback of PCA might be a potential for addiction. The potential, however, appears small, based on the Kentucky trials and the experience with more than 3,000 patients of another pioneer in studying PCA, Dr. Michael Keeri-Szanto of the University of Western Ontario in London. "This is the only way," he observes, "that patients can have a choice about their drug other than taking it or refusing it. Given a chance for a graded response, the normal nonaddicted patient will opt for a small amount of residual pain that he knows he can control." Most patients, Keeri-Szanto has found, do not seek complete sedation, much less euphoria.

Anesthesia, Topical
Rehabilitation aid for stroke and spasticity

A novel approach to controlling movements and gait patterns in patients with stroke and multiple sclerosis appears to be useful for rehabilitation.

The technique—which uses a common topical anesthetic to temporarily desensitize the skin—is being developed and has been used in early trials with some patients by Dr. M. A. Sabbahi and other investigators of Harvard Medical School, Massachusetts Rehabilitation Hospital, and Boston University, all in Boston, and the Liberty Mutual Research Center in Hopkinton, Massachusetts.

The anesthetic—benzocaine—when applied to the skin of an affected limb relaxes muscles and facilitates movement, doing so, the investigators believe, by affecting the central nervous system through the skin.

Although it is not a cure and has only temporary effects, topical anesthesia nevertheless may be useful in rehabilitation.

In every one of the first five patients—two with stroke, one with right-side paralysis because of head injury, and two with multiple sclerosis and consequent muscle hypertonicity (tightening) in both legs—the skin desensitization led to a substantial increase in the range of joint mobility, enabling the patients to perform movements they were previously unable to accomplish.

A Stroke Case.

The patient, a thirty-four-year-old man, had suffered a stroke nine months earlier, with sudden complete weakness in the left side of his body. Physical therapy over a four-month period led to improvement in the strength of upper and lower limb muscles, but the affected leg was spastic, the foot had become inverted, and he was unable to lift the foot off the ground and unable to fully straighten his knee while standing. There was still weakness in his leg, he needed a cane for stability, his gait was abnormal, and physical therapy had ceased to provide further improvement.

The patient, nine months after suffering the stroke, was placed on the same physical-therapy program he had been on at the beginning: movement training, bicycle exercise, and walking on a treadmill. But before each treatment session, benzocaine was applied to the skin of the leg and thigh. The procedure was repeated twice a week for six and a half weeks, a total of thirteen sessions.

The patient reported that the affected leg became "much looser" after application of the anesthetic and that he could better control the speed, direction, and magnitude of his movements. The effect of the anesthesia lasted about four hours, during which substantial progression toward a normal gait pattern was noticed. At the end of the thirteen sessions, the patient was able to walk without a cane.

Although the direct effect of the anesthetic is only temporary, the investigators report that during this time the patient can carry out movements and perform exercises previously impossible. And, they note, "It appears that this augmented exercise capability has a lasting effect in providing improved and more normal motor performance. These intriguing results could provide a basis for a novel approach which may help in the rehabilitation of spastic patients."

Angiography
(Blood-Vessel Imaging)
Conventional—and now computerized

For many years, physicians have been using standard angiograms (also called "arteriograms") to evaluate arteries when atherosclerotic disease and its narrowing of the vessels is suspected. Now coming into use and likely to replace standard angiography in many situations is a new procedure called "digital subtraction angiography." It is quick, painless, requires no hospitalization, and it is expected to make diagnosis easier for physicians, safer and more economical for patients.

Conventional Angiography.

In this valuable technique, a thin plastic catheter (tube) is inserted in an artery, usually in the groin area or in the crease of the elbow. With the aid of a fluoroscope, which provides live X-ray images, the catheter is guided to a suspected area in the same artery or up to another, more distant artery. An opaque dye solution, visible on X-rays, is injected into the catheter and when the dye reaches the area of concern, X-ray pictures are taken.

The pictures reveal any narrowed regions and allow the physician to visually estimate the degree and seriousness of the narrowing. Because the procedure is difficult and may occasionally lead to complications, the patient must be hospitalized overnight.

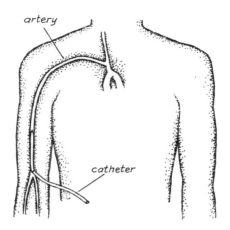

DSA.

DSA (digital subtraction angiography) provides a whole new approach to revealing narrowing or other problems in blood vessels. Instead of a long catheter inserted deep into an artery, DSA allows a shorter catheter to be inserted into a *vein*. Because the catheter is placed in the low-pressure venous system instead of the high-pressure arterial system, the procedure is simpler and safer for the patient. Additionally, DSA requires only about one-third the amount of dye necessary in standard angiograms. Although the contrast material is usually quite safe when monitored properly, use of the dye contains an inherent risk. The less dye the better.

DSA is distinguished, too, by its use of a computer to combine two images, in effect subtracting one from the other, eliminating irrelevant detail and providing a sharp picture.

First, before dye is injected, a fluoroscopic image is made of the area under study, enhanced electronically, and then stored in the memory of a computer. In the process, the information is digitized—that is, the image is divided into a grid of squares known as "pixels" (picture elements). Each of the several hundred thousand pixels is recorded as having a brightness ranging from black to white.

Once this preliminary or "mask" image is recorded, dye is injected into the vein and a second, "contrast" image is produced, enhanced, and recorded.

The computer then compares the two images, pixel by pixel, to produce a "subtraction" image. Where corresponding pixels in both mask and contrast images are identical, the pixel in the subtraction image is shown as a white dot. Where corresponding pixels differ in brightness, the pixel in the subtraction image appears as a shade of gray; the greater the difference, the darker the gray. A large difference is seen as a black dot.

The result is a canceling out of everything common to mask and contrast images, a subtraction of images of bones and soft tissues, leaving only what is really wanted: an image of the contrast medium in the vessels under study.

With DSA, physicians now can see blood vessels as small as one millimeter (1/24 inch) in diameter without directly injecting the artery. This clarity of vision is a significant advance.

From the Patient's Standpoint.

The majority of DSA studies can be performed on an outpatient basis. Reports Dr. Thomas Brandt of the Department of Diagnostic Radiology at Michael Reese Hospital and Medical Center, Chicago: "The patient saves the cost of a night in a hospital, and misses only one day of work. Since the procedure may take as little as an hour, it's perfectly conceivable for someone to come in on their lunch hour, have a digital angiogram, and go back to work."

In undergoing DSA, the patient, in a hospital gown, lies on an examining table. After an arm or leg is cleansed with an antiseptic solution and draped with sterile towels, a local anesthetic is injected to prevent pain. A catheter is placed in a vein, and in due course the X-ray contrast medium is injected through the tube.

The patient is asked to remain motionless and to hold the breath for about thirty seconds while the X-rays are being taken. The complete examination takes thirty to fifty minutes, depending on whether different views are needed. Afterward, blood pressure and pulse are monitored in the outpatient recovery area for fifteen minutes or more to be sure there are no side effects.

The procedure hurts very little. A brief stinging or pinching may be felt when the local anesthetic is injected, and there may be a feeling of warmth when the dye is injected. The heat, which is painless, disappears within ten seconds. A taste of metal in the mouth may also appear and disappear quickly.

In some cases, there may be side effects. A few people, sensitive to the dye, experience nausea. Occasionally the injection site becomes black-and-blue. About 10 percent of patients experience hives, which can be treated with antihistamines and are seldom a problem.

DSA Uses.

One of the major uses is in patients with symptoms of cerebrovascular (brain blood vessel) disease. DSA is particularly valuable for studying the carotid arteries running up the sides of the neck, a major source of blood supply for the brain and often the sites of blockages.

The technique is also useful in examining the kidney arteries. At the University of Arizona Health Sciences Center, Tucson, it has been used to evaluate kidney arteries of transplant donors, the blood vessels of the recipients, and for follow-up of transplanted kidneys. With potential donors, DSA can provide crucial preoperative information on the number, length, and position of the kidney arteries and the presence of any disease. After transplantation, the technique can determine whether the transplanted kidney arteries remain open and functioning.

DSA appears to have an important role in diagnosing many types of disease in blood vessels over two millimeters in diameter. It is as yet of no use in screening for disease of the coronary arteries, which feed the heart muscle, because of the small size of those vessels. The technique, however, is being used at the University of California-San Diego Medical Center and half a dozen other centers to detect ischemic (lack of blood supply) heart disease and to evaluate heart function.

Many clinical indications for DSA are still being evaluated. With more experience, improved equipment, and additional studies, further uses for the technique are likely to emerge. (Compare CARDIAC CATHETERIZATION.)

Antibodies, Monoclonal
"Medicine's new guided missiles"

Since the very first of them were produced in a laboratory in Cambridge, England, in 1975—not very long ago as major developments go —monoclonal antibodies have been causing increasing excitement in the medical world. They are being talked about as the realization of a century-old dream—of "magic bullets" that can provide ammunition against a wide variety of diseases, that can search them out and identify them at their start, and, going beyond, can selectively destroy the causes without harming normal cells and tissues.

"Key to a revolution in clinical medicine," the American Medical Association's journal, not ordinarily given to excitement, called them not long ago.

Among the uses foreseen for them—some already being realized, or coming close to realization:

- in laboratory tests of unprecedented accuracy for diagnosing diseases: hepatitis, cancer, and hundreds of others;
- in imaging, where, acting as homing devices in the body and tagged radioactively, they will locate tumors and other growths;
- in therapeutics, fighting disease on their own or delivering drugs, piggyback, to specific sites in the body.

What They Are.

The vast potential for monoclonal antibodies (also called "MoAbs") lies in the fact of their being antibodies, but pure ones, which can be manufactured in a remarkable new fashion by means of "hybridoma technology."

Every cell, microorganism, and virus has on its surface many identifying markers, called "antigens." The body's immune defenses are designed to attack and destroy anything with antigens different from the body's own.

Antibodies—Y-shaped protein molecules produced by white blood cells—are one component of the body's immune defense system. An antibody acts as a kind of "red flag," attaching itself to a specific foreign antigen and thus marking the invading cell, microorganism, or virus for destruction by the body's defense mechanisms.

Every type of cell, virus, or other organism has antigens unique to itself. On each antigen there are many sites where an antibody may attach itself. The interaction between an antigenic site and its antibody is highly specific: They match each other one-for-one, like a lock and key.

In a sense, the body's natural immune system is spendthrift. When a foreign antigen appears, the system calls up an army of antibodies, only one of which may be necessary.

Until the development of the hybridoma technique, researchers seeking antibodies had to inject animals with an antigen and retrieve the resulting antibodies from the animals' blood. What they got was a mélange, a mixed population of antibodies, often in small amounts.

The hybridoma technique provides, for the first time, a way to produce a pure antibody, readily and in large quantities. Hybridoma colonies pump out large amounts of pure—and potent—antibodies. For example, one antibody tested at the University of Texas M. D. Anderson Hospital and Tumor Institute in Houston was so potent that after being diluted 10 million times, it still worked to inactivate mouse breast-tumor virus.

As their name suggests, monoclonal antibodies are produced by identical descendants—clones—of a single cell.

How They're Made.

The hybridoma technique that makes monoclonal production possible starts with the injection of a selected antigen into a mouse. A few days later, the mouse's spleen—now containing large numbers of antibody-producing white blood cells—is removed and the white cells are retrieved. These white cells are then mixed with fast-dividing mouse myeloma (bone-marrow cancer) cells, along with polyethylene glycol, a kind of chemical glue.

The result is a hybridoma—a fusion combining the spleen white cell's ability to produce antibodies and the myeloma cell's ability to divide and reproduce rapidly almost forever.

Hybridomas thrive in a laboratory culture, spawning identical clones that produce a specific antibody.

Diagnostic Uses.

Among the first fruits of the new technique are medical diagnostic tests, more than twenty of which have been approved by the U.S. Food and Drug Administration.

Several pregnancy tests using monoclonal antibodies are now available to physicians and hospitals. They detect increased levels of the hormone human chorionic gonadotropin (HCG) and are reported to be as much as twenty times more sensitive than conventional tests—able to detect pregnancy earlier, ten days after conception and before the first missed menstrual period.

A useful new test measures levels in a patient's blood of theophylline, a drug frequently used to treat lung problems but one that has a narrow range of effective concentration. Because each patient breaks down the drug and excretes it at a different rate, the physician needs to measure its concentration in the blood in order to arrive at an effective dosage. Previous tests were unable to distinguish between theophylline and caffeine, which is very similar to the drug. The monoclonal antibody test can measure as little as a single microgram (one-millionth of a gram), even in the presence of several hundred times that much caffeine.

Although blood banks screen samples for hepatitis B virus before using them for transfusions, recent research has discovered that conventional tests fail to detect active or chronic hepatitis in some blood donors. A new monoclonal antibody test can do that.

Time savings with new monoclonal antibody tests can be critical in treating some serious infectious diseases, such as meningitis. Where previous methods required up to forty-eight hours before the causative bacteria could be identified, now it's a matter of fifteen minutes.

Each year in the U.S., there are 10 million new cases of chlamydia, the most common sexually transmissible disease. Once identified, it can be treated effectively with certain antibiotics (but not others, such as penicillin, effective though those drugs are for other sexually transmitted diseases). Where previous diagnostic tests required six days to perform, one monoclonal test requires two days, and another, now in development, is expected to take only twenty minutes.

Among other tests already available are one to detect and measure ferritin as an indicator of anemia; another for human growth hormone as an indicator of pituitary-gland functioning; another to assess allergic responses; and still another to measure a hormone, prolactin, for fertility studies.

Another highly useful potential for monoclonal antibody tests is in diagnosing and monitoring malignancies. Already available is a test that uses antibodies specific for an enzyme, PAP (prostatic acid phosphatase), to detect prostate cancer.

Well along in development are monoclonal antibodies that attach to specific kinds of white blood cells so they can be counted and used to diagnose immune-system diseases such as leukemia and acquired immune deficiency syndrome (AIDS).

There seems to be, too, a great potential in tagging monoclonal antibodies with radioactive materials so that once the antibodies target in on a tumor site, the concentrated radioactivity there can be detected with scanning devices. There have been promising preliminary results with a tagged antibody for melanoma and with tagged antibodies to detect cancer of the colon and rectum.

Guided Missiles for Treatment.

If monoclonal antibodies can transport radioactive tracers to tumors for detection purposes, they may also be able to deliver cell-killing agents—radioisotopes, drugs, or toxins.

Ricin, a highly toxic compound isolated from the seeds of the castor-oil plant, has been called the "assassin's drug." It gained notoriety in 1978 when a ricin-filled bullet was shot from the tip of an umbrella to murder a Bulgarian exile, Georgi Markoff. Just 100 micrograms will kill a human.

At the University of Texas Southwestern Medical School in Dallas, investigators have used a ricin/monoclonal-antibody combination to eliminate leukemia cells in mice. After bone-marrow cells were removed, the mice received very high doses of radiation to destroy the remaining marrow. Meanwhile, the removed cells were treated with the ricin-antibody combination, so ricin's deadly power could be aimed directly at the tumor cells, leaving healthy cells intact. The healthy cells then were implanted in the animals to restore a healthy marrow able to produce normal red and white blood cells.

Antibodies by themselves may lead to the killing of malignant cells, by setting off an immune attack on their targets. At Stanford University Medical School, Harvard Medical School, and the University of California-San Diego, investigators have used suitable monoclonal antibodies for small numbers of lymphoma and leukemia patients. The patients showed transient improvement in symptoms and decreased numbers of tumor cells in their blood or other tissues— enough improvement to encourage further research.

Among the most dramatic results thus far have been those with a patient treated at Stanford for a recurrent lymphoma. Researchers made a monoclonal antibody by combining his own cancer cells and those from a mouse. Treatment produced a remission that at last report had lasted for many months since therapy stopped.

How monoclonal antibodies will perform against most cancers is still uncertain. The need, not yet met, is to find in further research specific receptor sites for the antibodies on cancer cells—that is, receptor sites that do not appear on normal cells as well. Another need may be to make antibodies toxic enough to destroy large tumors entirely.

Still another problem to be overcome is that mouse-derived monoclonals may be recognized by many patients' immune systems as foreign, leading to inactivation. Researchers now are trying to produce human monoclonals, and, despite technical difficulties, there is some prospect of success.

Another area of research with monoclonal antibodies concerns the development of vaccines against some of the most devastating parasitic infections, including schistosomiasis and malaria. Such diseases, which afflict hundreds of millions throughout the world, are caused by parasites that go through many stages of development and have evolved many ways of getting around the natural defenses of the human body.

Groups of investigators at Johns Hopkins, New York University, and elsewhere are seeking out particular antigens on the parasites to which antibodies can be produced. Tiny spines on the surface of schistosomiasis parasites seem important in the infection process. At Johns Hopkins, antibodies to these spines have been produced, and some scientists are hopeful of a schistosomiasis vaccine within five years. A malaria vaccine is seen as another probable development.

Monoclonal-antibody research is still very young. Although many investigators are enthusiastic about the prospects of developing many, many diagnostic and therapeutic uses for the agents, including successful cancer therapy, none expects this to happen easily or without delays.

Antivirals

As far back as 1966, the first antiviral drug was licensed by the U.S. Food and Drug Administration. Called "amantadine hydrochloride," it was intended to block infection by influenza A and some influenza B virus strains.

Yet, until very recently, amantadine has had very little use. It was introduced at a time when doctors believed that there were no antivirals. A whole generation of physicians had been taught in the 1950s that antibiotics do not work and in fact should not be used for viral infections, and some experts believe that this lesson was mistakenly broadened to include all chemical agents.

Today, that attitude is changing rapidly. There are now a number of promising antiviral agents and the whole idea of combating viral diseases is more established.

Two Cousins.

In September 1982, Dr. Raphael Dolin, now professor of medicine at the University of Rochester but then at the University of Vermont College of Medicine, reported dramatic success against influenza with amantadine and rimantadine, a derivative of amantadine. He determined that while a flulike illness developed in 41 percent of a group of subjects receiving placebo, an inert preparation used for comparison purposes, only 14 percent of those given rimantadine and 9 percent of those receiving amantadine became ill. Accompanying that report in the *New England Journal of Medicine* was an editorial declaring, "Amantadine is a highly effective prophylactic agent against several strains of influenza. . . . In an epidemic of influenza, amantadine would be indicated for many persons."

Recent studies at Cornell University Medical College in New York City have indicated that amantadine is also effective in speeding recovery from established flu infections.

The influenza program of the National Institutes of Health is currently aimed at establishing the effectiveness of rimantadine in a variety of populations, particularly those considered to be at high risk for influenza, such as the elderly. Some of these studies will examine the therapeutic effect of the drug in patients already infected.

Ribavirin.

This is another antiviral agent that has been available for study for a number of years but has only recently begun to show promise.

Although poor results were achieved in trials where ribavirin was administered orally, it has lately been shown to be quite effective when delivered into the respiratory system as a water-borne aerosol. In a study by Dr. Vernon Knight of Baylor College of Medicine, Houston, college students with influenza A were treated for an average of twenty-three hours with ribavirin in aerosol form. The treatment speeded recovery and reduced the extent of viral shedding. The following year, Knight did a similar study on students with influenza B. Again, results were satisfactory.

Knight has also studied the value of aerosol ribavirin treatment against respiratory syncytial virus (RSV), which in winter months causes widespread community outbreaks of severe respiratory illness and is the most common cause of serious lower-respiratory-tract disease in infants and young children. The treatment proved to be of value, although not as dramatic as in the influenza studies.

The future importance of ribavarin therapy remains to be seen. One problem is that few young adults are likely to accept the benefits of more-rapid clinical improvement from flu or RSV at the expense of twenty or more hours of confinement for the treatment. However, further studies may demonstrate that shorter courses of treatment, perhaps on an intermittent basis, could prove effective. And there is also the possibility that simple hand-held aerosol devices could be developed, similar to those used to deliver medication to patients with asthma.

Another antiviral, enviroxime, has shown some preliminary experimental promise against rhinoviruses, one of several groups of viruses responsible for the common cold.

Other new agents are being developed for use against rhinoviruses and other viruses as well. Among them are dichloroflavan and nitrobenzonitrile, which are presently undergoing clinical testing.

The Search for a Herpes Cure.

Researchers are intensifying efforts to find agents effective against genital herpes, a venereal viral infection affecting Americans in epidemic numbers.

The herpes simplex virus that causes genital herpes is a tough foe. After an attack, which can cause blisters and flulike symptoms such as fever and headache, the virus lies dormant in the nervous system, hiding itself in host cells.

One antiviral agent, acyclovir, has been produced as an ointment. It hasn't been found to prevent or substantially alleviate recurring attacks, but it does speed the healing of sores and slows the spread of the virus during initial infections. And it acts only against infected cells, reducing risk of toxicity.

Meanwhile, an oral form of acyclovir is being tested with the hope that it will prove more effective against recurring attacks.

Combinations and Manipulations.

In many serious bacterial infections, combinations of antibiotics have been used effectively when any one agent proved inadequate. Taking a lesson from this, investigators now are studying combinations of antivirals. Moreover, scientists are learning how to manipulate the chemical structure of antivirals, just as they have done with antibiotics, to make them more effective against specific viral diseases.

Interferon.

This is another drug that has created a great deal of excitement—because of its action against both viruses and cancer.

Visualize a single small lump of sugar. It may weigh more than all the interferon given to people—possibly, 2,000 around the world—since its discovery twenty-five years ago. This is a measure of the potency of the substance, which is made naturally in the body to combat viruses and cancer.

Interferons (there are three major types) have passed tests for safety. They can sometimes produce side effects, mainly flulike symptoms, but these are temporary.

Although they are not cure-alls or miracle drugs, interferons are showing promise against cancers and viral diseases. They have shown activity against all of the types of cancers so far tested, but not for all patients with any particular type of cancer. Benefits have ranged from small to significant, with some complete remissions.

An interferon has been reported to be the best single agent yet found against the most common form of kidney cancer. It makes some other tumors more sensitive to radiation treatments. Although the original impure natural interferon was not impressive against melanoma, it is now producing more results when patients also take the antiulcer drug cimetidine.

An interferon is saving some children from choking to death from wartlike growths of the throat while avoiding repeated surgery for the growths. It is showing some remarkable effects against Kaposi's sarcoma, a cancer that has become epidemic among male homosexuals and also occurs in heterosexuals. Interferons are now also being tested against cancers of the brain and prostate gland, and are moving into other fields.

Immune interferon, now being tested in humans, appears to be more potent against cancers than are the other two types, the leukocyte and fibroblast interferons. In animal experiments, it greatly boosts the potency of the others when combined with them.

On the antiviral front, interferon has prevented common colds caused by one major class of cold viruses. It is helping to control hepatitis B, the dangerous liver disease. It prevents chickenpox, a viral disease, from killing patients whose immunity is lowered by cancers or by anticancer drugs. It is being tested against herpes viruses that cause cold sores of the mouth and sores on sex organs.

Significantly, too, in the last several years, the supply of interferons has been rising sharply and the cost falling dramatically as scientists have employed genetic-engineering techniques (see GENETIC ENGINEERING) to make bacteria churn out interferons in great quantity. For example, in the fall of 1978, when the American Cancer Society made its first $2 million purchase of natural leukocyte interferon from a laboratory in Denmark, it was only enough to treat about 150 patients, at a cost of about $30,000 per patient. Now it costs about $200 per patient for bigger doses of highly purified interferons produced in bacteria.

The mechanism of interferon action has also become clear in terms of viruses, leading it to be called a kind of "chemical Paul Revere."

When a virus invades a body cell, the cell's manufacturing facilities are converted from making proteins needed to sustain the cell and other parts of the body to producing carbon copies of the virus. Eventually, the cell becomes so filled with the viruses that it explodes and dies, and the spilled-out viruses promptly invade healthy cells to repeat the process and spread infection.

Interferon enters the picture when, somehow, the initial infection causes the first cell to produce the chemical. The interferon moves out of the cell, through the cell membrane, to become a messenger, warning nearby cells of the viral invasion. The latter respond by producing interferon so that an entering virus has less chance of multiplying and, if it does manage to reproduce, its offspring are left unable to leave the cell, thus breaking the cycle of infection.

How useful can interferon be against the common cold?

Recent experiments in Britain, at the Medical Research Council's Common Cold Unit at Harvard Hospital in Salisbury, have shown that pure interferon, made artificially, can be protective. Volunteers received nine doses of interferon by nasal spray, then a common cold virus by droplet, followed by several more days of nine interferon doses each. The virus used was one of about 100 rhinoviruses that are responsible for about half of all common colds. Not a single cold developed among the volunteers.

Going on from there, the British researchers are presently developing a self-treatment method that hopefully will be safe and practical.

Meanwhile, at a recent symposium under the auspices of the University of California-Los Angeles, researchers from around the world reported on preliminary trials of the use of interferon in small numbers of patients with various viral diseases.

Papillomavirus infections—from juvenile throat warts to warts of all sorts—were reported cured or well controlled in studies in Israel, Germany, and Sweden.

In a Stanford University study, children with chickenpox who received interferon less than seventy-two hours after symptoms appeared had less severe illness and got well faster.

According to a German report, herpes encephalitis, a viral infection of the brain and its coverings, can be treated successfully with interferon. This report also noted interferon benefits in cases of viral infections of the inner ear. One woman, after enduring virally caused deafness for twelve years, regained her hearing.

According to a report from Massachusetts General Hospital in Boston, interferon can prevent the cytomegalovirus infections responsible for the deaths of 2 to 3 percent of kidney-transplant patients.

Genital warts that resist other treatment may yield to interferon, according to a study at Duke University Medical Center. The warts, which occur in both men and women and are caused by a sexually transmitted virus, are often curable by local applications of liquid podophyllin or trichloroacetic acid. But in the Duke trial, interferon was used in a group of patients with warts unresponsive to standard therapy and persisting for at least six months. Ninety-four percent of the patients responded.

Much yet remains to be learned about interferon's potential, proper dosages, specific types of interferon to be used for specific diseases, and any possible undesirable effects that may as yet be unrecognized.

Apheresis
Cleansing the blood

Bloodletting existed as a medical treatment for some disorders for many centuries. But a new refinement, which differs markedly from the ancient technique, is now being used increasingly by modern medicine.

Called "apheresis"—from the Greek for "removal"—it removes not all of blood, as did the old treatment, but specific portions for specific purposes. It cleanses the blood of elements apparently involved with disease and returns the rest, using sophisticated equipment for the purpose.

A costly method (best used with discrimination when other measures have proved inadequate), it is being tried with varying degrees of success in dozens of serious problems, some rare and some common, for which cures are not available, such as myasthenia gravis, multiple sclerosis, rheumatoid arthritis, systemic lupus erythematosus, and aplastic anemia.

The Cleansing Process.

Apheresis procedures have many names—plasmapheresis, platelet-pheresis, lymphopheresis, and more—but all share basic principles:

Through a needle or catheter, blood is withdrawn from the patient and mixed with an anticoagulant to prevent clotting. The blood flows through a cell separator, a machine that spins the fluid so that centrifugal force can separate the components. The heavy red cells settle out first; next, the white cells; then the platelets that help blood clot; finally, the plasma, the fluid portion of the blood in which the components have been suspended and which also contains valuable proteins.

Once the undesirable component (the fraction suspected of containing harmful substances associated with the patient's disease) is removed, the remainder of the blood is returned to the patient. If the plasma is removed, it is usually replaced with varying proportions of saline and albumin, the latter being a major plasma protein.

The procedure usually takes three to five hours and is named according to the major blood component removed. If platelets are removed, the technique is called "plateletpheresis"; if white cells, or leukocytes, "leukopheresis"; if lymphocytes, a special variety of white cells, "lymphopheresis"; if red cells, "erythropheresis." In plasmapheresis, the plasma is removed; and when both plasma and lymphocytes are removed, the procedure is called "lymphoplasmapheresis."

Apheresis is now available at most major medical centers—but it's costly: A cell separator can cost as much as $30,000; a single session may cost the patient from $400 to as much as $1,600, and most conditions require several sessions—as many as twenty for rheumatoid arthritis, for example—spread over several weeks.

Possible Complications.

Apheresis is generally well tolerated, but in some cases there may be one or more complications or side effects.

Chills may occur while the procedure is being carried out. There may be dizziness and headaches, which respond promptly to injections of calcium. A few patients experience ringing of the ears. In a few, fast pulse or abnormal heart rhythms may require treatment.

Although the list of possible complications is a long one, apheresis, according to Dr. Charles Linker of the University of California-San Francisco Medical Center, "has proved to be a well tolerated and safe procedure." At his institution, just one significant complication occurred in a series of 300 procedures—a heart attack in an elderly woman who then recovered completely.

In a special report on apheresis, Dr. Linker goes on to note that

this excellent safety record both at our center and at large apheresis centers may be due in part to the care with which the procedure is carried out and the close supervision used. Apheresis in our institution is done by a small group of well-trained nurses, and all procedures are closely supervised by a physician knowledgeable in apheresis and immediately available on the premises. If apheresis procedures become more widespread and are carried out in a less careful fashion, the complications rate may increase substantially. . . . Finally, we must recognize that apheresis is a new field and that other complications may become apparent in the future.

Uses.

One of the most dramatic uses of apheresis is in treating thrombotic thrombocytopenic purpura. This is a disorder of blood platelets that leads to bleeding into the skin and formation of small, round, purplish-red spots, with nosebleeds and bleeding into the gastrointestinal and genitourinary tracts. As a result of bleeding, anemia may develop, producing weakness and fatigue. Severe kidney involvement occurs in more than half of all cases, and nervous-system complications are common. The disease has proved fatal in 80 percent of patients, but apheresis now is producing a recovery rate of 74 percent and up.

Only a small number of cases of autoimmune hemolytic anemia have been treated with apheresis, but with good response in eight of nine. This type of anemia is potentially lethal.

Systemic lupus erythematosus, a rheumatic disorder, can produce fever; abdominal, muscle, and joint pains; spleen enlargement; and congestive heart failure. The disease is an autoimmune one in which the body's immune system acts against the body itself and attacking immune complexes circulate in the blood. Occasionally, apheresis has led to dramatic responses in patients who were failing despite conventional treatment. Of forty-seven cases reported in the medical literature, 70 percent responded to apheresis.

There have been conflicting reports about the usefulness of apheresis in rheumatoid arthritis. In one early report, for example, all of six patients treated by lymphopheresis responded, and responses were maintained for three to five months. Later, however, the same investigators carried out a controlled trial with twelve patients. Six of the patients, serving for comparison, had only a small volume of plasma without lymphocytes removed; the other six had lymphocytes removed. Fifteen procedures were done over a period of five weeks. Although lymphopheresis was clearly beneficial, leading to a significant reduction in the number of swollen joints and in morning stiffness, the investigators concluded that the improvements were rather modest and probably would not justify such a cumbersome and expensive form of treatment.

Apheresis has great usefulness in myasthenia gravis. One study reported on five patients who were failing to respond to conventional treatment with thymus-gland removal and administration of drugs. All five responded to apheresis. Other investigators have confirmed the high response rate, and apheresis is widely accepted in the treatment of myasthenia.

Leukopheresis has been used mainly for chronic myelogenous leukemia, in which there are extremely high numbers of white cells in the blood. The high viscosity created by the mix of so many white cells with the red cells can be fatal. Leukopheresis can quickly reduce the white count, serving as an emergency lifesaving measure.

In acute blastocytic leukemias, when the white count is very high, leukopheresis before starting chemotherapy may be beneficial. The reduction of the leukocyte count beforehand appears to enhance the drugs' efficacy.

Leukopheresis has also been used with benefit in some cases of hairy-cell leukemia.

Erythropheresis has proved valuable in rapidly reversing life-threatening complications of sickle-cell crisis. It is not considered necessary for the usual symptoms of sickle-cell crisis, which can generally be managed by more conservative measures.

Apheresis is currently being studied for possible usefulness in many other disorders—among them, multiple sclerosis, some severe kidney diseases, and multiple myeloma, a malignancy originating in the bone marrow.

In Perspective.

Despite many enthusiastic reports, there is a consensus among experts that, as of now, apheresis is the primary treatment of choice in only a small number of diseases. In other situations, it may sometimes be of value as an added treatment. Dr. Richard J. Cohen, clinical professor of medicine at the University of California-San Francisco School of Medicine and chief of medical oncology and hematology at Children's Hospital of San Francisco, notes that apheresis "must be used with considerable discrimination. The risks and the costs are such that it should be employed only when more conservative measures are inadequate. When needed, however, it should be used without hesitation, as it can—and does—save lives."

Much more research must be done before the full usefulness of apheresis can be evaluated. And that research needs to be concerned not so much with the procedure itself as with gaining more-precise knowledge about the specific factors in blood and how and under what circumstances they become instigators or contributors to a wide variety of diseases.

Arthroscopy
For knee and other joint problems

Six years after tearing cartilage in his left knee, a young Chicago soccer enthusiast did the same to his right knee. The first time, the repair operation required general anesthesia, opening up the knee through a four-inch incision, four days of hospitalization, and six weeks of slow recovery. It was three months before he could play again.

The second time, fully alert, he watched on a TV screen as the surgeon looked into the knee with a small viewing instrument inserted through a quarter-inch incision and, working through the instrument and two half-inch incisions, did the repair. He was home a few hours later, out walking in three days, playing soccer a few weeks later.

The Viewing Instrument.

The innovative operative technique is called "arthroscopic surgery" after the viewing device, the arthroscope. First used in primitive form as a diagnostic tool in Japan in 1917, today's arthroscope is a needlelike metal instrument, 1.7 to 6 inches long and only 2 to 6 millimeters wide, with a fiberoptic light source inside. Inserted in a knee through a small puncture under local anesthesia, it can be moved about to show the interior from various vantage points and can be hooked up to a TV screen for viewing.

The knee is subject to everyday stress and to arthritic and other disease processes. There are more than fifty different possible reasons for knee pain. The arthroscope has helped raise diagnostic accuracy to 98 percent.

Operative Use.

The first application of arthroscopy in surgery was for sports-related injuries. Conventional open-knee surgery—arthrotomy—with its wide incisions and much tissue cutting, necessarily means slow healing, perhaps hobbling on crutches and canes for weeks. Muscle tone and coordination are lost and have to be laboriously regained.

With arthroscopic surgery's small puncture cuts—one for the scope; two or three others for slim surgical tools—a damaged piece of cartilage, the most common knee injury, can be snipped away from healthy cartilage and readily removed. Usually, hospitalization is not required and recovery is fast; many professional ballplayers have returned to play within two to three weeks.

The technique now is being used for amateur athletes and for the nonathletic, who, because of injuries, have required more than 223,000 knee operations yearly.

It is not without its critics. Some surgeons believe that open-knee surgery to remove all cartilage when a portion is torn reduces the chances of future complications from undetected tears. But advocates say those chances are minimal; that removing only the damaged portion of cartilage has the advantage of allowing the remainder to function as a stabilizer; and that arthroscopic surgery may in fact reduce the incidence of such complications as arthritic changes.

Uses in Other Joints and for Arthritis.

Use of arthroscopy is being extended to other joints—including ankle, hip, shoulder, and wrist—with problems similar to those of the knee. It also now appears—from experience at the University of Chicago Medical Center and elsewhere—that arthroscopy may be of value for arthritis sufferers.

The most common form of arthritis, osteoarthritis (also known as "wear-and-tear arthritis") involves wearing away of cartilage in a joint. Worn cartilage cannot be replaced, but other causes of pain may exist and can often be dealt with. There may be synovitis, an inflammation of the synovial membrane, which lubricates joint surfaces. In some cases, pain may be due to loose bodies—broken-off bits of bony spurs or lining or other structures.

The arthroscope is used to determine the cause of discomfort. If it is localized synovitis, the area of inflamed tissue can be removed; if it is a loose body, that can be removed. While such procedures do not cure the arthritis, they often relieve symptoms and allow renewed activity.

In rheumatoid arthritis, inflammation is a key factor. The synovial membrane may become so inflamed and swollen that it distends the joint, stretches and damages ligaments and tendons, and may end up causing deformity. Removal of the affected membrane through the arthroscope has been found to help.

Artificial Blood

On March 1, 1982, an Akron, Ohio, couple attempting to push their disabled automobile were struck down by another car and critically injured. The incident initiated a complex medical drama that would soon be played out some 370 miles away, at Michael Reese Hospital and Medical Center in Chicago.

Upon being transported to Akron General Medical Center, the couple, Jehovah's Witnesses, refused to submit to needed blood transfusions because their religion forbids receiving human blood. Even as the Akron hospital sought a resolution to the dilemma in court, the wife died of her injuries. The husband, now the sole surviving parent of six children, adamantly refused to reverse his decision.

The court ruled action must be taken to save his life: He was to be given the essential transfusions or treated with an artificial blood substitute being tested at Michael Reese, provided he could be safely transported to Chicago.

Under the surveillance of four doctors, he was flown to Chicago on March 2, arriving in critical condition, his right leg already amputated as a result of the accident, and with severe loss of blood. Over the next ten days, he received five liters (about ten pints) of an artificial blood solution, Fluosol—the maximum amount permitted under regulations of the U.S. Food and Drug Administration protocol for the Reese research. Its purpose was to keep him alive while his body generated new red blood cells. The solution did its job well, buying time, but the amount of time it gave him wasn't enough. By March 12 his body still hadn't generated adequate numbers of red blood cells and no more Fluosol could be administered. He still refused transfusion.

The choices facing Reese were clear: Transfuse against the patient's will; observe his First Amendment right to refuse therapy and allow him to die; or go to court in Illinois and let the court decide. On March 12 the court decided, observing that while it respected the man's religious beliefs, it felt the interests of his children must be protected.

A week after the court decision, the patient had received six pints of blood, was in fair condition, and the outlook was favorable. He was the first patient in the United States successfully treated with Fluosol under multihospital clinical trials.

The Solution.

Research for an artificial blood solution goes back a century. The "ideal" liquid would carry oxygen to body tissues and carry waste carbon dioxide away; would not require matching to antibodies; could be stored without refrigeration for long periods; could be given without supplemental oxygen; and would be free of toxic effects.

Fluosol—more technically, Fluosol-DA 20 percent—is a milky-white emulsion developed in Japan. It contains two perfluorochemicals, substances capable of carrying large amounts of oxygen. The perfluorochemical particles have to be very tiny—with diameters of about one-tenth of a micron (about 0.0000039 inch)—in order to pass through the tiniest blood vessels, the capillaries.

The emulsion has many, but not all, properties of the "ideal" liquid: It's nontoxic, carries oxygen and carbon dioxide, does not require matching to antibodies, and can be stored for prolonged periods. But it must be frozen for prolonged storage, and supplemental oxygen must be given to the patient.

The synthetic emulsion has undergone clinical trials in Japan with encouraging results. In one trial at the University of California-Los Angeles, it was used for seven patients who had lost blood, required surgery, and refused blood transfusion. Of the seven, two did not complete the treatment because they developed symptoms after test doses of Fluosol-DA. All five receiving clinical doses tolerated surgery well, although the most severely anemic patient died on the fifth postoperative day from a failure of several body organs that was judged to be unrelated to the emulsion.

Limitations and Potential.

At Michael Reese Hospital and Medical Center, Dr. Gerald Moss, chairman of surgery and a member of the research team evaluating the blood alternative, puts it into perspective:

"You must keep in mind," he notes, "that Fluosol only provides precious time. It's not a permanent solution for the patient. There's no substitute for blood. But this kind of temporary solution could prove invaluable in cases of religious objections to blood transfusions and in medical emergencies during which blood isn't available in sufficient quantities."

An editorial in the *British Medical Journal* sees these and other uses for Fluosol-DA and other perfluorochemicals: for immediate management by paramedical personnel of large numbers of casualties from disasters or armed conflicts; for replacing blood for priming heart-lung machines and for perfusing organs before transplantation; and for helping in the management of some severe infections caused by anaerobic organisms (organisms that flourish best in the absence of oxygen). Perfluorochemicals might also be tailored to remain in the circulation long enough to be of value in patients with thalassemia major (Cooley's anemia) or aplastic anemia, both of which can require repeated transfusions with risks of hepatitis or of overloading with the iron transfused in blood.

Fluosol-DA will not be in widespread use until further trials establish its safety as well as efficacy. It is not, in a true sense, artificial blood. Rather, as an oxygen carrier, it is a performer of just one function of blood; it cannot perform other vital functions, such as clotting.

Other Approaches.

Normal red blood cells are filled with hemoglobin, the complex molecule that actually carries oxygen as it is transported through the blood. The U.S. Army is currently developing a solution of free hemoglobin as a possible blood substitute. Going one step beyond that, University of California-San Francisco Medical Center researchers headed by Dr. C. Anthony Hunt are encapsulating hemoglobin to increase its lifetime in the body and improve its oxygen-delivering properties.

Hunt takes real hemoglobin, obtained from outdated or unusable human blood (or in the future even animal blood), and encapsulates it in microscopic bubbles of fat. The resulting "neohemocytes," as they are called, are only sixteen-millionths of an inch in diameter, twelve times smaller than a red blood cell, and thus can reach areas of the body inaccessible to red cells.

In studies with rats transfused with neohemocytes, 50 percent survived until their bodies were able to restore normal levels of red cells. All the rats given partial or total transfusions survived longer than they would have on a solution of hemoglobin alone. With further improvements, Hunt hopes to raise the long-term survival rate to 100 percent.

Neohemocytes, are designed solely as a temporary blood substitute, providing oxygen while the body works to replace its lost red cells. One of their advantages, however, is that they can be transfused into anyone, regardless of blood type. Another advantage is that they already have a shelf life of two months, twice that of whole blood.

Artificial Body Parts

In an eighteen-month period recently, a thirty-four-year-old victim of severe rheumatoid arthritis received an artificial hip, an artificial wrist, an artificial elbow, and two artificial finger joints. The debilitating effects of her twenty-three-year bout with arthritis had left her unable to hold anything in her hand or even to climb a street curb—so handicapped that she was afraid to leave her home.

"The first artificial joint," she recalls, "was scary, but after I saw the results of that one, I was ready to go for another. I've got a lot of joints to be replaced and they'll be done slowly but surely."

By the time doctors at Rush-Presbyterian–St. Luke's Medical Center in Chicago have finished with her, she will have nine more new artificial joints—in her knees, other elbow and hip, two shoulders, and at least three more fingers.

Artificial hips became practical in the late 1960s, knees in the early 1970s, elbows by the mid-1970s, and wrists by the late 1970s, and improvements continue to be made in their effectiveness. Artificial shoulders are promising but still experimental because, although they can relieve pain, they do not improve function significantly.

Other remarkable "spare parts" have been emerging: artificial skin, artificial blood vessels, microelectronically driven limbs for amputees, and even a rudimentary artificial heart. All told, the National Institutes of Health Office for Medical Applications estimates that several million artificial implants are now being used each year in the U.S. alone.

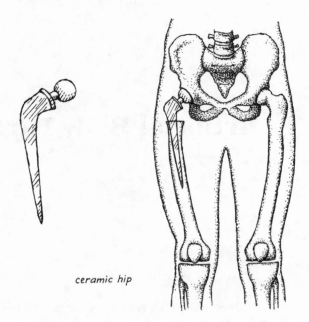

ceramic hip

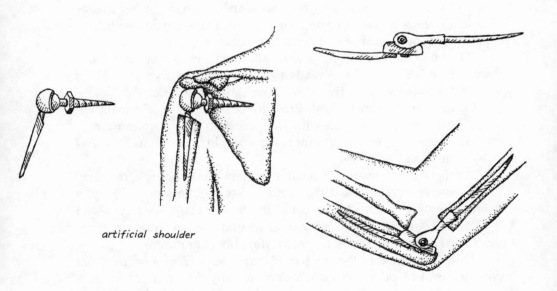

artificial shoulder

artificial elbow

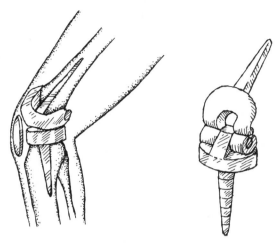

artificial knee

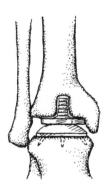
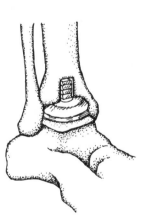

artificial ankle

Joint Replacements.

Satisfactory replacements for the hip joint have become commonplace. Each year, 100,000 Americans have a stiff, painful hip transformed into a pain-free joint. Ten years after they are inserted, 85 percent of the implants survive. Most failures result from loosening.

Until very recently, hip replacement has involved a metal and plastic prosthesis secured in place with a plastic cement. Now a new ceramic joint is considered potentially superior because it is implanted without cement, which sometimes tends to crumble. Totally compatible with the body, the new hip is screwed into place and new bone growth helps to anchor it firmly. It is expected to last a lifetime in most patients.

After implanting the device in thirty-one patients, aged twenty-one to seventy, Dr. William R. Murray of the University of California-San Francisco reported: "Patients were capable of pain-free motion in the artificial hip within hours after surgery and were able to walk normally without any limp after four months. Equally important is the life expectancy of the prosthesis. We anticipate that none of these patients will have to undergo another surgery for hip replacement because of fixation failure."

The earliest knee-joint replacements were simple metal hinges that often became loose and were difficult to salvage afterward. Now several types of improved artificial joints are available. With any of them, pain relief can be expected in 80 to 90 percent of cases, and the incidence of failure requiring replacement is as low as 5 percent.

Replacement of the elbow can provide worthwhile pain relief. Although the range of movement is not complete, the degree of bending is adequate for most everyday activities. Researchers at Rush-Presbyterian–St. Luke's are developing a new material for the artificial elbow that will not require cement. Called "fiber metal," it is made of porous titanium alloy that allows bone cells to grow into the metal, forming a stronger and more durable bond than that created by cement.

The shoulder has proved difficult to replace because of its complexity and wide range of movement. Rotation, the most useful movement of the shoulder joint, is usually restored, but rarely can the arm be lifted above shoulder level (fortunately of little functional importance).

Replacement of an ankle severely affected by rheumatoid arthritis usually provides good pain relief and satisfactory, though limited, range of movement—about 10° to 20° either side of neutral.

Rheumatoid arthritis often affects the finger joints, causing deformity and instability. Artificial joints correct deformity and restore stability. Deformities, however, may sometimes recur.

Artificial Limbs.

Microelectronics has made possible a new generation of artificial limbs for amputees.

Already in use, the Boston elbow or arm, developed by Boston universities and research centers, including the research center of the Liberty Mutual Insurance Company, is designed to allow above-elbow amputees to perform even heavy manual labor. The battery-powered, plastic and metal device has electrodes that pick up signals from the brain to the remaining arm muscles, enabling the elbow to move. To the elbow can be added an artificial hand, controlled by movements of muscles in the opposite shoulder via a cable and switch.

A promising new experimental artificial leg with an electromechanical knee controlled by the will of the wearer has been developed at the Rehabilitation Engineering Center of the Moss Rehabilitation Hospital in Philadelphia.

The leg is set in motion when the wearer consciously or subconsciously sends signals to the muscles above the amputation site. A computer connected to electrodes on the thigh senses the electrical activity of the remaining musculature. The resulting patterns of electrical activity about the leg are analyzed by a program, which signals the leg to react. A pneumatic-tube actuator provides the energy that enables the movement to take place.

According to Dr. Gordon D. Moskowitz of the hospital, because the leg is controlled by the will of the wearer, it can be sensitive to unexpected occurrences that can affect gait and cause stumbling, such as bumps in sidewalks or high curbs. The natural motion of the leg is also said to let the wearer closely simulate his or her normal gait and to lift and cross the limb in a smooth action.

A prototype model has been used successfully in tests. A clinical model may become available within a few years.

Skin Substitutes.

A severe burn can be doubly destructive: Without the protective layers of skin, vital fluids leak out of the body, and deadly bacteria have an easy entry. Skin grafts from cadavers and pigs have been used, but they may be rejected by the body's immune system (TRANSPLANTS).

Now several artificial skin substitutes that are nonrejectable have been developed. One is a clear polyurethane film called Op-Site, which can be laid over the burn site like a piece of gauze. It not only keeps the area moist so new skin cells can move readily over the wound surface to begin the healing process, but also allows oxygen to reach and sustain the white blood cells that protect the site from invading microorganisms.

Another skin substitute, Biobrane, is a silicone-rubber-nylon compound coated with chemicals from collagen (which is part of normal skin). Only one-hundredth of an inch thick, the material is nonrejectable and can be stored indefinitely.

A third substitute, developed at Massachusetts General Hospital and MIT, is two-layered like human skin. The top epidermal layer is made of silicone; the bottom, or dermis, of a mix of proteins from cowhide and shark cartilage.

The Artificial Heart.

On December 2, 1982, in Salt Lake City, Utah, an artificial heart was placed in the chest of a sixty-two-year-old dentist who had end-stage cardiomyopathy, a severe disease of the heart muscle. Three months later, the patient's mental status was normal, his appetite had returned, his activity level was increasing, and all surgical wounds had healed well, with no evidence of infection. Hospital discharge was anticipated. But on day 92 the patient developed a flulike syndrome, with vomiting; pneumonia followed as vomitus reached his lungs; severe intestinal infection developed. The patient died 112 days after the heart was implanted.

The design of the Utah heart is being constantly modified. In the 1982 operation, the patient's blood vessels were stitched around two fist-size aluminum and plastic chambers that were connected to a 375-pound air compressor. Within months after the 1982 operation, a portable drive system was under test. It weighs less than eight pounds and is about the size of a small camera case. The system is completely portable and has rechargeable batteries that provide power for up to three hours. Animals have exercised while using the system—with excellent results.

Electronic Vision.

Not long ago, at the University of Western Ontario Hospital, a Vietnam veteran blinded when a land mine exploded in front of him volunteered for a highly experimental procedure.

Under local anesthesia, a piece of bone was removed from the back of his skull and a one-square-inch wafer containing sixty-five platinum electrodes was laid gently on the visual center of his brain. When wires were attached to the electrodes and connected to a computer across the room, the patient saw the first light he had experienced since being blinded. He could identify simple visual patterns, letters, and geometric shapes.

The system is just one short step on the long road to providing useful vision for the blind. Sixty-four electrodes are too few to produce useful vision. Plans are to use at least four times that many in a device that would include a tiny camera mounted inside an artificial eye, with a microcomputer attached to an eyeglass frame and serving to determine which electrodes to stimulate in order to produce recognizable images.

Restoring Hearing.

Profound deafness, beyond help by ordinary hearing aids, afflicts several hundred thousand Americans. In many cases the problem lies with damage to delicate sensory hair cells in the cochlea, a spiral cavity of the inner ear, shaped like a snail shell.

The bones of hearing in the middle ear relay sound vibrations from the eardrum to the cochlea. There, the vibrations must be converted by the hair cells into electrical impulses that the auditory nerve employs to transmit sound to the brain.

Over the past dozen years, about 300 Americans, including about 70 children, have had implanted a kind of artificial ear called a "cochlear implant." The electronic device, which is surgically placed in one inner ear, is activated by sound and bypasses the damaged hair cells, electrically stimulating the auditory nerve.

The resulting hearing is far from normal—in most cases, speech cannot be understood. But recipients can, with practice, identify traffic noises, the ringing of a telephone or alarm, the honking of a horn, and the slamming of a door. They can distinguish voices from other sounds and, with practice, can lip-read more accurately. Hearing acuity is limited because the implant, developed by Dr. William House of Los Angeles, uses a single electrode. The electrode stimulates large groups of nerve fibers in just one way—unlike the complex stimulation that makes possible normal hearing.

There are now efforts to improve the quality of hearing with multielectrode implants and other refinements. Dr. Donald Eddington at the University of Utah has been working with arrays of six electrodes implanted in volunteers. Hearing is improved to the point where the volunteers are able to understand 40 percent or more of a list of two-syllable words.

Eddington's objective—and that of other researchers in the field —is to arrive at an implant that will allow a deaf person who has heard before to carry on a telephone conversation without difficulty and with full understanding. But how soon that goal can be reached is unknown. (Compare BONES OF THE EAR, REPLACING.)

Restoring Control.

A small, implantable urinary-control device is allowing many previously incontinent adults and children to lead relatively normal lives instead of being social cripples because of dependence on clamps, catheters, diapers, and rubber underwear.

The artificial urinary sphincter consists of a small, balloonlike fluid reservoir, an inflatable cuff that fits around the bladder neck or the urethra (the canal draining the bladder), a deflation pump, and a small control assembly placed in the groin.

During implantation, the fluid-filled cuff's pressure is adjusted to match the blood pressure of the patient. It gently squeezes the urethra closed so urine cannot escape from the bladder. Voiding (urination) occurs when the pump is squeezed several times to open the cuff.

About 2,000 patients have had the device implanted at Beth Israel Medical Center in New York City and elsewhere, with a success rate of about 85 percent. Among those helped have been patients with incontinence due to spinal injury, urethral surgery, failed stress-incontinence surgery, prostate removal, pelvic fracture, nerve-induced loss of control, and other disorders.

Other Replacements.

"Somebody is working on an artificial substitute for almost every organ in the body," remarks Dr. Carl Kjellstrand, the president of the American Society for Artificial Internal Organs. Researchers are trying to create hybrid organs that combine living tissue with man-made parts. Now in varying stages of development are hybrid kidneys, livers, and pancreases.

Artificial voice boxes have been developed for patients whose larynxes were removed because of cancer. The first was designed by Dr.

Mark Singer and speech pathologist Eric Blom of Methodist Hospital, Indianapolis. The prosthesis, an inch-long rubber tube, is fitted through a small surgical hole in the neck and the trachea, or windpipe, into the esophagus. The end in the esophagus contains a one-way valve that allows air to enter from the trachea but not to leak back. To speak, the user closes the neck hole with a finger and exhales. Air passing into the esophagus through an opening in the tube creates sound-producing vibrations in the tissues of the esophagus. A 90 percent success rate has been reported. Recently, too, the device has been refined so talking is possible without covering the neck hole with a finger. (Compare VOICE-BOX RECONSTRUCTION.)

There are even efforts under way now at Brown University in Providence, Rhode Island, to develop an implantable artificial lung. One model, which consists of an arrangement of coiled Teflon tubing fitted in what resembles a plastic sandwich bag, is being tested in animals.

Although human testing is still a long way off, the Brown researchers have high hopes for the artificial lung.

Auditory Feedback, Delayed
An aid for stutterers

Stuttering, which afflicts an estimated 2 million Americans, can be a painfully embarrassing problem—and more. For severe stutterers, any act of communication—talking on the telephone, ordering a meal in a restaurant, speaking up in a classroom or at a meeting, even introducing themselves—can be a nightmarish experience. When severe, the speech impediment may affect every aspect of life, leading to underemployment, even a hermitlike existence.

In recent years, a variety of therapies have been developed to help stutterers. In many of them, a device called a "delayed auditory feedback (DAF) machine" is employed, along with other measures. When the stutterer talks into a microphone, the DAF machine feeds his voice back to him through earphones after a short delay.

Commonly, stutterers try to talk rapidly. But when they do so with the machine, exceeding a speaking rate for which the machine is set, a disturbing echo is heard. They learn to get rid of the echo by slowing speech, stretching it out. The DAF is at first set for a 250-millisecond (thousandths of a second) delay, requiring the stutterer to talk with greatly exaggerated slowness. The delay is gradually adjusted to 200, 150, 100, 50 milliseconds, so that speech nears a normal rate.

Usually, within a period of about three hours, stutter-free speech has been established at each DAF delay level and the patient is able to maintain it as the therapist abruptly switches the machine to various levels—and then as the patient takes over operation of the machine and manages his or her own abrupt changes.

Therapists are quick to point out that slowing speech is not a cure-all for stutterers. But in many cases it helps because it allows the patient to feel a sense of control and because it facilitates other changes in speaking behavior.

Among other techniques often used with DAF to help stutterers speak more fluently are those designed to smooth out air flow and relax muscle tension in the vocal cords.

Balloon Therapy
For blocked arteries

It had begun for the fifty-two-year-old woman with numbness in her left hand. Over a period of several months, along with increasing numbness in the hand, she experienced severe pain shooting down her left arm. Finally, the arm became so swollen that getting clothes on was difficult. Now there was no pulse in the arm.

The diagnosis: a blocked subclavian artery under her collarbone.

She was informed that she could undergo the conventional surgical procedure to clear the blocked artery. That would mean general anesthesia, opening up the chest to get at the artery, and a hospital stay of at least two weeks. Or she could elect to try a new procedure.

She had the new procedure at a Boston hospital—with no opening of the chest and with only a local anesthetic. A catheter introduced through a small incision into a leg artery was maneuvered carefully, with X-ray guidance, all the way up to the site of artery blockage. Once there, a small balloon at the catheter tip was inflated to open up the constricted area. Almost immediately, a normal pulse could be felt in the arm.

Awake throughout the procedure, the patient could even watch what was going on on a video screen. In the midst of the procedure, she could feel sensation returning to her hand. After just three days in the hospital, she could go home and that same night cook dinner for her family.

Balloon dilatation therapy—more formally known as "percutaneous balloon angioplasty" (*percutaneous:* through the skin; and *angio-*

plasty: blood-vessel repair)—today is emerging as a major alternative to surgery in many situations. It is being used to open clogs in arteries of the arms, legs, and other areas—and, as an alternative in some cases to coronary bypass surgery, to open up blockages in the coronary arteries feeding the heart muscle. It has been adapted recently to opening up even diseased heart valves, replacing open heart surgery in children. And other uses as well are being found for it.

The Start.

It was less than twenty years ago when, at the University of Oregon Medical School Hospital in Portland, Dr. Charles T. Dotter, a radiologist, and Dr. Melvin Judkins, an associate, were faced with a frail, eighty-three-year-old woman with a clogged leg artery for whom leg amputation had been advised because of gangrene of three toes.

Rather than resort immediately to amputation, the two physicians decided to try a procedure they had long and carefully been working out in animal studies. They made a small incision through the skin into the artery, slipped in a thin coil-spring catheter, and moved its tip through the narrowed section of artery. Over the first catheter, they then moved in another, larger one, pushing the obstruction aside, allowing normal blood flow, and eliminating pain and the need for amputation. In the next year, nine patients underwent the same procedure, and six were saved from amputation.

There was no great enthusiasm for the procedure in the medical community, because of concern that it might cause bits of the linings of arteries to break off sooner or later and plug smaller vessels. But the work in Oregon did arouse research interest and, especially abroad, led to trials of the technique with gratifying results in hundreds of cases of leg-artery blockage. With major improvements in catheters—and with use of inflatable balloons in the catheter tips—a remarkable broadening of the scope of percutaneous angioplasty has been occurring.

Opening Fine Arteries and Long Blockages.

With improved catheters, angioplasty is being used with increasing success not only in larger leg arteries but also in finer leg, arm, and other arteries.

At Deaconess Hospital in Boston, Dr. Melvin E. Clouse reports successful use of the technique in leg arteries "right down to the ankles —vessels as small as 2 millimeters, less than a tenth of an inch." In one study at the University of Chicago Medical Center, newer balloon-tipped catheters were used for thirty seriously afflicted patients with blockages as much as eight inches long in various leg arteries. All were experiencing leg pain even at rest; surgical repair had been ruled out as virtually impossible; and all were considered candidates for amputation—six, in fact, had already had the other leg amputated. In twenty-five of the thirty patients, balloon angioplasty succeeded, avoiding amputation.

The first efforts to open up blocked kidney arteries were made about five years ago, and the procedure is now in increasing use. It was used recently for a young woman with high blood pressure that failed to respond to any kind of medication. X-rays revealed a marked narrowing of her right kidney artery. Twenty-four hours after balloon angioplasty opened up the narrowing, her blood pressure was down to a normal 120/80.

At Columbia-Presbyterian Medical Center in New York City, where the procedure was carried out in the young woman, the cure rate in the first fifty patients treated has been 80 percent, with patients entering the hospital one evening, being dilated next day, and going home the following day. The cost: about one-tenth that of kidney-artery surgery.

A beginning has been made in the use of balloon angioplasty for babies born with narrowing (coarctation) of the aorta, the main body artery. At Children's Hospital, Orange, California, the condition was diagnosed in a two-day-old infant. Medical treatment failed to help, and heart size and breathing rate increased abnormally in the next two weeks. After a balloon was introduced into a leg artery, maneuvered up to the aorta, and inflated there, normal breathing was restored, and the child has been doing well since.

Using Detached Balloons.

As many as two of every five men who are infertile may have a problem called "varicocele"—a scrotal mass composed of congested varicose veins. Surgery can correct the problem, but recently, at Johns Hopkins Medical Institutions in Baltimore, balloon angioplasty has been used successfully. After a balloon-tipped catheter is introduced into a leg vein and maneuvered up to the internal spermatic vein, the balloon is dropped off there and left in place to block the vein, causing the varicocele to shrivel and disappear. Requiring no general anesthesia, the procedure can be done on an outpatient basis, with the patient home within four hours afterward and able to return to full activity the following day. All of a first group of twenty patients have benefited.

In one of the first cases of the kind, a balloon was used at the University of Florida in Gainesville to plug a serious blood-vessel abnormality in the brain. The patient, a woman who had been shot in the head and stomach during a holdup, had needed surgery on her skull to relieve pressure around her left eye as well as an operation to remove part of her damaged large bowel. Later, it became apparent that bullet damage had caused another problem—an abnormal artery-vein connection inside the skull, above the eyes, which threatened blindness and stroke. Five days after a balloon-tipped catheter was inserted in a leg artery, moved up to the brain site, and inflated and detached to plug the abnormal connection, the abnormality was gone—as was the tiny balloon, absorbed by the body.

Opening Up Coronary Arteries.

Clogging of one or more coronary arteries—the vessels that nourish the heart muscle itself—leads to anginal chest pain and heart attack.

Years ago, soon after the work of Drs. Dotter and Judkins at the University of Oregon was reported, Dr. Andreas Gruntzig at the University of Zürich, Switzerland (now at Emory University, Atlanta), wondered if it might be possible to develop catheters useful for the coronary arteries. By 1977, Gruntzig had devised a catheter with a balloonlike, sausage-shaped distensible segment and, to go with it, an automatic pump that could produce the right amount of pressure to compress clogging material against an artery wall. Two years later, he could report on successful treatment of fifty-four of eighty patients. The procedure involved introducing the catheter into a leg artery, moving it up into a blocked coronary artery, and inflating the balloon tip to press aside the clogging deposits.

By June 1981, the U.S. National Heart, Lung and Blood Institute was collecting data from 125 teams using the treatment. In its first report, the institute found improved heart function during exercise in a group of fifty-nine consecutive patients undergoing coronary balloon angioplasty. In many of the patients, the artery blockage was reduced from 74 percent to 31 percent after the procedure, and in about half of them the improvement was sustained for more than six months.

Still better results came from a larger series and more prolonged follow-up reported by Dr. Gruntzig in 1982. Of 528 patients, including his first cases, the procedure was successful in 88 percent. Artery narrowing recurred in 22 percent of the patients, most of whom underwent a second procedure. The overall success rate—arteries remaining open after at least three years—including patients who had a second procedure, was 85 percent.

More recently, Dr. Jay Hollman, an associate of Gruntzig's at Emory, reported latest data. At Emory, 808 procedures had been done, and when combined with Gruntzig's earlier cases, the total was over 1,000. Overall success in dilating the narrowed arteries by balloon angioplasty was 85 percent. There were no deaths, but heart attacks requiring emergency surgery developed in 4.3 percent of the patients.

Significantly, however, complications decreased considerably in the most recently treated patients: In the last 100 cases, the success rate reached 93 percent and only one heart attack occurred. The improvements are attributed by Dr. Hollman not only to greater experience but also to technical developments—including a steerable catheter tip that can be rotated 360°—and to much clearer views of obstructions made possible by digital subtraction angiography (see ANGIOGRAPHY).

Recently, balloon angioplasty—originally limited to single coronary-vessel disease—has been used to open up several vessels. However, 8 to 10 percent of multivessel cases have not stood up over time and have required subsequent coronary bypass surgery.

As of now, it appears that most patients with coronary disease are still candidates for surgical coronary bypass if medication is unable to help them. Dr. Gruntzig now estimates that angioplasty is suitable for some 10 to 15 percent of patients; other estimates range up to 20 percent.

In patients undergoing angioplasty, surgical bypass is carried out if needed when complications arise during the procedure, or if blockage returns at a later date, or if angina persists or worsens.

Clearly, balloon angioplasty is a relatively new procedure and further experience is still needed to define its role in managing coronary artery disease.

For Heart-Valve Narrowing.

Each year about 1,000 children in the United States require surgery because of a congenital heart defect called "pulmonary valve stenosis" —a narrowing of the valve that allows blood to flow from the heart to the lungs to receive oxygen. The strain of pumping blood through the narrow valve causes a buildup of pressure within a heart chamber, which can lead to heart failure.

Now early experience at Johns Hopkins Children's Center in Baltimore suggests that balloon therapy may be a useful alternative to the open heart surgery previously needed.

A special balloon has been designed to open the narrowed valve. The deflated balloon, incorporated in the tip of a catheter, is introduced into a vein in the patient's leg and snaked through the veins into the heart and pulmonary artery. Once in place across the narrowed valve, the balloon is inflated several times until the valve is opened, after which the balloon catheter is removed from the body.

In its first year of trials at Hopkins, the procedure—called "balloon valvuloplasty"—has been used successfully in six children, ranging in age from three months to fourteen years. It requires three days' hospitalization, costs $3,000, has a very low risk of mortality, and is done with the patient under sedation, not general anesthesia. Open heart surgery requires ten days' hospitalization, costs approximately $20,000, leaves a scar, and carries a greater risk.

It will take four or five years of follow-up before there can be any certainty that valvuloplasty opens up the valve permanently.

"Band-Aid" Brain Surgery

The first sign of something wrong for a Grand Rapids, Michigan, woman came when she began losing side vision. Ophthalmologists and optometrists couldn't explain it. But in October 1981, a CAT scan (see CAT SCANS) gave a detailed X-ray image of a solid tumor, called a "craniopharyngioma," deep within the brain, pressing on the optic chiasma, the point at which the optic nerves cross and enter the brain.

In November 1981 an operation was performed, and for a time the patient's eyesight was good again. But in surgery of this sort, it is often impossible to remove all of the tumor. In January 1982, when the eyesight began deteriorating again, highly focused external radiation was applied, and again symptoms abated. But by the spring of 1983, eyesight again dimmed. Vision was down to 20/200 and 20/800, and a CAT scan now showed a fluid-filled cyst.

In July 1983, at the University of Michigan Hospitals in Ann Arbor, the woman became one of the first patients in the United States to receive a new treatment under development for a decade at the Karolinska Institute in Stockholm, Sweden, by Dr. Erik-Olof Backlund.

The procedure, performed in Ann Arbor by Dr. James A. Taren, a University of Michigan neurosurgeon who learned it from Dr. Backlund while on sabbatical, is expected to prove not only safer but also more effective than current therapy for some craniopharyngiomas and other tumors that may form fluid-filled cysts deep within the brain. It uses an accurate method of locating brain tumors and an injection of radioactive phosphorus. Because only a very small hole needs to be drilled through the patient's skull, the procedure has come to be called "Band-Aid" surgery by patients. The small hole greatly reduces risk and speeds recovery.

The Procedure.

The treatment requires a precision instrument called a "stereotaxic headpiece"—a metal framework that surrounds the patient's head, somewhat like the frame on a globe, and is firmly attached to the head at four points under local anesthesia.

With the frame in place, a detailed X-ray map of the brain is made by a CAT scanner. The headpiece contains markers that show up on the X-ray to provide reference points. The CAT scans clearly reveal the location and size of the tumor.

Again in the operating room, using the headpiece markers for reference, the surgeon can precisely locate the cyst. A tiny burr hole is drilled through the skull and a needle is then guided through the opening into the cyst. The accuracy is such that the needle can get within one-half millimeter (one-fiftieth of an inch) of the target point. The appropriate dose of phosphorus-32 is then injected into the cyst. The cyst is not drained, because its sudden collapse has been found to be dangerous. Instead, the cyst wall is destroyed by the radioactive phosphorus-32. The beta particles given off by the material penetrate only a few millimeters, just enough to destroy the cyst wall, with minimal danger to normal brain tissue or other people.

The radioactive phosphorus is in the form of a colloid—solid particles suspended in a fluid. As a colloid, the material disperses throughout the cyst, providing radiation to the entire circumference of the cyst wall.

Results.

Craniopharyngiomas can be very difficult to treat by any means. Because the tumors are deep in the brain, open surgery may injure or destroy healthy tissue, and mortality from conventional surgery has ranged from 8 to 40 percent. Also, the cysts tend to refill with fluid after open surgery and the procedure may have to be repeated. External irradiation may not control them well either.

The Swedish experience with stereotaxic treatment has been encouraging. "In a study of long-term effectiveness," says Dr. Taren, "a few patients died of unrelated causes, but the majority were alive and well and not disabled."

Meanwhile, over the short term thus far, the Grand Rapids woman is doing well. At a follow-up visit, her eyesight had returned to 20/30 and 20/25 and her peripheral vision had improved. She reported that she was able to see everything and read and drive again.

Other Uses.

At the University of Michigan Hospitals, the stereotaxic device is now being used to biopsy other brain tumors, including cancers. Also under way is a research project to test the effectiveness of phosphorus-32 against some other brain tumors.

Another research project is being developed for gliomas, the most common malignant tumors of the brain. The plan is to use stereotaxic techniques to inject phosphorus-32 into gliomas that form cysts and to introduce "seeds" of radioactive iodine-125 into solid tumors to provide more potent doses of radiation than can be delivered to such tumors from outside the skull.

Beyond X-Ray: The New Image Technology

	Analyses include	Technique
BEAM (Brain Electrical Activity Mapping) (page 65)	Brain lesions and tumors; some mental depressions; schizophrenia; epilepsy; Alzheimer's disease; mild head injuries.	Data from an electroencephalogram is converted by computer into colored topographical maps of the brain's electrical firings. Different contours and colors show different degrees of activity, producing a movie of the brain's workings.
Cardiac Catheterization (page 107)	Heart abnormalities; artery obstructions; valve disease; congenital defects.	A catheter, guided through a blood vessel and into the heart, allows an X-ray-sensitive dye to be injected, showing the blood's circulation through the heart and coronary arteries. Somewhat risky and expensive.
CAT Scans (Computerized Axial Tomography) (page 111)	Brain abscesses, hemorrhages, injuries; neuroblastoma tumors; parasitic infestations; congenital heart defects and valve disease; osteoporosis and bone deformities; hydrocephalus; heart attack risk.	An X-ray camera rotates once a second around area to be studied, creating hundreds of individual images. A computer reassembles the data into one changing cross-sectional image. Can discriminate between fat, fluid and gas, and can show the shape and size of organs, tumors, and many internal injuries.
Electroretinography (page 182)	Evaluation of retina in cases of cataracts, eye hemorrhages, retinitis pigmentosa.	A special contact lens, fitted with an electrode, records impulses produced by the retina, which are then translated into data by computer.
Endoscopy (page 184)	All gastrointestinal disorders; removal of polyps, swallowed objects and obstructions; biopsies; gastrointestinal bleeding; bile and gallstones; esophagus disorders.	A flexible, fiberoptic instrument, no wider than a pencil and containing a light source. Allows direct inspection of the gastrointestinal tract.
Mammography (page 272)	Breast cancer	Soft tissue X-ray that often can detect breast cancer before a lump is big enough to feel, making curable 85-95% of all cases.

Beyond X-Ray: The New Image Technology *(Continued)*

	Analyses include	Technique
NMR (Nuclear Magnetic Resonance) (page 286)	(Enormous potential—research just beginning.) Spinal, cranial and blood vessel interiors; neural sheaths (multiple sclerosis); psychiatry (schizophrenia, depression, dementia, Tourette's syndrome); brain tumors.	An extremely powerful electromagnet "charges" the hydrogen atoms of the body's water; when weak radio waves are bounced off the charge, structure and function of body tissue can be analyzed from a computer-generated image. Extremely safe and very expensive
Nuclear Imaging (page 282)	Gallstones; liver lesions; bile duct obstructions; artery diseases; heart function; bone cancer.	Radionuclides administered to the patient emit energy rays which are scanned by a gamma camera, producing very speedy images of the heart and other organs.
PET Scans (Positron Emission Tomography) (page 303)	(Just now under development and not yet out of the lab.) Brain activity and neural response; neurological disorders (Huntington's disease, Parkinson's disease, Alzheimer's disease, narcolepsy, Lou Gehrig's disease, epilepsy, stroke, sleep disturbances, schizophrenia, central nervous system tumors).	Radioactive versions (isotopes) emit positron particles from the area to be studied. Analyzed by computer to create a metabolic "portrait" of organs and tissue: how they process biochemical materials.
Ultrasound (page 351) and Echocardiography (page 166)	Unborn fetuses and problem pregnancies; liver, gallbladder, pancreas and kidneys; larger blood vessels; retinal tumors; ovarian cysts; aneurysms; heart abnormalities; brain tumors, prostate tumors, head wounds.	High-frequency sound waves are bounced off the area to be studied and converted into either a photograph or a video picture. Derived from wartime use of underwater SONAR.

BEAM (Brain Electrical Activity Mapping)

In Boston recently, a psychiatrist was confronted with a puzzling case —that of a young man experiencing auditory hallucinations, the kind to be expected with schizophrenia, but who failed to respond to any of the medications often of value for the mental illness.

It was a new technique called BEAM (for brain electrical activity mapping) that revealed what was really wrong. It showed that the man's brain waves looked more like those of an epileptic than of a schizophrenic. Indeed, when he was placed on anticonvulsant medication for epilepsy, his inner voices disappeared and for the first time in four years he was out of the mental hospital and back in the community holding down a job.

BEAM makes remarkable colored pictures of brain activity in the form of topographical maps of the brain's electrical firing. Created in the laboratory of Dr. Frank Duffy at Harvard Medical School over the past decade, BEAM was first used to help physicians at Children's Hospital Medical Center in Boston define a characteristic brain-wave signature of dyslexia, a common reading disability. It is now coming into use for diagnosing and evaluating a wide variety of otherwise difficult-to-assess problems.

BEAM pictures have begun to add to physiological understanding of schizophrenia, assist in diagnosing epilepsy and brain tumors, and help identify neurological problems in some depressions. At New York University Medical Center, BEAM is used to evaluate alcohol-related disruptions in functions, mild head injuries, and presenile dementias such as Alzheimer's disease—and, in the operating room, to warn neurosurgeons of very early indications of brain damage.

The Technique.

BEAM builds on the electroencephalogram (EEG), which records changes in electric potentials in various areas of the brain via electrodes placed on the scalp and connected to a system that amplifies the impulses more than a million times. BEAM uses the EEG to obtain the raw data.

As usual, a standard EEG grid pattern of twenty electrodes is applied to the scalp. Ordinarily, with an EEG, the slight voltage and frequency variations in the electrical firing of the billions of brain cells are translated into sawtoothlike lines on paper, and a trained physician, painstakingly examining reams of printouts by eye, interprets the meaning. An epileptic's brain waves, for example, often can be identified by spikes or broad wiggles in the EEG lines. But for most abnormalities and diseases, it is extremely difficult to spot discontinuities by eye. BEAM uses a computer to automatically convert the output of the EEG to a series of color contour maps of the brain's electrical activity; different shades are used to represent different degrees of activity. The BEAM computer displays the images in rapid sequence, producing a movie of brain activity.

The Usefulness.

BEAM is valuable in diagnosing maladies when there is no apparent anatomic problem. For example, certain kinds of epilepsy often are not detected in EEG examinations. The symptoms of one of these, temporal lobe epilepsy, can sometimes be mistaken for schizophrenic behavior. Once the patient lands in a mental hospital, unless he has a seizure, no one may ever think of epilepsy. But a BEAM map will show the epilepsy.

Another BEAM province is in quick diagnosis of recurrent brain tumors. Although CAT scans (see CAT SCANS) are often effective in locating tumors, they are not as useful in detecting recurrences. BEAM's topological mapping can find regrowths before irreversible damage occurs.

For example, until recently one highly malignant tumor, glioblastoma multiforme, was often lethal within months. At Massachusetts General Hospital in Boston, a newly devised treatment has led to reasonably good survival rates of one to two years, but the tumor eventually recurs and the efficacy of retreatment depends on how quickly the recurrence can be detected.

One puzzling case was that of a seven-year-old boy with headaches and behavioral disturbances. Although other diagnostic measures, including CAT scans, gave no clue to tumor, BEAM studies did by showing a striking change in his brain-wave patterns, allowing prompt surgical removal.

BEAM is also useful in following other kinds of lesions over time —those caused by stroke and multiple sclerosis, for example.

Many mentally depressed persons may also benefit from the mapping. In a Harvard study, a large number of depressed patients turned out to have surprisingly abnormal brain waves. Of those with abnormalities, a subclass showed signs close to the brain-wave patterns of epilepsy. In nearly half the cases, symptoms were relieved by anticonvulsant medications.

Although approximately 10 percent of school-age children are thought to have dyslexic reading disability—a disorder of the brain causing letters to be confused or the order of letters in a word to be altered—dyslexia is not always easy to diagnose. The CAT scan is characteristically normal. A recent BEAM study of dyslexic children, however, has found specific brain-wave abnormalities that can aid diagnosis. And since there has been some success in treating the condition —often by specially equipped teachers—accurate diagnosis is very much worthwhile.

To learn more about various learning disabilities, Harvard investigators are now following very young children in studies funded by the National Institutes of Health. One of the studies is concerned with determining whether brain-wave activity can be used to predict which of 200 preschool children will have difficulty in school. The objective is to facilitate early identification of those who would profit from intervention before they fail in the first grade.

The second study is following 120 children from infancy to age seven, to determine how well brain-wave activities picked up by BEAM compare with classic neurological examinations as predictors of later performance. Currently, neurological examinations are able to pick out only those who are severely damaged. "It is possible," says Dr. Duffy, "that we could push the frontiers of early diagnosis back to the newborn period."

Bench Nephrectomy
And other kidney-cancer progress

When a sixty-five-year-old New York man developed kidney cancer, the circumstances were among the most dangerous possible. He had just one kidney—and to make matters worse, the tumor was growing in the center of the kidney, an area that does not lend itself to conventional surgery.

The case, the first of its kind in the New York area, called for bench nephrectomy, a procedure in which the kidney is totally removed from the patient and placed on a perfusion machine. The machine keeps the organ alive while the delicate task of separating cancerous tissues from blood vessels is completed.

"There are many advantages to this procedure," according to Dr. Carl Olsson, director of urology service of the Presbyterian Hospital, New York, who devised the technique and performed the operation. "They include improved access to the area being operated on, reduced blood loss, lessened potential for spilling of the tumor cells into the bloodstream and the ability to carry out microsurgical repair of affected blood vessels."

The patient, although he now has only half of one kidney, has normal kidney function and is actively enjoying his retirement.

Spread to the Heart.

Each year, 16,000 to 18,000 cases of kidney cancer occur in the United States. Typically, a cancerous kidney is removed by surgery. But some cases present especially complex problems.

When she was admitted to the Presbyterian Hospital, a forty-three-year-old schoolteacher had a cancer that not only occupied her entire right kidney but also extended up the vena cava (a major vein that returns blood from the body to the heart), reaching to the right atrium (upper chamber) of her heart. The only hope was to put her on cardiac bypass, allowing a machine to do the work of the heart by maintaining blood circulation. That would permit surgeons not only to remove the affected kidney but also to work on the blood vessels, extracting tumor tissue from the vena cava and removing a portion of the already diseased major vein. It could also help assure that a piece of the tumor would not break away and travel to the lungs.

The procedure was carried out by the urologist, Dr. Olsson, working with cardiac surgeon Dr. Fred Bowman. Once all malignant tissue was removed, blood flow was reestablished from the patient's remaining kidney to the vena cava. The patient is now in excellent health and working on a Ph.D. thesis.

Beta-Blocking Drugs

An unusual step was taken not long ago by the National Heart, Lung and Blood Institute when it curtailed a major trial of a drug nine months ahead of schedule—because the results were so good.

There were 3,837 heart-attack victims, aged thirty to sixty-nine, in the study, all enrolled within five to twenty-one days after surviving their coronaries. They were randomly assigned—some to receive a drug, propranolol (tradename Inderal), and some to receive, for comparison, a placebo (a similar-looking but inert preparation). The objective: to determine whether the active agent would have any value in reducing the likelihood of a second heart attack.

The study was stopped early when, after two years, there were 183 deaths in the placebo group, an incidence of 9.5 percent, versus 135 deaths in the propranolol group, an incidence of 7 percent—a difference of 26 percent.

Propranolol—also being used for lowering high blood pressure, relieving anginal chest pain, and for other purposes including migraine prevention—is one of a class of drugs called "beta blockers."

How They Act.

The beta blockers act at specific sites called "beta-adrenergic receptors" located on heart cells and other cells. The receptors are readily stimulated by chemicals secreted by nerves in response to stress or excitement. In response to the receptor stimulation, the heart beats faster, labors harder.

By blocking the receptors to some extent so the chemicals can't induce so much stimulation, propranolol slows the heart rate and reduces the heart's work load, reducing the heart muscle's need for oxygen and thus often preventing the anginal chest pain resulting from insufficient oxygen. This, it's believed, may be a reason, too, why the drug reduces the risk of heart attack. The drug also relaxes arteries and thus reduces blood pressure by decreasing the resistance against which blood has to be pumped by the heart.

Other beta blockers have similar activity and usefulness. Timolol (trade name Blocadren) has also been found to cut second heart attacks. It has been used, too, in drop form for glaucoma, lowering the high pressure within the eye that is characteristic of that disease. Still other beta blockers that have been found useful include metoprolol (Lopressor), nadolol (Corgard), and atenolol (Tenormin).

Like many, if not most, drugs of any kind, the beta blockers can have side effects. They make some patients feel sluggish, drowsy, or weak, and may sometimes lead to gastrointestinal upsets or mental depression. Often, such undesirable effects can be relieved by adjusting the dosage or switching to another, similar agent.

Biofeedback

They might seem to have little in common: a Wisconsin boy of eight, with day and nighttime incontinence, hampering his activities and embarrassing him at school; a woman with the cold hands of Raynaud's phenomenon; a migraine victim; and a patient needing rehabilitation after a stroke. Yet all have been helped by a technique called "biofeedback," which teaches how to control unconscious bodily processes.

Biofeedback uses electronic or electromechanical instruments to measure and feed back to a patient an indication of body activities of which there is usually no awareness, so the patient may have the opportunity to develop desired control over these activities.

When investigators discovered in the 1970s that it is possible to exert a degree of control over some body functions once considered totally involuntary and beyond any conscious control, a rash of excitement broke out. Very quickly, the extravagant claims of hucksters made it difficult for legitimate researchers and health professionals to get a fair hearing for biofeedback as a valuable therapeutic tool. Nevertheless, serious research has been going on in many institutions, with increasing reports of excellent results in the use of biofeedback for many health problems.

The Principle.

Although simple in principle, biofeedback may be one of the basic medical discoveries. In effect, it extends the normal way we learn.

Our learning depends on the "feedback" cues we get from various sources—our eyes, ears, hands, feet. Swing a golf club, for example, and you feel your arms move, see how the club hits the ball, watch where the ball goes—all cues that guide you in correcting your swing next time for better ball placement.

Usually, the cues we get from inside the body are limited: We have no awareness of ups and downs of blood pressure, changes in brainwave rhythms, fluctuations in the state of muscles, and many other events. Such awareness, however, can be provided by sensitive electronic equipment. With electrodes attached at various points on the body, tiny internal fluctuations can be detected, amplified, and displayed in the form of sound beeps or light flashes. It is possible then to learn to exercise control.

Overcoming Headaches.

Both migraine and tension headaches are being treated successfully with biofeedback.

Migraine is believed to result from pressure when blood vessels in the head dilate. In a technique developed at the Menninger Foundation in Topeka, Kansas, a migraine patient sits before a biofeedback machine with temperature sensors taped to finger and forehead. A meter on the biofeedback unit shows the difference between head and hand temperature. While watching the meter, the patient is asked to do such things as relax while repeating a calming phrase (such as "I feel quiet"). The objective is to relax blood vessels in the hands so that more blood can flow there and hand temperature will increase. When the patient succeeds, the meter needle moves. With the relaxation and warming of the hands comes a redistribution of blood that reduces pressure in the blood vessels in the head, ending the migraine headache.

Once a patient develops the ability to move the needle while sitting at the machine, the same technique can be used without the equipment to cut short a migraine episode.

Menninger investigators have reported that almost three-fourths of patients—74 percent—have gained the ability to increase blood in the hands and relieve migraine in almost 100 percent of the situations in which they detect the onset of an attack.

For tension headaches—the most common kind, caused by contraction of forehead, scalp, and neck muscles—cure or alleviation rates of 75 to 80 percent have been reported.

A patient with tension headaches has sensor electrodes applied to the forehead to record muscle tension. If the tension level is high, the biofeedback machine emits rapid beeps that are heard through earphones. As tension is reduced, the beeps come more slowly.

Biofeedback gives tension-headache patients a precise measurement of their physical state as it pertains to headaches, and offers sufferers the gratification of knowing that they can alter that state, taking charge.

Cold Fingers.

It's known as "Raynaud's phenomenon," but many sufferers call it "cold fingers." Their fingers turn white and blue when exposed to cold and can become quite painful. Numbness, tingling, and burning sensations are common, and sometimes the finger tissue dies. About half of 1 percent of the population has the problem. Victims range from teenagers to people in their eighties, and 70 percent are women. Although it can occur spontaneously, the condition is often associated with rheumatoid arthritis and scleroderma, a form of arthritis in which the skin becomes thin, hard, and brittle.

At Vanderbilt University, biofeedback has proved superior to all conventional therapies in helping Raynaud victims. Patients are hooked up to biofeedback equipment and asked to increase their skin temperature. The machine provides positive feedback in the form of a temperature meter, light display, and audio speaker. Patients know they have successfully raised their skin temperatures when the meter needle deflects to the right, the red light remains on, and the low tone sounds get deeper and lower.

One patient, a twenty-seven-year-old woman with scleroderma, had a finger temperature before treatment of only 68° F and had ulcers where her finger tissue had died. With biofeedback training, she was able to raise her finger temperature to 94° F and the ulcers cleared up without further treatment. Two years later, she still is able to raise her finger temperature at will.

Heartbeat and Hypertension.

Promising studies have been carried out at Baltimore City Hospital with patients suffering from premature ventricular contraction, a heartbeat irregularity. Through electrodes taped to the chest, heartbeats trigger lights. When a patient sees a green light, he knows he needs to try to speed his heart rate; a red light indicates he should slow the rate. After about ten hour-long sessions, many patients can change their heart rates on command and can do the same at home without the equipment.

Similar techniques have been used at Boston City Hospital and elsewhere for patients with high blood pressure, with decreases of as much as thirty-three points being obtained in systolic pressures.

Bladder Control.

A portable biofeedback unit for home use, developed at the Medical College of Wisconsin in Milwaukee, has been used effectively to treat a series of patients, mostly children, with detrusor sphincter dyssynergia, an inability to properly coordinate the action of the bladder and the sphincter muscle that governs the release of urine. The condition is often accompanied by chronic urinary infections and incontinence (inability to control urine excretion), and if left untreated may lead to bladder or kidney damage.

The eight-year-old boy mentioned earlier is one of those who have responded well to the Wisconsin program after years of medication failed to help. Like other children with the condition, his tests showed no neurological or urologic damage to which the problem could be attributed. But somewhere along the line, for reasons that are unclear, the signals that control bladder/sphincter coordination had become confused. (In adults, detrusor sphincter dyssynergia is usually acquired and can often be traced to surgery or an accidental injury. Biofeedback enables them to relearn proper coordination for bladder control.)

In the biofeedback therapy, the activity of the sphincter is recorded by surface electrodes placed just in front of the anus. Leads from the electrodes are fed to a biofeedback unit worn on the waist. A green light indicates the sphincter is relaxed; red that it is contracted. A range of audio signals simultaneously provide the same information—a low, quiet tone indicating relaxation; a high, loud tone denoting contraction.

Once patients have learned to use biofeedback in the hospital, they are discharged to continue the training at home. With the device, the eight-year-old boy has been able to overcome his problem, retrain himself to go to the bathroom, and can sleep at friends' homes without worry about waking up wet. The home training allows children to conquer their problem without disruption of normal activities.

Stroke and Quadriplegia.

Biofeedback training may help some stroke victims regain motor control of their arms and legs, and may enable some people with paralysis of all four limbs (quadriplegia) to take advantage of the slight sensation-detecting function remaining in their hands. As many as a third of all patients who have had strokes could benefit from biofeedback, according to a recent report by Dr. John V. Basmajian, who has applied it to 500 patients, beginning at Emory University in Atlanta and continuing at McMaster University in Hamilton, Ontario, where he is now a professor of medicine and director of rehabilitation services.

Basmajian has used biofeedback chiefly to correct foot-drop, which develops after more than half of all strokes and involves foot dragging. He has employed a miniature device that, when hooked up to paralyzed muscles, detects very subtle muscle activity that normally would go unnoticed. When the activity begins, a buzzer sounds. Patients learn to make the buzzer sound and make use of dormant abilities that cause muscle movement. Many patients have learned to pull up their feet at the ankle and keep them from dragging on the ground, and some are able to walk without braces.

Basmajian has also found biofeedback helpful in rehabilitating some 200 hemiplegic patients with paralyzed arms. He reports: "We never succeed in restoring function to normal. But we can at least restore useful bimanual function, such as holding a piece of paper in place with one hand while writing with the other hand."

The use of biofeedback for quadriplegics is very new. Dr. William Finley of Children's Medical Center in Tulsa, Oklahoma, has recently reported on its use in five quadriplegic men who had suffered spinal-cord injury at least one year previously. The goal was to increase remaining sensory function in the patients' hands—function still present at very low levels, unknown to the patients.

First, by electrically stimulating their hands, Finley showed the patients on video displays that the nerve signals actually traveled up to the brain. Then, while watching the sensory signals, patients were instructed to increase them. After the biofeedback training, the patients reported being able to feel pressure exerted on their hands and being aware when a hand was moved without having to look at it.

It is hoped that biofeedback enhancement of sensation will allow physical therapy to produce results more rapidly.

Other Uses.

Reports from the Institute for the Crippled and Disabled in New York City indicate that biofeedback training may be helpful in cases of severe muscle spasm.

Some patients with torticollis (wry neck), a muscle-spasm disorder that twists the head and neck into an abnormal position, have responded. One man for three years had his chin pointing 90° to the right and was unable to straighten his head despite desperate efforts. Within eight weeks after he began three half-hour biofeedback training sessions a week, he learned to control his neck muscles, was able to keep his head in neutral position, and could return to work.

Biofeedback has also helped to decrease the frequency and severity of epileptic seizures, even in patients not helped by medication, according to the Brain Research Institute at the University of California-Los Angeles, the Children's Medical Center in Tulsa, and the University of Tennessee in Knoxville.

Biofeedback has come a long way in a relatively short time. As new medical developments go, it is still very much in its infancy and may hold much greater promise in the future, given continuing research and careful evaluation of results by serious investigators.

Biopsy by Needle
Easing diagnosis

In her shower one morning, a Philadelphia woman experienced an anxiety known to many women. She had discovered a lump in her breast. Yet by late afternoon that day, her anxiety was over. A biopsy done right in her physician's office had revealed that the lump was benign. The biopsy, performed with a needle instead of a knife, took the physician two minutes and the lab ten minutes.

The same kind of biopsy was able to provide quick reassurance to a man after a routine chest X-ray disclosed something that looked like lung cancer. It wasn't.

Now coming into wider use, the innovative diagnostic technique —called "fine needle aspiration biopsy"—is based on a simple principle: Much as a baker uses a toothpick rather than a carving knife to determine whether a cake is done—by looking at what sticks to the toothpick after it is pushed in and pulled out—so a fine needle often can be used instead of a scalpel to determine whether a patient has cancer. The needle can withdraw small amounts of fluid from a suspicious area, and examination of cells in the fluid can point to the diagnosis.

There is minimal discomfort for the patient: The biopsy can be carried out with a local anesthetic or even without anesthesia. The cost —which can be under $100—is much less than for a surgical biopsy since there are no hospitalization and operating-room charges. Accuracy has proved impressive in studies such as those at Lankenau Hospital in Philadelphia, where it has run as high as 96 percent in 9,000 cases.

Even when it is positive for cancer—breast cancer, notably—needle biopsy has another advantage. "The surgeon and the patient," observes Dr. Donald Henson of the National Cancer Institute's Breast-Cancer Program, "can then discuss the options—a larger biopsy, mastectomy, radiation therapy. The use of needle biopsy gives the woman more time to consider treatment options and assist her physician in management of the disease. The woman can have a part in planning the treatment."

Refinement.

First suggested more than fifty years ago by physicians at what is now Memorial Sloan-Kettering Cancer Center in New York City, needle-aspiration biopsy had obstacles to overcome.

One was a fear that malignant cells might be spread by needle insertion. There were in fact a few cases of such dissemination, but they came early on, when relatively large needles were used. Since then, with use of fine needles, dissemination has not been reported as a problem.

Another obstacle was the well-established position of conventional biopsy—removal of an entire section of tissue for microscopic examination. Physicians were accustomed to it and relied on it.

More recently, however, escalating medical costs have helped focus attention on needle biopsy. New advances in cell study have added to reliability, and there have been highly encouraging findings that the very fine needles can safely pierce even delicate organs, such as the spleen and major blood vessels.

Uses.

The technique is being used by more and more physicians both for superficial masses that can be felt and for suspicious internal lesions turned up by X-ray or other means.

Prostate enlargement, common in men over fifty, is usually benign. But about 10 percent of men who have undergone simple prostate removal for apparently benign enlargement have turned out, upon examination of the removed tissue, to have cancer. In such cases, simple prostatectomy not only may have some potential for disseminating malignant cells but may interfere with treatments such as radical prostatectomy or radiation. Obviously, it is desirable to identify men with occult prostatic cancer from the start—and that can be done with needle biopsy in the doctor's office.

In patients suspected of having lung cancer, a long, fine needle can penetrate the chest wall and, with fluoroscopic guidance, sample the lung area. Similarly, other masses in the chest can be sampled. Accuracy as high as 97 percent has been reported in aspirations from such internal sites as the liver, spleen, pancreas, adrenal glands, kidney, pelvis, and bony structures.

Despite its accuracy in most cases, the procedure is not always conclusive. But even when it fails to provide a diagnosis, little if anything is lost. As Dr. Charles Carney, director of cytology at North Carolina Memorial Hospital in Chapel Hill, has remarked, "Failure to make a diagnosis just means that the diagnostic process is set back one day, and the patient has to be worked up in the traditional manner. But that's better than overdiagnosing in the first place."

Bladder Substitute

Each year about 10,000 of the 30,000 Americans found to have bladder cancer require surgical removal of the bladder. For some of them—and for some other patients with other bladder problems that may cause incontinence—a new procedure that forms a substitute internal bladder, eliminating the need to wear an external urine bag, may hold promise.

The Ileal Bladder.

Called the "Kock continent urine reservoir" after the Swedish surgeon Nils G. Kock of the University of Göteborg, who developed it, the substitute bladder is made from a segment about twenty inches long of the ileum, a portion of the small intestine that can be spared.

The segment is folded to form a pouch. Ureters, which conduct urine from the kidneys to the bladder, are implanted. A nipple valve prevents reflux or return of urine to the kidneys, and another valve for continence is constructed in an ileal segment opening in and flush with the skin. Patients catheterize themselves—inserting a tube to withdraw urine—three to six times a day and then cover the opening with a small gauze pad that is readily concealed under a bikini or swim trunks.

The pouch is especially appealing to patients who have psychological or sexual difficulty adjusting to an external appliance. But it is not for everyone. According to Dr. Donald G. Skinner, professor of surgery and head of urology at the University of Southern California, it is best suited to young, active patients who don't want to wear an external appliance and can withstand the added operating time. It takes at least two and a half hours to construct the pouch, and this, added to the four and a half hours required for removal of the bladder, makes a lengthy operation much longer. Skinner hesitates to do the operation on very ill patients, those over fifty-five, and cancer patients who have received high radiation doses to the lower bowel.

Results.

Swedish surgeons have performed the operation on twenty patients since 1975 and have been able to follow fourteen of them for periods of one to seven years since surgery. For eight of the fourteen, the procedure was used to correct previous urinary diversions that had failed; for the other six, it was a primary procedure. Results have been good. The first patient in the group had been chronically ill and "socially crippled" before the procedure. She is now working comfortably as an occupational therapist.

Dr. Skinner at the University of Southern California has done the operation on a first group of seven patients—five with bladder cancer and two with other incontinence-causing disorders—with good results. Reoperation was required in only one, in order to drain an abscess. He does, however, believe that more follow-up time is needed to see if any complications develop.

Also at the University of Southern California, Dr. Alex Gerber has done seven of the operations. He finds that the ileal bladder prevents ureteral reflux (abnormal movement of urine back up from the bladder into the ureter connecting to the kidney) and ascending infections, which sometimes occur with other procedures. He concludes from his experience that the operation "provides a more ideal substitute for the lower urinary tract than any procedure thus far described."

"Bloodless" Surgery

"Bloodless" surgical techniques developed for adult Jehovah's Witnesses, whose religion forbids blood transfusions, have been effectively adapted for use even in infants and small children undergoing delicate open heart procedures—with significant advantages.

In first trials at Children's Hospital in Buffalo, New York, forty-eight youngsters, including a three-month-old infant, successfully underwent complex surgical correction of such congenital heart deformities as "hole in the heart" (atrial septal defect and ventricular septal defect), transposition of the great arteries, and tetralogy of Fallot, in which combined ventricular defect and constricted pulmonary valve cause "blueness." In only four of the children did any blood at all have to be transfused.

The Combined Techniques.

The Buffalo procedure combines features of two earlier techniques.

One is dilution, which was first used in the mid-1960s to permit operations on Jehovah's Witnesses without violating their taboo against transfusion. The children's blood was diluted with an equal or greater amount of a standard hospital solution of water plus minerals, starch, or other nutrients during the open heart procedures. The dilution reduced the patients' hematocrit (the proportion of oxygen-carrying red cells in the blood) to a minimum of 13 percent, lower than ever before reported.

The second technique used, with a modification, is "total hypo-thermic circulatory arrest," in which body temperature is drastically lowered and circulation stopped entirely during surgery. In the Buffalo procedure, the children's temperatures were lowered, but not as far as in total circulatory arrest.

The heart-lung support devices—equipment that removes blood from the body, oxygenates it as the lungs normally would, then returns it for circulation throughout the body, thus bypassing heart and lungs during the surgery—had been originally developed for adults. They were scaled down as far as possible to adjust to the low blood volume of children in comparison with adults. But because of limits on the miniaturization of equipment, a far greater dilution of blood was re-quired than with full-size patients.

Despite the high dilution, the children (median age, twenty-eight months; youngest, three months; oldest, eight years; median weight, less than forty-four pounds; tiniest infant, ten and a half pounds) toler-ated the procedure well. Only four of the forty-eight required trans-fusion to keep red-cell concentrations from going below a set mini-mum.

According to a report to the American Heart Association's Scien-tific Sessions by Dr. Sambamurthy Subramanian, chief investigator and professor of surgery at State University of New York-Buffalo and chief of cardiac surgery at Children's Hospital, none of the children ex-perienced clotting difficulties or problems with kidney or lung function, and oxygen uptake by tissues was "excellent" despite the massive dilu-tion of blood. In comparison to a matched group of other children receiving conventional transfusion therapy to keep their red-cell levels near normal during similar procedures, the children on dilution therapy lost less blood and hospital stays for the two groups were almost identi-cal.

A major advantage of the dilution technique, the Buffalo investiga-tors have reported, is that it allows complex procedures to be performed on small children without exposing them to possibly contaminated donor blood. Moreover, thinned-down blood actually circulates more easily through body tissues than does blood of normal concentration. Use of fluids as a blood substitute also offers advantages when a patient has a rare blood type, or when the correct type is unavailable, or when antibodies in a child's blood cause difficulties in matching it with that of a suitable donor.

Dilutional therapy may be useful in other types of procedures as well. "If it can be used in acute heart surgery patients," observes Dr. Subramanian, "then I'm sure it can be used in other patients, too. All our studies have shown that the procedure not only is safe; it may actually be positively beneficial."

Bone Healing with Electricity

A bone fracture, as any victim knows, is no minor affliction. A broken leg, for example, may have to be in a cast for six months before the body makes full repairs. And some fractures stubbornly refuse to heal.

After breaking two bones in his left leg in a fall, a New York building contractor was in and out of the hospital more than twenty times over the next ten years for surgery to implant pins, nails, and bone grafts, all to no avail. Not until weak pulses of electric current were applied through his leg cast each day did healing take place, allowing him to get back to work.

Bone healing through electricity is aiding a rapidly growing number of patients with "nonunion" fractures—those that haven't healed in a year of treatment—as well as those classified as "delayed healing" after four months.

Two Methods.

In applying electrical stimulation, the physician now may use one of two methods to pass harmless amounts of electrical current across the nonunion site of the bone. In one method, developed by Dr. Carl T. Brighton of the University of Pennsylvania-Philadelphia, what amounts to a self-contained electrical circuit is placed beneath the patient's cast. A small battery anchored in the plaster emits a steady twenty microamperes to an electrode implanted near the fracture during a minor outpatient operation. A number of such cathode electrodes may be used, depending on the extent of the nonunion. A single anode electrode is placed on the skin surface to complete the circuit. The minute, imperceptible current is then applied twelve hours a day, usually at night, for twelve weeks while the patient goes about his daily routine. The electrodes and cast are removed after about three months and the patient is usually completely well.

In the second method, developed by Dr. C. Andrew L. Bassett of Columbia-Presbyterian Medical Center in New York City, two soft plastic pads containing enclosed wire coils are strapped to two sides of the fracture site. An external power mechanism, plugged into a household wall socket, sets up an electromagnetic field in the wire coils. Treatment is usually carried out on an outpatient basis for ten or more hours daily, usually at night. The pads are removable when treatment is not in progress. Healing can take place within a few months, but sometimes takes as long as a year.

Success Rates.

The *Journal of the American Medical Association* has called electrical stimulation a major advance in traumatic orthopedic surgery. Physicians are not certain why it works, but many speculate that the currents stimulate osteocytes (bone cells) and may change the structure of the cell wall, enhancing bone union.

In one of the first studies of the Brighton technique with 210 patients at the University of Pennsylvania and a dozen other centers, healing occurred in 172 of 213 nonunion fractures, an 81 percent success rate. The average time of nonunion had been 2.6 years, and the patients had averaged 2.1 prior surgical procedures.

A recent check of results with the Bassett procedure shows successful promotion of bone healing in 834 of 1,078 patients worldwide —a virtually comparable success rate of 77 percent and in fact the success rate for 220 patients treated at Columbia-Presbyterian was 81 percent.

Each procedure has its advantages and possible disadvantages. The significant advantage of the Bassett procedure is that it is noninvasive and carries no known risk. It can be started and completed entirely on an outpatient basis. A drawback is that the method is not applicable for spine or trunk problems.

The Brighton procedure can be carried out on an outpatient basis but usually will be started with a hospitalized patient because of image-intensification equipment needed to determine the appropriate placement of electrodes. This technique is invasive but does not necessitate open surgery.

Success with Another Problem, Too.

Congenital pseudoarthrosis has been a frustrating and disabling condition. In pseudoarthrosis, mineral elements of bone are lost, leading to bending, fracture, and inability of the fracture to heal for lack of real bony structure. Bone grafts and other treatments often have failed. Each electrical method has been effective for pseudoarthrosis.

Bone Lengthening

Injury to a bone is usually much less serious for a child than for an adult. Young bones are less likely to fracture and more apt to heal quickly. But children's growth plates are susceptible to injury. These plates, at both ends of many bones, are responsible for most longitudinal growth. The plates may also be damaged by infection. In either case, growth may be halted permanently in the affected bone.

Now, however, both for youngsters with injured plates and for others with congenital shortness of one limb, a new procedure that can lengthen the affected extremity has been used for more than 100 children at the Presbyterian Hospital in New York City.

The Three-Step Procedure.

The first step in the lengthening process involves cutting the affected bone, usually in the middle. Next, an external cranking device is pinned to the two halves of the bone and gradually the separated portions are cranked apart. The limb is lengthened at the rate of about two millimeters (roughly four-hundredths of an inch) a day. The maximum separation is about two inches. Once desired length is achieved, bone fragments taken from elsewhere in the body are used to fill in the space and fuse the parts. The lengthened bone, according to Dr. Harold Dick, chief of pediatric orthopedic surgery at Presbyterian, has normal strength after a few months.

Although well over 90 percent of limb-lengthening operations involve the legs, the technique can be applied to the arms as well. It was in the cases of two children, a thirteen-year-old girl and an eight-year-old boy with injured growth plates resulting from a benign tumor and infection, respectively. Each had a two-inch discrepancy in arm length. Both were successfully lengthened.

Arm lengthening is usually not performed unless the discrepancy is significant. While a leg-length difference can affect the spine and the rest of the skeleton adversely, there are no such repercussions when the arms don't quite match in length.

Bone-Marrow Therapy

When a forty-eight-year-old woman in Milwaukee suffered a relapse of her small-cell lung cancer, she was well prepared to renew the fight against it. Physicians at the Medical College of Wisconsin (MCW) had previously removed some of her bone marrow and frozen it. The availability of this replacement marrow made it possible now to administer the massive doses of chemotherapy needed to gain control of the recurrent tumor even though much of the bone marrow in her body would be destroyed in the process. The retreatment was successful; periodic blood tests and chest scans continue to show complete disappearance of malignant cells.

A relatively new procedure, freezing bone marrow for subsequent infusion is, as Dr. Ross Abrams of MCW puts it, "one more tool, one more option that will make a difference with some malignancies."

Cancers particularly suited for marrow therapy are those fairly easy to treat at first occurrence but difficult to manage when they recur. Among them are small-cell lung cancer, lymphoma, some testicular malignancies, leukemia, and brain tumors.

Commonly, there is a direct relationship between the dosage strength of anticancer drugs and their effectiveness: The stronger the dosage, the better, until the larger doses begin to destroy healthy tissue. Bone marrow is generally the first to be destroyed, and removing a portion beforehand, which is saved to be restored later, provides an extra margin of effectiveness for chemotherapy.

The Procedure.

In the fairly typical case of the lung-cancer patient, about 10 percent of her bone-marrow cells were removed while her cancer was in remission. After being obtained, under general anesthesia, from her pelvic bone, the marrow was processed at a blood center, where sophisticated equipment separated and removed white cells and red cells no longer capable of dividing. The important cells still capable of dividing were isolated and placed in special plastic bags able to withstand temperatures as low as − 196°C. A solution containing dimethyl sulfoxide was used to stabilize the cells against injury during freezing. Once frozen, the bags were placed in liquid-nitrogen tanks where there is no risk of thawing.

When the patient's lung cancer recurred, the intensive chemotherapy essential to kill the tumor was used, destroying virtually all the bone marrow in her body in the process. It was then that her stored cells were reinfused—by vein and at her bedside while she was awake. Bone marrow is essential to fight infection and prevent bleeding, and the next several weeks were critical because reinfused bone marrow needs at least three to four weeks to multiply and restore the blood count to normal. The patient was hospitalized during this time—a period of seven weeks.

Frozen bone marrow is known to remain useful for a minimum of two years, and is probably useful even longer.

Bones of the Ear, Replacing

A new technique to replace nonfunctioning ossicles (middle-ear bones) —which, when normal, transmit sound vibrations to the inner ear and on to the brain—has been developed at the University of California-Davis Medical Center (UCDMC).

For more than two decades, both American and European physicians have been trying to develop an appropriate material and procedure to replace and/or continue the function of the ossicles. The prostheses that have been tried—some made of bone, some of plastic—tended to be rejected as foreign objects (see ARTIFICIAL BODY PARTS). They also lost the ability to vibrate if they touched and subsequently adhered to the side wall of the ear.

A Bolt of Cartilage.

Now the problems with earlier devices appear to have been solved by Dr. Richard Chole of UCDMC. Going a step or two farther than previous researchers, Chole chose for his device a "self-stabilizing" bolt-type shape that had already been found to be effective, and made the prosthesis totally out of human cartilage. The cartilage, supplied by the Lions Eye and Tissue Bank at UCDMC, is not difficult to obtain, is easy to "sculpture" to shape, and may be stored indefinitely in a simple alcohol solution.

In the first twenty-three patients who have been followed for at least two years, none of the devices has been rejected. In addition, the cartilage, because of its flexibility, has kept vibrating even upon touching an ear wall. In most cases, patients have regained and retained at least 85 percent of their normal hearing, Chole reports.

The procedure, called "ossicular replacement," usually takes one hour and can be done under local anesthesia. The results are immediate, with hearing actually restored while surgery is still under way.

Bony-Ridge Augmentation
For denture wearers

Until recently, the only solution for thousands of denture wearers who suffer from a condition known as "ridge atrophy" was to undergo painful and costly rib or hip graft surgery. Now a synthetic bone material, hydroxylapatite (or hydroxyapatite), has been found to dramatically reduce need for major bone-graft surgery, allowing oral surgeons to correct the condition through a relatively simple outpatient procedure.

Many people, especially the elderly, have difficulty wearing dentures or have problems keeping them in place. Because they are unable to chew well and often develop a jut-chinned appearance, both nutrition and self-esteem may suffer.

Most denture wearers' problems occur with the lower plate. That is because the upper teeth stay in place by suction while the lower false teeth are difficult to stabilize. Action of tongue and cheeks may continually dislodge them during eating and talking. Subjected to these stresses, after years of denture wearing, the alveolar ridge—the area that supports the dentures—tends to wear down, leaving no place for the dentures to set.

The New Procedure.

To use the synthetic bone material—crystals of hydroxylapatite that resemble sugar granules—the oral surgeon makes two small incisions in the ridge, usually under local anesthesia, and injects the crystals via syringe into the resulting pockets. Malleable at first, the implant crystals are molded by the surgeon's fingers. The procedure may take about an hour, and the crystals are kept in place by plastic splints for two to three days until they completely harden. Within four to six weeks, the crystals have been completely incorporated into the ridge and new dentures can be fitted. According to Barry Hendler, D.D.S., M.D., director of oral and maxillofacial surgery at the Medical College of Pennsylvania in Philadelphia, the implants usually can be expected to last about five years, when the procedure can be repeated.

"Because hydroxylapatite avoids major surgery," reports Dr. James Quinn, an oral surgeon at Louisiana State University, where the initial clinical program on use of the material was developed, "the advantages are especially dramatic for the elderly, the most common sufferers of ridge atrophy [who] are also in the highest risk category when major surgery is involved." Moreover, adds Dr. Quinn, "In 60 percent of the rib or hip bone graft cases, the transplant is resorbed into the bone, necessitating another graft. This does not happen with the use of hydroxylapatite since the material is nonabsorbable. So, in essence, we may be avoiding not just one operation, but perhaps two."

The material provides other benefits, according to Dr. Daniel Waite of the University of Minnesota, another center for hydroxylapatite research. "Hydroxylapatite improves the ridge height and serves as an increased surface area for denture support. This minimizes the pain and discomfort of a denture resting on the small ridge covered with sensitive, thin tissue of the mouth."

It's expected that the new procedure may allow many people previously unable to wear dentures to be fitted for their use.

Botulinum Toxin
Sword into plowshare

Botulinum toxin is the most poisonous substance known to man, capable of causing rapid death by paralyzing muscles needed for breathing. But in Atlanta, an Emory University ophthalmologist, Dr. Allen Gammon, injected one-billionth of a gram of the poison into the eye muscle of a twelve-year-old girl to correct a form of strabismus ("crossed" eyes).

Since an international research project began in 1978, *botulinum* neurotoxin injections have been used on more than 200 patients worldwide. But the Emory patient is the first to have been treated with the toxin for cyclic strabismus, a little-understood condition in which the eyes cross at regular intervals of roughly every other day.

Seven months after the one injection, her eyes look and work in perfect unison and she need no longer see the world through double vision.

Strabismus occurs when one of the muscles holding the eye in place is too tight and pulls it to one side. When the imbalance does not correct itself naturally or through prescribed exercises, the usual solution is to loosen the overly active muscle by attaching it to a different part of the eye globe. The surgical procedure is designed to balance the forces between the two opposing muscles on either side of the eye.

The *botulinum* treatment is an alternative method to achieve the same balance. The poison, injected by needle into the overly active muscle, temporarily paralyzes it. The muscle on the opposite side of the eye then takes up the slack, tightening more in order to make the eye move. By the time the injected muscle begins to recover from its tiny dose of the poison, the other muscle will have become more contracted and stronger, thus better able to keep the eye in position.

Cyclic "Crossing."

Strabismus affects approximately one in 100 people, but cyclic strabismus is considerably more rare. Why one muscle should begin to tighten after years of balance—and why it should tighten one day, release one day—is not understood.

Although the change in her eye was probably gradual, the Atlanta child herself refused to admit anything was wrong. A bright child who had begun reading at three, she compensated for her double vision by sitting up closer in the classroom and listening harder. Her brain also compensated by making one eye work harder to focus. Eventually it became obvious that her eyes were increasingly crossed—but not crossed at all times. Cyclic strabismus was diagnosed when daily photographs were taken and the girl's mother charted the days of crossing.

THE TREATMENT AND COURSE.   The treatment itself was simple, says the youngster. Seated in a chair in the examining room, she leaned her head back. When anesthetic eye drops were applied, she clutched her father's hand and admitted, for the first time, she was scared. But she held perfectly still when the needle with the poison was actually injected.

The dosage had to be, and was, carefully controlled. There was no undesirable systemic response, not even headache or nausea. But, as expected based on years of animal studies, the dosage needed to temporarily paralyze the muscle had an impact on adjacent muscles and the next morning the eyelid could not be opened. On schedule, however, over the next few months, it regained its strength.

Only one injection was needed in this case. Some patients, because of the amount of muscle error or because their work will not tolerate even temporary loss of the use of an eye, have several injections, each altering muscle tension just a little.

Although the girl's eyes are well aligned now, with no tendency to turn separately, Gammon and other researchers cannot yet be certain of permanent cure. The research is still young. But because there are no known irreversible ill effects, the treatment could be repeated—even at regular intervals like "booster" shots, Gammon notes. And, of course, other methods, such as lengthening the eye muscle, could be added.

For some forms of strabismus, such as that caused by heavy scar-tissue buildup due to accidents, the *botulinum* treatment would not be appropriate. In other cases, however, there is some likelihood that the still experimental treatment could prove to be a powerful sword turned into a medical plowshare.

Brain-Oxygen Monitor

A new, noninvasive monitoring device that can show within two to three seconds whether the amount of oxygen available to the brain is sufficient now can make surgery safer. It may have other valuable uses as well, including helping premature infants.

It is the first means of meeting a long-felt need in the operating room—the need for continuous, instantaneous readouts of oxygen in the brain during anesthesia.

Inadequate Body Signals.

Most anesthetic injuries—patient deaths or severe brain damage—occur when the supply of oxygen to the brain is insufficient for any reason. Three minutes is about the maximum time the brain can go without oxygen and not be permanently damaged. Lack of oxygen supply to the brain can leave a patient in a vegetative state. Anesthesiologists have used blood pressure, heart rate, and electrocardiogram readings of the heartbeats to monitor a patient's condition. But those body readings, while useful to a point, fall short of being ideal warning signals to the anesthesiologist because they are indirect indicators.

The Niroscope.

The new instrument, developed by a Duke University Medical Center professor of physiology, Dr. Frans Jobsis, is called a "Niroscope" for "near infrared oxygen sufficiency scope." It works by shining near-infrared light (just beyond the darkest red color visible to the human eye) of different wavelengths through the skin and skull into the brain and measuring how much of that light comes back out.

Jobsis discovered two important facts: that infrared light can penetrate skin and bone tissue much more easily than ever thought before, and that brain tissue changes its absorption of this kind of light depending on the amount of oxygen available to the nerve cells.

The infrared is carried through hairlike strands of glass fibers bound together in flexible "bundles." A tube containing these bundles of optical fibers directs the beam of light into the patient's forehead with a simple headgear.

"There is no risk to the patient," reports Dr. Elizabeth Fox, associate professor of anesthesiology at Duke. "You get about the same amount of infrared exposure as you do when walking around on a sunny day in North Carolina."

In use in the operating room at Duke since April 1982, the instrument has proved its value. For example, when a patient undergoing neck dissection for a thyroid mass experienced a sudden drop in blood pressure and brain oxygen supply, the Niroscope detected the problem within seconds, allowing quick remedial action.

Future Uses.

Duke researchers expect that the monitor, after further trials, could have many potential applications in the delivery room, coronary-care unit, and neonatal intensive-care unit. Animal experiments indicate that the instrument may be useful in diagnosing brain lesions, spotting hemorrhages within the brain in premature infants, and determining precisely the right amount of oxygen a newborn needs.

Calcium-Antagonist Drugs

Early in 1982, when the Food and Drug Administration approved a drug called "nifedipine" (trade name Procardia), the way was opened for use of a group of heart agents anticipated by U.S. physicians with some excitement.

The drugs are known as "calcium antagonists"—and are sometimes referred to as "calcium channel blockers." Others include verapamil (trade names Calan and Isoptin) and diltiazem (Cardizem).

The calcium antagonists may well help lower death rates from heart attacks and almost certainly will improve the outlook for many patients suffering from anginal chest pain by providing a basic new approach to treatment.

How They Act.

The drugs work against a mechanism only recently recognized widely as a major contributor to chest pain and heart attack.

Angina pectoris, according to some estimates, affects 4.5 million Americans. The constricting pain is a warning signal from the heart that the heart muscle is not getting adequate amounts of oxygen-rich blood.

Angina was once thought to stem from a single cause: the buildup of fatty deposits on the walls of the coronary arteries, limiting blood flow. But it is now clear that an involuntary spasm—a sudden contraction of a coronary artery—can occur with or without fatty-deposit buildups, impairing blood flow to the heart muscle.

Actually, as far back as 1959, Dr. Myron Prinzmetal of Los Angeles had reported on a group of patients who experienced angina at rest, unlike many others who developed chest pain only with exertion. That led him to believe that the chest pain stemmed from coronary-artery spasm. Years later, physicians at UCLA Medical Center, in the midst of an operation to bypass a clogged coronary artery in an elderly woman, were the first to actually witness a spasm.

"Surgery was proceeding normally," one of them reported, "when, suddenly, the artery, which had been soft and pliable, went into an intense constriction until it felt like a piece of tough rope or twine."

It soon became clear that brief spasms could account for angina at rest not only in patients with partially clogged arteries but also in those with clear arteries. And spasm, if prolonged, could lead to heart attack, again both in a patient with clogged arteries and one with no clogging.

Calcium antagonists enter the picture because calcium is very much involved in the process of muscle constriction. For constriction to occur, calcium from blood must enter cells in artery walls. The entry is by way of special channels in the cells—and it is these channels that calcium-antagonist drugs close, keeping out quantities of calcium and helping to prevent spasm and its consequences.

In one of many studies, Harvard Medical School physicians gave nifedipine, a calcium antagonist, to 127 patients with spasm-associated angina. Most had failed to respond to beta blockers and other medications, and they were averaging sixteen angina attacks a week. Almost two-thirds of the patients had complete relief; another quarter had a 50 percent or greater reduction in the number of attacks.

Calcium antagonists are also proving useful for activity-induced angina, although physicians are not certain why. One possibility is that spasm may be involved in classic angina. There is also another possibility. In addition to acting against spasm in the coronary arteries, the drugs also tend to dilate other body arteries, thus reducing resistance against which the heart must pump blood, and, in doing so, lowering its work burden and oxygen need.

Studies carried out at eight medical centers with 150 patients found calcium-antagonist treatment producing at least a 50 percent decrease in angina and marked improvement in tolerance for exercise.

Side effects of the drugs can range from minor light-headedness and flushing to headache, weakness, muscle cramps, and wheezing. Often these disappear as treatment continues or dosage is modified.

Carbon-Fiber Implants

To regrow severely torn
ligaments and tendons

Some victims of severe knee and shoulder injuries—massive tears of
ligaments and tendons previously almost impossible to repair—are
moving their limbs freely and without pain because of new carbon-fiber
implants. The strands of fiber provide a scaffold for regrowth of tissues
torn, most often, in auto accidents and athletic mishaps.

A ligament links one bone to another; a tendon connects muscle
to bone. In many cases, a torn ligament or tendon can be repaired
surgically by simply sewing the torn ends together. But in many other
instances, the tear is so massive that not enough ligament or tendon is
left to rejoin.

For years, researchers have been frustrated in efforts to find an
effective permanent prosthetic replacement for tendons and ligaments.
The carbon-fiber implants, which are expected to help as many as
100,000 Americans a year, are the result of a different approach to
solving the problem. That approach was taken by Dr. Andrew B.
Weiss, professor of surgery, and Dr. Harold A. Alexander, a mechanical engineer, at the University of Medicine and Dentistry of New
Jersey, in Newark.

The Lattice.

The hope of the Newark team was to find some material that could be
sewn in and around a massively torn ligament or tendon, not as a
permanent replacement but to temporarily connect and reinforce, and

to provide a lattice into which the body's own connective tissue could grow. If the connective tissue could move into the rift, the result might be a reconstructed ligament or tendon virtually identical to the original.

There were many efforts to find a suitable material. Carbon fibers were a candidate because research had shown that the fibers are compatible with the human body. One problem, however, was that when British investigators had experimented with the fibers in sheep, the material had looked promising for a time but then had degraded. Another problem was that the fibers were brittle, difficult for a surgeon to handle.

Finally, Alexander and his associates hit upon the idea of coating the fibers with polylactic acid—a plastic made up of long chains of lactic acid. Polylactic acid gave the fibers a pliable structure that could be attached to surgical needles. Moreover, because lactic acid is a natural product of body processes, it can be broken down by the body and eventually eliminated. Hopefully, that would leave the carbon fibers to serve as a scaffold.

Proof.

Testing the coated carbon-fiber implants in animals, Weiss and Alexander found that the novel coating improved the fibers' handling ability during implantation. Most important, after two weeks in the body, the coating biodegraded, leaving carbon as a support mesh into which connective tissue began to grow. After nine to twelve months, the connective tissue had filled in the rift in the ligament or tendon and the reconstructed ligament or tendon not only was almost identical to the original but provided desirable joint stability and function.

The Procedure.

The implants are made up of 3-foot-long bundles of 10,000 filaments of carbon, each hair-thin, about seven-millionths of a meter in diameter. After being sprayed with polylactic acid, the bundles are flattened into ribbons. Surgical needles are attached at both ends and the ribbon is sterilized.

The end result is an easily maneuverable strand that can be woven in and around injured tissue to connect and reinforce, and if necessary can be threaded through holes drilled in bone to replace tendons. The entire operation requires from one to two and a half hours.

The first human trials started in April 1981 and were carried out in sixty patients, ranging in age from eighteen to fifty-seven years. All had injured tendons or ligaments in the knee or leg, which had persisted for an average of 5.2 years. They'd had an average of 2.5 previous operations for repair, which had failed; some had endured as many as 13 operations. There have been follow-ups of up to eighteen months thus far since the implantations. All patients have experienced improvement—in some cases, dramatic improvement—in joint strength and/or motion as measured by physical-therapy machines and orthopedic evaluation.

On the basis of these results in New Jersey, the Food and Drug Administration approved further testing in a multicenter trial. Results at Stanford University Medical Center, the University of Texas Health Science Center in Dallas, and elsewhere have been comparable to those obtained in Newark.

One of those who received implants at Michael Reese Hospital and Medical Center, Chicago, is a man whose legs are paralyzed as a result of poliomyelitis. When he ruptured a shoulder ligament, it became extremely difficult for him to get about on crutches. Within three months after the implant, he had recovered a full range of motion and was able to do everything he had done before the shoulder injury.

Thus far, in no case—either in animal or in human trials—has there been any rejection of the carbon-fiber implants.

If all should continue well, other possible applications for the material are foreseen. One could be its use in treating degenerated ligaments in rheumatoid arthritis. Produced in sheet form, it may also have value in hernia repair.

Cardiac Catheterization

This is a procedure used to visualize the heart's chambers and the course of blood flow through them, and to determine what the pressure is within the chambers. It may also be used to study the coronary arteries that feed the heart muscle.

The Procedure.

Usually carried out in a hospital cardiac-catheterization laboratory, the procedure can provide otherwise unavailable information in many types of heart disease. It is used when noninvasive studies such as electrocardiography or echocardiography (see ECHOCARDIOGRAPHY and ELECTROCARDIOGRAPHY) have not afforded a diagnosis, when more precise definition of the extent and severity of a heart lesion is sought, or when medical treatment is no longer effective and surgery may be contemplated.

The patient lies on a table, receives a local anesthetic, and a small incision is made into a blood vessel, often in either the groin area or the crease of the elbow.

A catheter—a long, thin, flexible plastic tube—is inserted in the blood vessel and slowly guided up through the vessel and into the heart while its progress is watched via a fluoroscope that provides an image on a television screen. The patient feels little if any discomfort while this is going on. There is the brief sting of the anesthetic, followed by numbness.

Once the catheter is in place in the heart chamber, a chemical dye that is visible on X-ray films in injected into the tube and soon reaches the heart. As the dye is injected, the patient may feel a brief sensation of warmth.

As the dye circulates through the heart, X-ray movies are made. If the catheter is also placed so that the dye can be injected into the coronary arteries, the movies can reveal the state of the arteries.

Blood samples are taken through the catheter to determine how much oxygen is present in the blood in different chambers of the heart. The pressure of the blood in the different chambers can also be measured.

The procedure may take from one and a half to three hours, depending on whether the coronary arteries also are studied. Afterward, the catheter is gently removed, a dressing is placed on the incision site, and the patient is taken back to his room, usually to remain in bed for six to twelve hours. There are usually no aftereffects.

The Movies.

After the X-ray films are developed, they are studied carefully by a team that may consist of a cardiologist, radiologist, and heart surgeon. The movies, which can be stopped at any point for close scrutiny, can reveal any changes in the heart muscle and any obstructions in the coronary arteries. They can indicate whether one or both coronary arteries, or one or more branches, are obstructed, the site and extent of the obstruction, and whether it is because of spasm or involuntary contraction or atherosclerotic deposits. They can also confirm the presence of valve disease or congenital defects.

Catheterization has some drawbacks. It is expensive and requires hospitalization. Some risk is involved: The procedure may sometimes disturb heart rhythm; rarely it may cause a heart attack; still more rarely, it may result in death. In expert hands, in institutions where at least 200 to 300 catheterizations are performed yearly, the mortality rate is 0.2 percent (2 in 1,000) or less.

The procedure is clearly a very valuable one when there are proper indications for it and when other, less expensive and perhaps less risky tests do not provide the information the physician needs.

Cardiobeeper/Medication Pen
Reducing heart-attack risk

A new patient-activated system developed by State University of New York-Buffalo and University of Rhode Island physicians in conjunction with a Maryland firm has been shown to effectively reduce deaths from repeat heart attacks. It allows patients who have had previous attacks to immediately transmit their hearts' electrical activity over telephone lines to trained personnel for interpretation when they suspect another oncoming heart attack—and, when necessary, to take immediate corrective action on their own, using a little medication pen.

Answering a Need.

As many as 60 percent of deaths following a heart attack occur in the first few hours after symptom onset. A major reason is the development of abnormal heart rhythms. Although many cities now have excellent rescue and ambulance squads that can transmit a patient's electrocardiogram for interpretation, valuable time may be lost getting the squad to the patient.

With the new system, however, the patient can have his or her heart's electrical activity "read" immediately over the telephone and, if necessary, can self-inject arrhythmia-correcting lidocaine while awaiting the ambulance.

Results.

In a study carried out in Buffalo and Providence, 164 patients who had suffered previous heart attacks received wallet-size cardiobeepers capable of detecting heart activity and transmitting the information by telephone. Along with a beeper, each patient carried at all times a pen-size device that, when pressed against muscle, delivers a needle with premeasured 300 milligrams of lidocaine.

A second group of 127 patients—whose age, sex, and risk for heart attack were similar to those of the first group—did not receive cardiobeepers or medication pens, and thus served as a control or comparison group.

At the end of the three-year study, none of the patients in the first group using the system died of heart attack, while eight in the control group did. The system also significantly reduced prehospital delay time after onset of symptoms from an average of 24.6 hours for the controls to only 4.6 hours for the group using the system.

There was another benefit, an unforeseen one. Reports Sandy Van Every, nurse coordinator in Buffalo: "Patients who have already suffered a heart attack are typically fearful of having another, and their fear may be so intense that it considerably alters their whole life-style. They may become afraid of any exertion and be 'crippled' from their fears."

Patients in the first group appeared to be reassured by the system, knowing they were only a telephone call away from immediate help. "They seemed to have fewer fears of subsequent heart attacks and were more able to resume their normal activities because of the cardiobeeper, the premeasured lidocaine they carried with them, and the instruction they received about the system prior to joining the study."

Another Application.

The two-unit system was developed by Dr. John Visco of the University at Buffalo and Dr. Robert Capone of the University of Rhode Island, along with Survival Technology of Bethesda, Maryland. Another study is under way to pinpoint further the extent to which the system cuts the death rate for those who have suffered previous heart attacks.

Dr. Visco sees another potential use: "The system might ideally, in the future, be extended to patients who have not had previous heart attacks but are shown statistically to be at considerable risk."

CAT Scans
The computerized super X-rays

In 1979, the Nobel Prize in medicine was awarded to the inventors of CAT scanning in recognition of the technique's significant contribution to diagnostic medicine.

Called both CAT (for "computerized axial tomography") and CT (for "computerized tomography"), the imaging was first applied to the head and then, more recently, to the rest of the body. With a whole series of improvements in the original technology, it has become increasingly valuable for more and more purposes and is employed not only for detecting and diagnosing dozens of conditions but also for observing the effects of therapy and following up on the results of operations.

The Way It Works.

The technique uses a computer to interpret many X-ray images and reconstruct a cross-sectional image of any area of the body.

After the patient is placed in the scanner, an X-ray source rotates rapidly—almost once a second in current CT machines—making hundreds of individual pictures. The pictures at each point are electronically recorded and stored by a computer. The computer can then reassemble the data into thin cross-sectional "slices."

The CT scanner can assess the composition of internal structures, discriminating between fat, fluid, and gas. It can also show the shape and size of various organs and lesions, and is sensitive enough to detect abnormal lesions as small as one or two millimeters.

Scanning the Brain.

In 1981, only eight years after the first use of CT for brain scanning, a National Institutes of Health panel of thirteen experts—radiologists, neurologists, neurosurgeons, and others—reported that the imaging technique had "transformed the diagnosis and much of the management of structural disease of the brain and its surrounding tissue."

CT, the panel found, is the tool of choice in diagnosing suspected brain abscess, intracranial (within the skull) masses, and intracranial hemorrhage. In patients with head injuries, CT scans allow rapid identification of lesions causing increased pressure, thus allowing early surgical treatment of hematomas (blood masses) and limiting unnecessary surgical exploration. The scans improve management of patients with brain abscess by speeding diagnosis, allowing quick start of antibiotic therapy, and determining more accurately if and when surgical intervention is needed.

CT can precisely detect and localize small brain tumors, making surgery more precise and safer, and hospital stays shorter. The scanning is also valuable for diagnosing many other brain conditions—hydrocephalus ("water on the brain"), herpes encephalitis, parasitic infestations, progressive degenerative diseases—and is useful as well for pinpointing sites in the brain that may be responsible for some types of epileptic seizures.

Scanning the Body.

CT is being used to diagnose disorders in the lungs, the gastrointestinal tract, the blood-vessel system, and more. Emergency rooms often find the scanning valuable for diagnosing abdominal trauma. CT of the spine can be used to diagnose back ailments without the painful injection of contrast media (dyes).

One example of CT's value is in the detection of neuroblastoma, the most common solid malignant tumor in children outside of tumors of the head. Neuroblastomas may be located in the chest or abdomen, usually in the adrenal gland atop a kidney or in the sympathetic nervous system along the spine. Two percent of children's deaths associated with cancer are from neuroblastoma; it is fatal to 70 percent of those who have it.

Recently, University of California-San Francisco Medical Center physicians presented the results of a five-year study showing that neuroblastoma can be detected with 100 percent accuracy with the use of CT. The advantage of such accuracy, the investigators noted, is that the physician can immediately determine what kind of tumor it is, even if it is quite small, and can then determine what combination of therapies would be most effective, speeding treatment and, hopefully, saving lives.

Scanning the Heart.

Until recently, the heart has been the only organ to elude the CT scanner. Because the heart beats several times as the scanning X-ray detectors rotate around the body, each individual view was out of sync with the others, and the computer was unable to assemble them all into a clear, composite image.

One solution to that problem is a new "gated" CT scanner being used at the University of California-San Diego Medical Center, which instructs the rotating X-ray detectors to "snap" each view at the precise instant when the heart is motionless, just before each beat. The resulting identical views can then be assembled by the computer.

One patient, whose heart was compressed by an abnormal buildup of fluid in the pericardium (the heart's surrounding sac), recently was spared major chest surgery after physicians were able to determine the exact location of the fluid with the aid of the gated scanner; they could then insert a needle into the pericardium and drain the fluid without endangering vital structures less than an inch away.

The gated scanner also can be used to view enlargement of heart chambers (a result of heart-valve disease) and congenital heart defects. Another use is in determining the size and location of areas damaged by heart attacks, information helpful in treatment.

A further refinement in the gated scanner is the programming of its computer to predict the minimum number of views needed to obtain a clear image of the heart. When the rotating scanner has taken enough images, the computer tells the doctors to stop the scanner, reducing radiation dosage to a minimum.

Another potentially significant new development for heart imaging is an unusual electron beam scanner that, for the first time, can image the beating heart in three dimensions and measure heart-muscle blood flow directly. Called the Cine CT scanner, the device can take twenty-four images per second as opposed to the conventional one picture every one to five seconds. In addition to its speed, the Cine CT can take exposures of the heart at eight anatomical levels, instead of the one level or one slice at a time of conventional CT systems. For the first time, the entire heart can be scanned as it actually beats.

The Cine CT scanner may be the only imaging technique that can picture blood flow within the walls of the heart. According to Dr. Martin J. Lipton, one of the developers of the device at the University of California-San Francisco Medical Center, it also provides a remarkable display of the heart walls so that thinning and thickening can be measured. It may enable physicians to detect patients at risk of a heart attack before it occurs. It may also, Lipton believes, reduce the need for cardiac catheterization in some patients.

Scanning Bone for Osteoporosis Prevention.

Osteoporosis—the loss of mineral content and the thinning of bone— affects one of every four women after menopause and can lead to spinal and other fractures. Now, however, a new CT scanning technique that allows measurement of the mineral content of the spine—also developed at the University of California-San Francisco Medical Center— is expected to make a major contribution to osteoporosis management. The new technique requires only slight and relatively inexpensive modification of existing CT machines and already has been used to show the difference in bone-loss rate between healthy postmenopausal women and those with osteoporosis.

Although the decline in estrogen production following menopause is known to contribute to bone loss, and estrogen-replacement therapy has been well documented as effective in preventing the loss, few physicians place all postmenopausal patients on estrogen, because of possible increased risk of uterine cancer. However, if they could routinely determine which women are losing dangerous amounts of bone, they could place only those women on estrogen, because in such cases the benefits of preventing fractures would outweigh the relatively small risk of cancer.

3-D CT Images.

A new computer program, without requiring any additional computer hardware, can manipulate CT scan data into three-dimensional images that simulate the skin, muscle, and bone surfaces that will be encountered during surgery. Developed by Dr. Michael W. Vannier at Washington University Medical Center in St. Louis, the program was first used in more than 100 cases of reconstructive surgery to predict the type of reconstruction needed and allow surgeons to know in advance the exact "spare part" requirements. It also has been used in nearly 150 other patients to evaluate brain tumors, head and neck malignancies, cervical (neck area) spine injuries, pelvic fractures, and deformities of the hands and feet. The program is reported to reduce operative time and improve surgical results.

Chemonucleolysis
Injecting the slipped disk

Of the more than 1 million Americans a year who suffer herniated disks, about 200,000 undergo an operation known as "laminectomy" to correct the problem. Many of these now will be candidates for a newer technique, chemonucleolysis, in which a chemical, chymopapain, is injected to dissolve the cause of pain.

Between each vertebra and the next in the spine is a disk, a circular cushion of connective tissue and cartilage, which serves to absorb the impact of body weight and movement. If the tough outer covering of a disk is severely injured, suddenly or over a period of time, gelatinous material within the disk may pour out much like toothpaste from a tube when the tube develops a small hole. If the material is extruded at a site where it presses on a nerve root, there is pain.

Most often, the disk between the fifth lumbar and first sacral vertebra low in the back is involved and pressure is on the sciatic nerve, which feeds the legs. Pain is felt down the back of the thigh and usually into the foot. Usually the leg pain comes first; it may be followed by numbness and weakness of the leg, then low back pain.

Conservative treatments such as traction and bed rest help most herniated-disk patients. Only a minority have required surgery. Surgery may be carried out under spinal or general anesthesia through a four- or five-inch incision in the back over the herniated-disk area. The disk material may sometimes be removed without removing any part of the vertebra bone, but in other cases a laminectomy, with removal of part of the bony ring, may be needed to get at and remove the material.

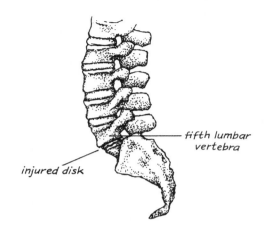

fifth lumbar
vertebra

injured disk

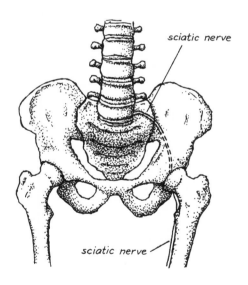

sciatic nerve

sciatic nerve

The Fruit Derivative.

Chymopapain is an enzyme derived from the papaya plant. A sister enzyme, papain, is commonly used as a meat tenderizer. Chymopapain, in experiments going back to the early 1960s, proved capable of dissolving herniated disk material. Late in 1982, after many trials had shown efficacy, the U.S. Food and Drug Administration approved the use of the chemical.

In the chemonucleolysis procedure, the patient goes to sleep under anesthesia. Guided by images on a fluoroscope, the surgeon inserts a needle into the gelatinous core of the disk and injects about a third of a teaspoon of chymopapain. Quickly, the chemical begins breaking down the pulpy tissue, relieving nerve pressure. Blood absorbs the tissue particles, which are then removed in the kidneys, and excreted in urine.

The entire procedure takes forty-five minutes to an hour. Patients usually remain in the hospital for two to five days, and most return to a full work schedule within two months. By contrast, a laminectomy requires ten to fourteen days in the hospital and three to six months for full recovery. Another advantage is that chemonucleolysis may cost about $4,000, about half the cost of a laminectomy.

In FDA-approved studies in which more than 15,000 patients had chymopapain injected into their disks, the chemical proved to be as successful as laminectomy in relieving pain. About 70 percent of patients improved with either therapy.

Safety.

Use of chymopapain is not without drawbacks. It is possible for the chemical to trigger potentially fatal anaphylactic shock, which can lead to collapse of the respiratory and cardiovascular systems. In one clinical trial with more than 1,400 patients, anaphylaxis occurred in only 1 percent of cases, and of these just two patients died. That death rate is no higher than for spinal surgery.

About 1 percent of patients may suffer other reactions, such as rash, itching, headache, dizziness, or nausea. These complications often disappear.

Chemonucleolysis is hardly a procedure for automatic use, any more than is laminectomy. By no means does a backache invariably mean a herniated disk. In the vast majority of cases, the problem is one of muscle strain, not herniation. And it's important to remember that even when herniation occurs, most patients can be helped by conservative measures.

As the FDA points out, doctors should use chymopapain only when conservative measures fail. In many, perhaps even most, such cases, the new procedure may avoid need for surgery. But in very severe, complicated cases, surgery will still be needed. (See also MICROSURGERY.)

Childbirth Chair

Return—with refinements— to vertical delivery

Although most mothers today deliver their babies while lying on their backs, it wasn't always so. Until two centuries ago, vertical delivery was the rule. The ancient Greeks used a birthing chair with a crescent-shaped opening. There were later variations, among them a V-shaped stool used in sixteenth-century Venice.

Horizontal delivery became the custom during the eighteenth century when physicians began to replace midwives for childbirth. Such positioning made it easier for a physician to listen with a stethoscope to the infant heartbeat or to apply forceps when necessary to help bring the child out of the birth canal.

Now the ancient sitting-up practice is being revived—with modern refinements.

The New Chair.

Today's birthing chair—introduced less than half a dozen years ago and now installed in several hundred hospital delivery rooms—is made of high-impact plastic, with molded knee braces and adjustable footrests, and is motorized so it can be raised, lowered, or tilted.

Upright delivery has several potential advantages, to which the modern chair adds others. As some physicians point out, delivery of a baby is most naturally accomplished in a sitting or squatting position. In that position, the force of gravity can augment natural uterine contractions, often reducing the time required for delivery.

With its molded contours, the modern chair supports and takes the pressure off a woman's back and may reduce the pains that often follow conventional delivery. With a place to rest the legs, it's easier to push. There is some indication, too, that risk of blood clots in the legs is reduced.

For some women, there may be psychological benefits. "When you're supine, you feel vulnerable," one mother has observed. "In the chair, you feel more in control." A "plus" for another woman was the ability "to see everything better looking down instead of up."

Not all women who have tried the chair are enthusiastic. At one Miami Beach hospital, 40 percent of women didn't like it—perhaps, however, because obstetricians there were not very positive about the value of the chair and used it only for delivery, not for labor as well.

Some obstetricians object that the chair allows less room to maneuver forceps. But there are many enthusiasts, such as an obstetrician at a major New York City hospital who remarked, "It's embarrassing for us doctors to finally learn what nature told us many years ago. Most of womankind will give birth in the vertical position if there's no interfering physician to make them lie down."

Chorionic-Villi Sampling
For early (first trimester)
prenatal diagnosis

Detection of fetal defects as early as the tenth week of pregnancy has been made possible by a relatively simple new technique that largely may replace amniocentesis (see AMNIOCENTESIS), presently the standard test for such conditions.

Known as "chorionic-villi sampling," the procedure not only can be done earlier than amniocentesis, which cannot be performed until the sixteenth week of pregnancy; it can provide results within twenty-four hours where test results from amniocentesis are not available for two or more weeks. Unlike amniocentesis, too, the new method does not require penetration of the wall of the abdomen or uterus or invasion of the amniotic cavity.

How It Is Done.

Chorionic villi, which provide the fetal cells for analysis in this procedure, are hairlike projections of the membrane surrounding the embryo early in pregnancy. At about ten weeks, the villi begin to disappear as part of that outermost membrane, the chorion, thickens to become the placenta (the "afterbirth").

The sampling, which is optimally done between eight and ten weeks of gestation, is carried out this way. Using ultrasound for guidance (see ULTRASOUND), a physician moves a thin plastic catheter (tube) through the vagina into the uterus and up to the chorionic villi. Approximately thirty milligrams—a tiny fraction of an ounce—of tissue is suctioned out for study. The tissue consists of rapidly dividing fetal cells that can be analyzed immediately for any defects. With amniocentesis, the fetal cells are so dilute in the amniotic fluid that they must be grown for several weeks in culture before there are enough of them for analysis. Analysis of the chorionic-villi sample takes five to ten hours and results may be available the same day, with confirmation within three to five days. The whole procedure is painless, requires no anesthesia, and is performed on an outpatient basis in less than thirty minutes.

First to use the sampling technique in the U.S.—in 1983—has been Michael Reese Hospital and Medical Center in Chicago, following its use in some seventy-two women at the University of Milan in Italy and in several dozen women in England and Scotland.

Actually, in the late 1960s, Swedish and Danish researchers showed that they could get tissue from chorionic villi for prenatal diagnosis, but because amniocentesis was being developed and put into use at about the same time, they did not follow this up.

In 1975, Chinese investigators reported using the technique to determine fetal sex. They did not use ultrasound guidance for the risky job of placing the catheter, nor did they have the facilities to look for fetal abnormalities. According to a World Health Organization report, the Chinese stopped doing the sampling because they could not get medically useful information and because they found that many women were using the sex identification to abort female embryos. The Soviets, too, briefly tried the technique, also using the method only to determine sex.

Risks.

Because the procedure has not been done in enough women, the risks have not yet been well defined. For amniocentesis, there is a small risk (about 0.5 percent) of infection, needle damage to mother or fetus, cramping, or miscarriage. The risks of villi sampling are believed to be much the same.

Costs.

The charges for villi sampling set at the beginning at Michael Reese are about the same as for amniocentesis—about $800. They may eventually be lower, however.

Who May Benefit.

Chorionic-villi sampling, according to a U.S. pioneer in its use, Dr. Eugene Pergament, director of medical genetics at Michael Reese, is appropriate for most women who fit the present criteria for prenatal genetic diagnosis: those over age thirty-five and/or those who are known carriers of certain chromosomal abnormalities or inborn errors of metabolism.

Some women who otherwise fit these criteria may not be suitable for various reasons—among them, pregnancy beyond ten weeks, a history of bleeding during pregnancy, a desire primarily to know the sex of the fetus.

The new technique cannot completely replace amniocentesis. It cannot detect neural-tube defects—serious problems such as openings in the spinal cord or the skull resulting from failure of the neural (nervous system) tube to close properly early in embryonic life. A fetal material called "alpha-fetal protein" flows out of the neural-tube opening into the amniotic fluid, where it can be detected. A new multistage test, recently approved by the Food and Drug Administration, uses a blood test and ultrasound examination at about sixteen weeks to provide indications of a neural-tube defect, which then may be confirmed by amniocentesis.

Future Prospects.

A major immediate advantage of chorionic-villi sampling is that it is done early in pregnancy when, if a woman should choose to abort, it is safer to do so. But some investigators are confident that the technique's most exciting potential is for great improvement in fetal treatment.

Currently, only a few rare biochemical defects can be treated in the uterus. The new technique could change that outlook, spurring research, making it possible to detect defects early, start treatment early, and then check later with amniocentesis to determine whether the treatment is working.

For example, phenylketonuria (PKU), with its serious danger of mental retardation, is now treated by a restricted diet from infancy onward. Starting the pregnant woman on that diet early in pregnancy might improve the baby's chances for a normal life.

Experts note, too, that many other genetic disorders do their damage because the baby lacks some enzyme or other substance, or because of abnormal accumulations of some substances. Early detection of such problems in the fetus might allow them to be overcome with treatment in the uterus that could compensate for deficiency or dangerous excess.

Although much yet remains to be learned about the new technique, its discovery, says Dr. Leon Rosenberg, Yale University's distinguished geneticist, is "a *major* event."

Clock, Personal Rhythm
A computerized bedside aid
for family planning

A battery-powered clock that uses a high-precision thermometer and a built-in microcomputer to signal the onset of a woman's infertile period is being marketed after recent approval by the U.S. Food and Drug Administration. Not much larger than a pocket calculator, the bedside device was developed by scientists in England with the aid of a University of Florida College of Medicine physiologist, Dr. Robert Abrams.

How It Is Used.

Once batteries are inserted and the clock is set, the user routinely takes her oral temperature each morning upon awakening, placing a small probe attached to the clock console under her tongue for about three minutes until the unit emits a beeping sound to indicate it has recorded the temperature. By pressing a button on top of the clock, she can determine whether or not she is in the infertile phase of her cycle. A pattern of six bar lines is displayed on the face of the clock on each day of the infertile period; the display window is blank on fertile days.

The clock's microcomputer is programmed to make adjustments for normal time-of-day variations in body temperature and for menstrual cycles that may be shorter or longer than usual.

Tests.

Early data from clinical studies in England—among middle-class clients of the Natural Family Planning Centres in Birmingham, Liverpool, and Wigan—suggest that the clock is reliable and well accepted by women who previously practiced natural family planning by recording and interpreting charts of their daily temperatures to determine periods of fertility and infertility. Further studies to establish reliability are under way at the University of Florida in Gainesville. In these trials, women are using both the clock and a standard thermometer, keeping a log of temperature readings by the latter method, so researchers, analyzing the results, can compare reliability of the two methods.

Future Prospects.

Developers of the instrument believe it will find acceptance by those who, for religious or other reasons, prefer something other than the birth-control pill or barrier methods of contraception. The computerized system, according to Dr. Abrams, "is designed to take away much of the guesswork in the thermal method of family planning and thus give women greater confidence in this approach." With proper use, he expects it to be as reliable as condoms and diaphragms for family planning.

The clock, made by the P. K. Morgan Company of Kent, England, is expected to sell for about $100.

Collagen-Implant Therapy
To correct facial scars

A thirty-six-year-old woman was one of the first to undergo this new procedure. Beneath the deep scars left on her face by acne, a Duke University Medical Center dermatologist inserted a material through a needle to partially raise the levels of the skin indentations. After three more such treatments, each lasting fifteen minutes, the indentations were virtually gone.

Approved not long ago by the U.S. Food and Drug Administration, Zyderm Collagen Implant, the material that makes the procedure possible, is expected to be of benefit to many. In addition to deep acne scars, other abnormalities—caused by infection, injury, aging, or birth defects—are common. Until now, many people have had to live with unsightly depressed scars. Age-related wrinkles may also respond to the new implants.

Natural Material.

Collagen is a normal body material—the chief structural building block found in cartilage, bone, tendons, ligaments, and body organs. Only recently, however, did researchers at Stanford University and the Collagen Corporation of Palo Alto, California, find a way to adapt collagen from cattle for use as a human tissue replacement.

The highly purified cattle collagen is suspended in a saline solution containing lidocaine, a local anesthetic. After injection, the fluid is absorbed and the collagen, activated by body temperature, becomes a fleshlike material that does not migrate. It serves as a structural framework as the body proceeds to infiltrate it with cells and blood vessels, turning it into a living part of the skin. (Compare CARBON-FIBER IMPLANTS.)

Experience with thousands of patients indicates that best results usually are obtained with two to six treatments administered in a doctor's office at intervals of at least two weeks. Although the anesthetic lidocaine helps lessen the pain of injections, there is a brief aftermath of mild soreness, redness, and swelling at injection sites.

Efficacy.

In one of the first studies, 89 percent of patients, most of whom had acne scars, showed significant improvement, with maximum benefit achieved after three to five treatments. Results were similar in large-scale trials by fourteen California plastic surgeons and dermatologists under the auspices of the Food and Drug Administration.

At Stanford, Dr. Ernest Kaplan has found that many wrinkles respond well and that the implants can alter the look of bad burn scars and improve the appearance of children who have had surgery for cleft lip.

More recently, a two-year study by Dr. Sidney Hurwitz, associate clinical professor of pediatrics and dermatology at Yale University School of Medicine, found two-thirds of 109 adolescents and adults treated for acne scars showing 80 to 90 percent improvement. Also, forty-nine patients with other types of scars, including superficial chickenpox and postsurgical scars, improved 60 to 70 percent.

Before collagen implants are used, a patient should be tested for possible allergy to the material. How long results will last is not yet known definitively. Follow-ups of some of the earliest treated patients for up to eighteen months have shown 30 percent maintaining all correction during that time while 70 percent have required minor supplemental treatment at intervals of six to eighteen months.

Latest estimates are that more than 3,000 plastic surgeons, dermatologists, and head and neck specialists nationwide are using the collagen-implant procedure.

Coronary Bypass Surgery
For coronary artery blockage

Coronary bypass surgery has become the most common open heart operation, with more than 150,000 of the procedures being performed yearly in the United States, at a cost per operation of $15,000 to $20,000, not including professional fees.

Background of the Operation.

As performed today, the operation builds on many past efforts. Coronary artery disease—in which fatty deposits accumulate on the inner walls of one or more of the small coronary arteries that do the vital job of nourishing the heart muscle itself—can lead to anginal chest pain and to heart attacks. As far back as 1929, an effort to overcome advanced coronary artery disease was made by a distinguished surgeon, Dr. Claude Beck, who tried irritating the heart with talc and scraping procedures in the hope that the irritation might lead to formation of new blood channels to increase flow to the heart muscle. But the amount of increased blood flow, if any, could not be determined.

In the early 1940s, a procedure for using the internal mammary artery to supply more blood to the ailing heart was devised by Dr. Arthur Vineberg of the Royal Victoria Hospital in Montreal. The internal mammary runs down behind the chest wall, providing blood for certain chest areas—but because other arteries also supply the same areas, the internal mammary could be spared.

Vineberg's plan was to free the artery from its chest-wall attachment, bring it over to the heart muscle, and place it in a small tunnel made in the heart muscle. Hopefully, there, the internal mammary would give rise to small collateral vessels that would hook up to unblocked branch coronary vessels, providing blood for the heart muscle through a new network.

Over a period of many years, Vineberg was able to show, in experimental animals and then in very sick human patients, that this sometimes does happen. But as long as six months may be needed before the new network is established and the patient begins to benefit.

Other techniques were tried, including opening a blocked segment of a coronary artery and reaming out the clogging material. But relatively few patients had obstructions limited to short lengths of artery.

Then in the late 1960s came the idea for saphenous-vein grafting, the technique now in wide use.

The saphenous, a large vein running the length of each leg, returns some of the blood from the leg to the heart. Because other veins can take over its function, it can be spared—and in fact is the vein often removed in varicose-vein surgery.

After being removed from a leg and tested to make certain it is in good condition, the vein is cut to suitable length and used as a bypass. To understand the bypass process, it's helpful to realize that the aorta is the major trunk artery emerging from the heart; other arteries branch off from the aorta to supply all parts of the body, and it is from the aorta that the coronary arteries, which feed the heart muscle, also branch off. When one end of the length of saphenous vein is attached to the aorta and the other end is attached beyond the obstructed area in a coronary artery, fresh blood from the aorta is carried around the obstruction, bypassing the block, to nourish the heart muscle. Several such bypasses can be made when more than one coronary artery is affected.

Another bypassing technique employs the internal mammary artery—but unlike the Vineberg procedure, the internal mammary is attached in the same way as a saphenous vein. In some cases both the saphenous vein and internal mammary artery may be used.

How the Operation Is Done.

Typically, before the surgery, catheterization with X-ray movies is carried out (see CARDIAC CATHETERIZATION) to show where a coronary artery obstruction is located and to allow the surgeon to plan ahead.

In the operating room, the surgeon is assisted by a sizable team that may include assisting surgeons, anesthesiologists, nurses, a heart-lung-machine technician, and a technician for the patient-monitoring electronic equipment used throughout the procedure.

Once the patient is anesthetized, an incision is made in a leg to remove a length of saphenous vein, and at the same time the patient's chest is opened. After the vein has been tested and prepared, the patient is placed on the heart-lung machine, which temporarily takes over the work of both heart and lungs, removing carbon dioxide from the blood, adding oxygen, and pumping the blood through the body. Electrodes now may be briefly touched to the heart to stop it so the surgeon has a quiet field in which to work. The vein is then sewn in place with suture (stitching) material as fine as a human hair.

When bypassing is completed—one or several, if necessary, are carried out in the same way—the patient is disconnected from the heart-lung machine and instruments measure the improved blood flow to the heart muscle through the bypass or bypasses.

The total procedure, including closure of the patient's chest, may take three to six hours or even more.

Afterward, the patient is monitored continuously for several days in the intensive-care unit to make certain that complications do not occur—and that if they do, they can be dealt with immediately. Length of hospital stay can vary, being as short as ten days or even less in some cases.

The operation is, of course, a major one with risks. The risk of death may be less than 2 percent, depending on the skill of the surgeon and on the individual patient's general condition. During the operation or immediately afterward, 10 to 15 percent of patients have experienced a heart attack, not necessarily fatal. There is also the possibility of infection, and a very few patients may experience a lung, kidney, brain, or liver complication.

The CASS.

The CASS (Coronary Artery Surgery Study), the first major comparative study of patients undergoing the operation and similar patients treated only with medication, shows, as reported late in 1983, that the surgical patients experienced a significantly improved "quality of life" by most—but not all—yardsticks. They had less chest pain and fewer activity limitations, needed less medication, and performed better in exercise stress tests. But the systematic study of 780 patients for an average of 5.5 years found no significant differences in employment and recreational status.

CASS was organized by the National Institutes of Health as a major collaborative effort involving fifteen medical centers in the U.S. and Canada. The study drew from a registry of 24,959 consecutive patients who underwent coronary artery X-ray examinations between 1974 and 1979. From that patient pool, 780 patients with 70 percent or more blockage of at least one coronary artery were chosen for the study, and 390 were assigned randomly to each group for either medical or surgical therapy.

Forty-one of the 390 surgery-group patients refused the surgery initially, but ten ultimately underwent it. Also, 100 of the 390 originally placed on medication were later recommended by their physicians to have the surgery. During the course of the study, sixty-five patients died —twenty-nine in the surgery group and thirty-six in the medical group.

The following other findings were reported by Dr. William J. Rogers of the University of Alabama-Birmingham, and other CASS investigators:

· A "substantially greater" number of the surgical patients were free of chest pain at one-, three-, and five-year intervals.
· There were "highly significant" differences in activity levels between the two groups, with more surgery patients reporting no limitations on activity.
· Both groups increased the time they could spend exercising on a treadmill, but the surgical group increased "much more dramatically."
· The percentage of patients working, full- or part-time, decreased slightly in both groups, and no difference in ultimate employment status was noted.
· There were no significant differences in the groups' recreational status, either at the start or at the end of the study.
· Drug treatment with beta blockers declined "dramatically" in the surgical group while it increased in the medical group, and use of long-lasting nitrate-type drugs also dropped among surgery patients while remaining constant in the medical group.
· Few among the 41 percent who were cigarette smokers in the medical group and 39 percent in the surgical group stopped smoking during the course of the study. No changes were noted in other heart-disease risk factors such as high blood pressure, high cholesterol, and overweight in either group.

The CASS researchers conclude from the study that for patients without symptoms after a heart attack or who have chronic stable anginal chest pain of mild to moderate severity, surgery, "when com-

pared to medical management, offers no advantages in terms of pro-
longing life.

"Surgery, however, may offer advantages in terms of improving
the quality of life through reduction in chest pain, improvement in both
subjective and objective descriptors of activity, and reduction in the
need for daily drug therapy. . . . However, neither medical nor surgical
therapy appears to offer a significant advantage in helping patients
return to work or in modifying recreational status."

In view of the findings, the CASS team observes, patients who have
no symptoms after a heart attack or who have mild chronic chest pain
should be treated medically at first to prevent or control symptoms.
"Should the symptoms worsen or should dissatisfaction arise with limi-
tation on lifestyle imposed by symptoms or by need for drug therapy,
surgery can be performed electively with the reasonable expectation
that it will improve quality of life."

Risk Factors After Surgery.

Almost at the same time that the CASS results were being reported, the
results of another study were published. These strongly suggest that
patients who undergo bypass must control their risk factors for heart
disease afterward or the grafts may close down, again placing them at
risk for heart attack.

A team of pathologists examined at autopsy the forty-four bypass
grafts of twenty-four patients who had undergone surgery from one to
fourteen years before death. The scientists—Dr. James Atkinson of
Vanderbilt University in Nashville, and others from Vanderbilt's Department of Pathology and the Armed Forces Institute of Pathology in
Washington, D.C.—correlated the atherosclerosis and other lesions
they found in the grafts with some of the major risk factors for coronary
artery disease: high blood pressure, high blood cholesterol, and diabetes.

The researchers found three types of lesions. Twelve grafts with
the first type—total closing of the graft by fibrous tissue—were eliminated from the study because these probably occurred due to a clot soon
after surgery.

Eleven grafts had the second type of lesion—atherosclerosis similar to that found in native coronary arteries. The atherosclerosis totally
blocked five of the grafts. Fifty-five percent of the patients who had
atherosclerosis in their grafts had diabetes, 36 percent had high blood
pressure, and 36 percent had high cholesterol levels in their blood.

In twenty-one grafts, the third type of lesion was found—an increase in smooth muscle and fibrous tissue in the inner layer of the vein, causing narrowing and thus reducing blood flow. Fifty-seven percent of patients with these lesions had high blood pressure, 29 percent had diabetes, and 9 percent had elevated cholesterol levels.

The results suggest that what happens to coronary bypass grafts may depend strongly on whether patients control their blood pressure, diabetes, and cholesterol levels.

"If you have bypass surgery, you are certainly not immune from having further problems," reports Dr. Atkinson. "The bottom line is that some of the risk factors that predispose an individual to clogging of the coronary arteries also seem to predispose to clogging of bypass grafts."

In fact, several studies have shown that atherosclerosis progresses more rapidly in grafts than in native coronary arteries. "It may take a person 50 years to build up enough atherosclerotic plaque to clog the coronary arteries," observes Dr. Atkinson, "whereas it may take only three or four years to clog bypass grafts. Probably the best theory is that the veins we use as grafts are more susceptible to injury which is probably accelerated in the presence of risk factors."

Cryosurgery
Trading scalpel for icy probe

The use of ice or snow or some form of refrigerant for medical therapy goes back as far as the ancient Greeks. The father of medicine, Hippocrates, recommended ice for bleeding, pain relief, swellings, and gouty joints. Baron Larrey, Napoleon's army surgeon, reported that cold and frost had an anesthetic effect during amputations.

In modern medicine, cold has been used by dermatologists for the treatment of many skin disorders—among them, acne scars, keloids, warts, and skin tags. The latter are little outgrowths from the skin, benign but sometimes unsightly when they occur on the eyelids and the neck. A single thirty-second freezing with liquid nitrogen of an eyelid skin tag is often followed within seven days by disappearance of the tag.

Cryosurgery—surgery in which decreased temperature is used—has also been effective in the treatment of skin cancers and some other malignancies.

Skin Cancer.

This is the most common of all human malignancies, and many ways have been developed for its treatment: surgical removal; curettage with electrodesiccation (surgical scraping and destruction of tissue with short, high-frequency electric sparks); radiation; and Mohs's chemosurgery, a technique in which tissue samples are removed in thin slices and checked for cancer under a microscope until no more malignant cells are found.

Cryosurgery offers another means of treatment; and according to a most recent report, freezing of skin cancers can produce a high rate of cure—between 96 and 97 percent, based on the findings of an eighteen-year study involving more than 3,000 skin-cancer patients.

In addition to its high cure rate, cryosurgery is an office procedure featuring simplicity, superior cosmetic end results, and moderate cost, reported Dr. Setrag A. Zacarian of the Yale University Medical School faculty.

The procedure involves the use of a liquid-nitrogen-filled probe or an open spray of the refrigerant. When applied to the skin, the probe emits liquid nitrogen that freezes and destroys a skin cancer. The depth and width of the freezing are determined on the basis of the tumor's location and size.

After the cancer is removed, there is some swelling and some oozing of fluid from the cryosurgical site and eventual sloughing off of dead skin. Usually the freezing process removes pigment from the area permanently, which means that the site of the skin cancer will be lighter in color.

From his study of 3,022 patients and a review of other studies, Dr. Zacarian recommends that cryosurgery be used for skin cancer that is nodular or ulcerated, has a well-defined border, and is on top of bone or cartilage or on the eyelid or nose.

Of the 3,022 patients treated in the Zacarian series, 3.6 percent experienced recurrences. Nearly half of these appeared during the first year after cryosurgery, and nearly another half appeared during the second and third years. All skin-cancer patients should therefore be followed for five years, recommends Dr. Zacarian, so any recurrence can be detected and retreated.

Other Cancers.

For the past twenty years, a group of pioneering Buffalo surgeons has been showing skeptical colleagues that in certain cases of oral cancer the scalpel can be safely traded for the cryoprobe.

The efficacy of cryosurgery in such conditions is now being investigated by researchers around the world, who—like Dr. Andrew A. Gage and his associates at the State University of New York-Buffalo School of Medicine—are continuing to identify appropriate freezing agents as well as temperatures and number of freeze-thaw cycles that must be achieved in order to kill different types of malignant tissues.

Although it has been known that cryosurgery can be safely used to treat a variety of inflammatory lesions, benign tumors, and precancerous conditions of the oral cavity, Gage's current research suggests it can be an appropriate therapy for certain malignant oral conditions.

Gage's criteria are stringent: Cancerous growths should be in the small-to-moderate range, preferably adjacent to bone (which limits spread of the disease), and with heart, lung, or blood-clotting problems in the patients as indications for cryosurgical rather than excisional removal.

A five-year study of eighty-two oral-cancer patients who fit the criteria showed a 73 percent survival rate after three years and 56 percent survival at five years. Deaths after the third year, however, were nearly always due to conditions other than the cancer.

Gage used a cryoprobe containing liquid nitrogen to achieve temperatures of $-40°$ C or colder in all malignant tissue. Biopsies (removal of tissue samples for microscopic examination) a few weeks after treatment revealed any missed sections, which then could be refrozen and allowed to heal.

The study found that results were most satisfactory when the cancer overlay bone, which limited its penetration. Less satisfactory results were obtained when the malignancy occurred on the floor of the mouth or on the back third of the tongue. The survival rate, Gage notes, is comparable to that for surgical excision—and in those patients in whom bone was adjacent to the cancerous tissue, freezing did not damage the bone to the extent that surgical excision would have.

Conservation of the bone, reduced operative mortality, more-quickly regained function, and the suitability of cryosurgery for patients who would be at high risk with excisional surgery—all make the technique useful for many patients. And for those with extensive oral malignancies for which neither cryosurgery nor conventional technique can be curative, reports Dr. Gage, freezing and sloughing of the diseased tissue can reduce pain as well as rid patients of the bulkiness of tumors that interfere with talking.

Much of the Buffalo cryosurgery research has dealt with malignancies that could be treated equally effectively with excisional surgery. But Gage and his co-workers have found that cryosurgery may be the only effective way to deal with liver cancers. The liver, Gage points out, does not lend itself well to control of hemorrhage that occurs in excisional surgery, nor are most liver tumors suitable for surgical removal.

The Buffalo surgeons have begun to use cryosurgery on patients with liver tumors, but long-term benefits cannot yet be evaluated.

Another area in which the Buffalo workers are demonstrating the value of cryosurgery is in removal of pilonidal cysts.

A cyst is a liquid-containing sac or capsule. A pilonidal cyst, which may be present in as many as one of every twenty people, is located in the middle of the lower back just above the cheeks of the buttocks. It is present at birth and is believed to result from an infolding of skin in which hair continues to grow. It may remain entirely symptomless and unnoticed until adolescence or adulthood, when, as the result of irritation and entrance of microorganisms, it may become a small lump exuding a yellowish discharge. Sometimes a cyst may become severely abscessed and require lancing to permit escape of pus. After that, the cyst can be removed surgically. The incision may be 2 to 4 inches long and up to an inch wide, and all the tissue beneath the skin, including the cyst, is removed.

The Buffalo workers report having been able to reduce recurrence of the cysts from 30 percent to 6 percent by freezing an area 3 to 5 millimeters with liquid nitrogen after a small incision has been made to allow entry of the cryoprobe.

In cryosurgery, the freezing rate, coolest temperature produced, length of freeze, and thawing rate are all important factors. If tissue is not adequately frozen so it is in fact killed, it will return. But if the tissue is overfrozen, unnecessary damage may be done to nearby areas.

In animal research, the Buffalo workers are seeking to determine optimal combinations of factors that may make cryosurgery still more effective.

Customized Support
For the severely disabled

An easily assembled and inexpensive means of sitting upright for comfort and for more independent functioning is designed to help many severely disabled people, including those with cerebral palsy, spina bifida, spinal-cord tumors, osteogenesis imperfecta, muscular dystrophy, and others. Developed jointly by the University of Alabama Center for Developmental and Learning Disorders and the Southern Research Institute of Birmingham, the support can be fabricated to individual need by a therapist or orthotist using a small portable vacuum pump and a kit of materials consisting of a premeasured amount of adhesive, paint, and an elastic bag filled with polystyrene foam pellets.

Based on testing done at the Arkansas Orthotic Center in Little Rock, Rancho Los Amigos Rehabilitation Hospital in Los Angeles, two county school systems in Alabama, and elsewhere, the support, according to Dr. Joan Bergman of the University of Alabama, should enable "untold thousands of severely and multiply disabled individuals around the world [to] undertake on a routine basis such normal functions as sitting at a dinner table or at a workdesk."

Adds Dr. Gary Edwards, also of the University of Alabama: "People who have been confined to beds or wheelchairs for years can now go to school, to ballgames, and undertake many other activities and thus be seen by their families and others as more normal and able to be integrated into more independent living situations."

The Customizing.

The support can be molded into a variety of seating bases, including children's wooden chairs, wheelchairs, corner chairs, travel chairs, Hogg chairs, high chairs, and infant seats.

The customizing begins when a therapist pours the premeasured adhesive into the elastic bag filled with polystyrene foam pellets. The therapist kneads the mixture and forms the bag to the general shape of the patient with the aid of a vacuum pump. The disabled person is then positioned and the bag is shaped as desired for maximum support. After the material has hardened, the elastic is peeled off and the shape is refined and smoothed as needed. Holes can be made for toileting or for placement of support and restraining devices. Several coats of latex paint are applied, leaving a lightweight but durable, washable, and urine-resistant seat.

The seat conforms perfectly to the individual's body and thus is not likely to cause pressure sores. Moreover, while providing total support through close contact, the seat is not hot, thanks to the pebbly texture of its surface.

The kit is being marketed by a newly formed company, DESEMO, Inc., of Savannah, Georgia, under license from the university and Southern Research. Cost ranges from about $100 to $200, depending on size.

Other Uses.

At the University of Alabama Comprehensive Cancer Center, radiation therapists are currently using the custom-molded supports to allow patients to be precisely and repeatedly positioned. They are reported to be especially valuable for positioning children and for radiation of head and neck tumors in adults.

Cyclosporine
Transforming transplant medicine
(See also TRANSPLANTS)

In the last several years, a drug with humble beginnings—derived from a Norwegian soil fungus and intended to be a potent antibiotic but proving not to be—has been revolutionizing virtually all types of organ transplantation. The drug, cyclosporine, may also be used to treat a variety of serious autoimmune diseases and some major parasitic infections of worldwide importance.

Its remarkable effects on organ transplantation were highlighted in 1983 at congressional hearings before the House Committee on Science and Technology. In testimony before the committee, Dr. Thomas Starzl of the University of Pittsburgh, long a pioneer in efforts to achieve successful liver transplantation, reported that after almost twenty years of near-frustration, cyclosporine now is producing 65 to 70 percent liver-graft survival during the crucial first year—"results so encouraging that at the University of Pittsburgh liver transplantation is now considered a service as opposed to an experimental procedure."

Dr. G. Melville Williams of The Johns Hopkins University, testifying about kidney transplants, said, "Four centers in this country have had experience with the new immunosuppressive drug cyclosporine and all of these investigators agree that many of the practices we have applied to increase graft survival may prove to be obsolete." Indeed, 80 to 90 percent of all cadaver kidney transplants succeed with use of the drug, whereas without it only about 50 percent have done so.

At the University of Minnesota, Dr. John S. Najarian has found that cyclosporine kidney-transplant patients have only one-third as many episodes of threatened rejection, half as many infections, and the mean cost per transplant has been cut by $9,000.

At Stanford University, reported Dr. Norman Shumway, not a single instance of rejection of a transplanted heart has occurred since use of the drug began in December 1980 on an experimental basis.

The Remarkable Characteristics.

The unusual properties of cyclosporine were discovered by Dr. Jean Borel, a Swiss researcher at the Sandoz Corporation, a pharmaceutical firm in Basel.

The company, like many others in the drug industry, makes it a practice to ask employees on trips abroad to bring back handfuls of dirt. The reason: Such valuable drugs as the antibiotic streptomycin often come from microbes living in various types of soil.

In 1970, Sandoz microbiologists, screening soils collected in Wisconsin and Norway, discovered new strains of fungi that produced the substance now known as cyclosporine. When tested for antibiotic (bacteria-killing) activity, it proved to be of little value. But carrying on other tests, Dr. Borel was greatly surprised to find that the substance had a remarkable effect on the immune reaction that is responsible for rejecting foreign tissues such as transplants. Even as it suppressed the part of the immune system responsible for rejection, it left intact the part of the system that acts to prevent infection, a leading cause of death among transplant patients.

Although Sandoz had recently set up new goals for its research efforts—goals that did not include immunology research—Borel convinced the management to allow him to continue to develop the drug.

Trials.

In 1977, British investigators at Cambridge University carried out a trial of cyclosporine in rats receiving heart transplants. Its success in preventing transplant rejection was striking. Trials then proceeded in other animals and with various kinds of transplants, including kidney, liver, skin, pancreas, small bowel, and muscle—again with impressive results.

Still other trials with animals, including rhesus monkeys, demonstrated that, unlike many other immune-system-suppressing drugs, cyclosporine did not kill bone-marrow cells—cells from which all blood cells are derived and whose loss makes patients susceptible to infections and increases their risk for cancer.

Trials in human patients followed. In an eight-center European study, 73 percent of 117 patients receiving cadaver kidneys and treated with cyclosporine still had their grafts after one year, compared with 53 percent of 115 other patients given other drug treatment to prevent rejection. A multicenter trial in Canada yielded even better results: 83.5 percent survival among cyclosporine-treated kidney-transplant patients.

At the University of Minnesota, investigators found that cyclosporine-treated patients experienced one-third as many rejection episodes and half the number of infections of other kidney-transplant patients.

There have been gratifying results as well in patients receiving liver and heart transplants, as noted above in the congressional testimony of Drs. Starzl and Shumway. At Stanford, too, the drug has been used in eleven recipients of heart-lung transplants, eight of whom are alive and leading normal lives.

Side Effects.

Few if any drugs are entirely free of undesirable effects, and cyclosporine is certainly no exception. A major concern is that in about 10 to 15 percent of patients, it seems to affect the kidneys. These patients have increased levels of creatinine in their blood, which is an indirect indication of abnormal kidney function. What part of the kidney is affected and how are unknown. Reportedly, some patients in England have been taking cyclosporine for as long as five years and their creatinine levels have been consistently elevated, yet their kidneys seem to be working normally.

Other possible side effects include increased hair growth, overgrowth of the gums, increased sensitivity to heat and cold, transient fatigue, and tingling sensations about the lips.

Additional Uses.

Outside the field of transplantation, the drug may have many other potentially important uses, according to preliminary studies.

One whole area could be in the treatment of many diseases known or suspected to be autoimmune diseases—brought about when the body's immune system mistakenly attacks the body's own tissues.

Among these diseases are uveitis, myasthenia gravis, multiple sclerosis, systemic lupus erythematosus, Hashimoto's thyroiditis, type 1 diabetes, and rheumatoid arthritis.

Uveitis, an eye inflammation, often results from an autoimmune reaction and, when severe, may lead to blindness within three years if not treated successfully with immune-suppressing drugs. At the National Eye Institute, after successfully using cyclosporine against uveitis in animal studies, Dr. Robert Nussenblatt undertook a pilot study in human patients, limiting the study to only those who could not tolerate or were failing to respond to conventional drugs. Of thirty-one patients who have taken cyclosporine in the pilot study, all appear to be doing well, with improvement in eye inflammation, no further deterioration of vision, and in some cases actual improvement in vision.

At University Hospital in London, Ontario, Dr. Calvin Stiller and other investigators are cautiously optimistic about other possibilities for the drug. After finding that it prevents diabetes in rats otherwise genetically prone to the disease, they have given cyclosporine to more than twenty patients with newly diagnosed type 1, or juvenile, diabetes, which is suspected of being an autoimmune disease. Of those treated within the first six weeks after diagnosis, all were able to reduce their insulin dose by at least half, and three were able to stop taking insulin entirely.

Stiller and his colleagues are starting pilot studies of the drug for other autoimmune diseases including multiple sclerosis, inflammatory bowel disease, and the kidney disease glomerulonephritis.

Among the newest findings about cyclosporine, and apparently unrelated to its effects on the immune system, are its antiparasitic effects. In experimental animals, the drug has been effective against schistosomiasis and malaria, two diseases believed to affect about a billion people throughout the world.

Schistosomiasis, which is caused by blood flukes, is endemic in Africa, the Middle East, Cyprus, some West Indies islands, the northern part of South America, Japan, central and south China, and the Philippines, and occurs in some Puerto Ricans living in the United States. Infection develops from bathing or other contact with swimming parasites that penetrate the skin. A skin outbreak is followed by fever, hives, possibly bladder inflammation, or chronic dysentery.

At The Johns Hopkins University School of Medicine, Dr. Ernest Bueding found to his surprise that cyclosporine kills schistosomes, the flukes or worms that cause the disease. He and his colleagues went on to discover that the drug acts against an enzyme in the worm needed to degrade blood hemoglobin on which the fluke feeds. The drug is effective against all species of schistosomes, including those most resistant to conventional drugs. And in testing cyclosporine derivatives, the Johns Hopkins workers have found several that do not suppress the immune system and yet are effective against schisotomiasis.

Cyclosporine also has cured as well as prevented malaria in animals. In the animal studies, it proved as effective against malaria strains resistant to the antimalarial drug chloroquine as against those sensitive to the latter. The suspicion, yet to be confirmed, is that here, too, cyclosporine may work against an enzyme the parasites use to break down blood hemoglobin. And just as with schistosomes, derivatives of cyclosporine that have no effect on the immune system kill malaria parasites.

The biggest problem with cyclosporine research now, as a report in the journal *Science* observed, "is to keep things under control. The drug seems so amazing and its possibilities are so great that many researchers can hardly wait to get their hands on it."

Devices for the Disabled

In Seattle not long ago, at the University of Washington Hospital's Rehabilitation Medicine Division, a forty-year-old woman, paralyzed from the neck down by an accident and no longer able to speak, became one of the first to use a powered wheelchair controlled by a computer that also lets her "talk."

She wears a light detector fitted to her headband and points the detector to a display board mounted on her wheelchair. The board includes letters of the alphabet, numbers, and key phrases (such as "Don't bother me now" and "I'm hungry"). The board also has wheelchair speed and direction controls. When the light detector is pointed at a letter, number, or other square on the display board, the computer types the message on a small screen. The message can also be printed on ticker tape or spoken by the computer.

The system, although advanced, is still slow, but it makes the woman an independent communicator. Previously, she was dependent on a chalkboard and a partner. The partner would point to letters of the alphabet in sequence on the board, she would nod when the desired letter was selected, and in this way she and her partner composed messages letter by letter.

According to some estimates, there may be as many as 35 million Americans who are handicapped in one way or another. For many, such simple tasks as eating a meal, dialing a telephone, or saying hello may be impossible without help from others. Disabilities take a toll on victims who want more independence and on families who often must cope with the emotional strains and demands of caring for them. Increasingly, engineers and medical researchers are working to lessen that burden, adopting some of today's most sophisticated technologies to create aids for the handicapped.

Here is a sampling of some of the many newer developments.

Wheelchairs—Remarkable and Varied.

Recently, the National Aeronautics and Space Administration reported the development of a voice-controlled wheelchair and manipulator for the paralyzed and other severely handicapped. The system—based on robot and other technology devised for space programs—has at its heart a voice-command analyzer and a minicomputer. After a patient has repeated a command several times into a microphone connected to the computer, the analyzer thereafter recognizes commands only in the particular speech pattern of that patient. It translates the commands into electrical signals that activate appropriate motors, which in turn cause the chair to move as desired and the manipulator arm to pick up objects, open doors, turn knobs, and perform other functions. The system responds to one-word commands such as "Go," "Stop," "Right," "Left," "Backward," "Forward."

Another "talking wheelchair" system, devised at Stanford University Medical Center, uses technology developed for advanced aircraft communications. Mounted on the wheelchair are a word processor, a video screen, a voice synthesizer, and a computer program that tells the synthesizer how to produce intelligible sounds in response to user commands. The patient, depending on his or her disability, can use a simple switch, stick, or keyboard to produce message units. The completed message appears on the video screen, and the patient then activates the speech synthesizer, which speaks the message. The tone is somewhat mechanical, and continuing research is aimed at development of a more natural tone, but with the keyboard an experienced user can construct messages as rapidly as thirty words a minute.

Still another kind of wheelchair recently reported by NASA is actually a wheelless chair—an adaptation for crippled children of a walking vehicle devised for possible use as an unmanned instrument carrier for exploring the moon's surface. The eight-legged vehicle moves with stepping motions and can clear curbs, climb stairs, and traverse rough or sandy terrain that would thwart an ordinary wheelchair. Its sole control is an upright stick, which can be modified with a chin cup for children unable to use arms or legs and needing to steer with their heads. The chair, which has two speeds forward and in reverse, can be guided by simply pushing the stick in the desired direction.

For Paralyzed Drivers.

With the aid of federal funding, Nelson and Johnson Engineering of Boulder, Colorado, has employed the technology used in NASA's moon buggy, with which astronauts toured the lunar landscape, to convert an ordinary van. Steering, accelerating, and braking mechanisms are all in a single "joy stick" mounted to the right of the driver. Although some driving systems for the handicapped already exist, the new one is for the severely handicapped with little use of their bodies. The joy stick can be manipulated readily with two fingers.

Another development, from the University of Michigan, is designed to eliminate the need for a paralyzed driver to get in and out of a wheelchair. Instead, a special hydraulic suspension system lifts the driver into the car.

Communication Aids.

At the Harvard-MIT Rehabilitation Engineering Center, communication aids for the nonverbal, the severely motor-handicapped, and the blind have been developed in several projects.

A Universal Communicator (UNICOM) is intended for people suffering major muscle paralysis including loss of speech. The most common version of UNICOM uses a TV screen on which a cursor constantly circulates, waiting for the user to select a letter, number, or word for formulating a message. Depending on the user's ability, the machine can be activated by a knee, an eye movement, a head stick, or a sip-and-puff device. Those with greater motor dexterity can move the cursor themselves or use the machine like a typewriter.

Another system is putting blind people to work as telephone operators. A microcomputer connected to the standard telephone switchboard converts signals that ordinarily operate the visual alphanumeric display and illuminate buttons into the equivalent messages by means of twelve braille English letters. The system has also been combined with an alternate approach using synthetic (artificial) speech and is now being produced commercially.

Recently, the UNICOM system has been adapted to the needs of two spinal-cord patients, who activate the keys by blowing into a series of tubes. Both patients continue to use UNICOM for conversational exchange and as a means of taking correspondence courses.

Crawling Aid.

Learning to crawl—the first step toward mobility—is impossible for some brain-injured children because of the problem of weight bearing and the friction caused by gravity. However, an effective new crawling aid now is in use as part of an overall rehabilitation program at the Institutes for the Achievement of Human Potential in Philadelphia.

Originally conceived for frictionless systems designed to simulate the motions of satellites in space, the device is a rounded plywood frame large enough to support a child's body, leaving arms and legs free to move. On its underside are three aluminum disks through which air is pumped to create an air-bearing surface with less friction than a film of oil. The upper side contains the connection to the air supply and a pair of straps that restrain the child and cause the device to move with him.

The intent is to re-create the normal nerve connections between brain and muscles—connections impaired by the brain injury. When the child makes a movement that causes him to slide forward on the frictionless surface, he gets a positive mental feedback and is encouraged to repeat the movement. With repetitive use of the device, he develops his arm and leg muscles as well as coordination.

In one test case, for example, a four-year-old boy who had needed sixteen hours to crawl just twelve inches was able, after a month on the device, to crawl sixteen feet in twenty-five minutes without the device. Children are given alternating therapy, with and without the crawling aid, until eventually the device is no longer needed.

Sight Switch.

A switch that is actuated just by movement of the eyes was originally developed for NASA as an aid to astronauts in situations where high G-forces might make them unable to move arms or legs. It's an ingenious device in which light sources, mounted on each side of a pair of eyeglasses, bounce light into the wearer's eyes and detect the difference between the reflection from the whites and from the darker pupils. Whenever the pupils move across the light beam, the reduced reflection activates an electric switch.

The switch can be employed in many ways by patients unable to move hands or legs. For example, it can operate a machine to turn book pages and to switch room lights, thermostat, and TV set on and off. With modifications, it is expected to find use in operating industrial machines, electric typewriter keyboards, and other machines.

Bypassing Damaged Spinal Cords.

More than 200,000 Americans are paraplegic because of spinal-cord injuries. Each year there are 10,000 to 15,000 new victims as the result of motor-vehicle, sports, and other accidents. What is especially tragic is that the average age of the spinal-injury patient is only nineteen, and although the victim is very likely to survive, it will be without ability to function.

Paraplegics are unable to walk because their cord injuries prevent necessary messages from going from the brain to the legs. There is no feeling in the legs, but the muscles aren't damaged—although they may be atrophied or wasted from lack of use.

Dr. Kate Kohn of Michael Reese Hospital and Medical Center, Chicago, and Dr. Daniel Graupe, Illinois Institute of Technology professor of electrical engineering, have devised an electrical system that promises a practical approach to easing the immobility of paraplegics and giving them control over their movements. Dr. Graupe adapted the system from one he helped the U.S. Navy develop to detect and analyze sonar signals from enemy submarines. In the new experimental system, similarly weak signals, from unparalyzed muscles above the spinal-cord injury, are detected by two electrodes. The signals are sent to a computer, which analyzes them. The computer then bypasses the spinal lesion and sends commands to an electrostimulator within electrodes in specific leg-muscle groups, producing movement.

Of the first half-dozen patients to use the system, three have walked, if somewhat haltingly, for up to twenty-five minutes. It's expected that with further research and refinements, the system could get 35 to 50 percent of lower-thoracic spine-injury paraplegics back on their feet. For the system to be useful, the spinal-cord break must lie somewhere within a foot-long span in the middle back. If the break is higher, upper body muscles will be too weak; if lower, leg braces will be more effective.

Although the Chicago investigators doubt that the system could help anyone with a chronic disease such as multiple sclerosis or muscular dystrophy because there cannot be permanent damage to muscles, they are hopeful of adapting it to stroke victims paralyzed on one side (hemiplegics), using undamaged shoulder muscles to permit lower arm movement.

At Case Western Reserve University in Cleveland, Dr. Hunter Peckham and his colleagues are seeking to help quadriplegics. Most quadriplegics, although paralyzed in all four limbs, have partial control of their shoulders and upper arms. The Cleveland researchers insert tiny electrodes into key muscles of the hand. By using shoulder or neck movements to control electrical impulses from a computerized transmitter, patients can pinch and grasp well enough to feed themselves, use a telephone, and comb their hair. Before the system can become practical, however, it must be made totally implantable and portable so there is no need to wear electrodes taped to the body and to be hooked up to the transmitter each day.

A system that may prove to be even more dramatic is an electronic prosthesis that hopefully will allow patients to walk. Being developed at Wright State University in Dayton, Ohio, by Dr. Jerrold Petrofsky and Roger Lazglar, it consists of groups of electrodes strapped to hip, knee, and ankle joints, and connected to a microcomputer programmed to transmit a complex series of electrical signals to the muscles.

In studies with dozens of paraplegics, the system has allowed exercising the legs by weight lifting and has produced marked increases in lifting strength. The system also permits patients to ride stationary bicycles. Equipped with the system, one coed, paralyzed in a car accident, rides a special tricycle around the Wright State campus. She is the first patient to stand up on her own with the aid of the system, and even has been able to take some halting strides.

Much more research is needed before electronic aids for the paralyzed become widely available. The budget of the National Institutes of Health for spinal-injury programs is growing year by year. And a recently formed organization, the American Paralysis Association, is devoted to fostering research—and raising money for it—to help overcome the idea that a spinal disability is forever.

Nor is the possibility of actual regeneration of nerves in the cord to be dismissed out of hand. When peripheral nerves, such as those in the arm or leg, are severed, they do grow. It now appears that their regrowth is made possible, at least in part, by non–nerve cells known as "Schwann cells."

The spinal cord has no Schwann cells. But now, in animal studies, investigators at McGill University in Montreal are grafting peripheral-nerve tissue into damaged cords with the hope that the Schwann cells may stimulate regrowth. In a few cases, some spinal-cord fibers have grown into the grafts. The big question is whether such fibers can be made to form the reconnections needed to restore function.

Diabetic Sentry

A new device could be valuable for many insulin-dependent diabetics, enabling them and their families to sleep a little easier. Worn as a wristwatch during the night, the Sleep Sentry sounds an alarm when it detects perspiration or a drop in skin temperature, two common symptoms of hypoglycemia (low blood sugar).

The Need.

By day, diabetics can recognize low-blood-sugar symptoms—perspiration, sleepiness, weakness, dizziness, and hunger—and can correct the problem by taking rapidly absorbed sugar.

Day or night, if the hypoglycemia is not corrected in time, the patient can become unconscious or have a seizure. Frequent episodes of hypoglycemia can worsen diabetic control and may lead eventually to serious nervous-system complications.

Historically, it has been believed that patients experiencing low-blood-sugar symptoms during sleep wake up and can take action. But recent tests, using reagent strips that measure blood sugar, have shown that diabetics often sleep through a low-blood-sugar episode and its symptoms, which may result from an insulin reaction.

Efficacy.

While the device is not 100 percent accurate, it is the only instrument available that can detect over 90 percent of hypoglycemia episodes, according to Dr. Stephen C. Duck, associate professor of pediatrics at the Medical College of Wisconsin and director of the diabetes program at Milwaukee Children's Hospital.

To study its effectiveness, Duck tested it for a year on twenty-four insulin-dependent children aged three to eighteen. The youngsters wore the device at home for a total of 1,444 nights.

The alarm sounded forty-two times in forty-six recognized hypoglycemic episodes, missing four actual cases. It also gave out 150 false alarms. In seven of the twenty-four patients, there were no false alarms. Of the 150 false positives, over half were associated with excess perspiration.

The device, therefore, may not be useful for diabetics who perspire excessively or, according to the manufacturer, for those whose skin temperature drops for other reasons such as fever, menopause, or medication side effects.

The $175 instrument—marketed by Teledyne Avionics of Charlottesville, Virginia—has permanent moisture sensors. When the unit, which operates on two hearing-aid-type batteries, is turned on by two control push buttons, sensors are automatically set to the patient's individual skin temperature.

Parents of children using the alarm in the study saw it as a distinct advantage even though it occasionally awakened child or parent when there was no drop in blood sugar. Observed one parent of a diabetic son: "You want always to be on the lookout and [you] never get a good night's sleep. The device relieves some of the pressure."

Drug Delivery Systems
New methods

Most drugs in use today are in dosage forms dating far back. Ointments, inhalations, and suppositories were described before 1500 B.C. The first tablet was produced in the late tenth century, and the capsule was invented in France in the nineteenth century.

Pills, capsules, and other old forms of drug delivery aren't museum pieces yet, but new delivery systems are appearing, and many more are in development. They aim at controlling drug release, putting medication where it is actually needed, avoiding as much as possible the sudden peaks of drug levels and evening out the availability. The more efficiently this is accomplished, the more likely it is that efficacy will be increased, undesirable side effects reduced, and the frequency of dosage reduced.

These are among the newer developments:

Transdermal.

Aboard the space shuttle *Columbia,* when the astronaut who was to pilot it to a landing on a dry lake bed in California became anxious about developing motion sickness (at least a third of astronauts flying in space have experienced nausea and dizziness), he reached into the shuttle's medical kit and took out a flexible patch resembling a Band-Aid. Peeling back the protective coating from the thumbnail-size disk, he placed its adhesive side on the skin behind his ear. Hourly thereafter, while the patch was in place, it dripped five micrograms of scopolamine —a drug that combats the symptoms of motion sickness—through his skin into his bloodstream. Illness was avoided.

Transdermal (through the skin) drug delivery of scopolamine has begun to come into increasing use in the 1980s among astronauts, yachtsmen, and just ordinary occasional travelers. It had to wait for the technology to solve the problem of controlled release. Although scopolamine is one of the best available drugs for motion sickness, too much of it can cause many undesirable effects, including hallucinations. The need was to find a way to trickle just the right amount through the skin over the right period of time.

The scopolamine disk is a four-layered affair consisting of an impermeable backing, a very thin "reservoir" layer impregnated with the drug, a microporous membrane to control the rate of the drug's release, and an adhesive surface that fastens to the skin. When put in place several hours before motion starts, the disk's action lasts as long as three days.

The same disk has proved highly effective in reducing nausea and vomiting in patients following surgery. These have been major complaints of patients since the earliest days of surgery and anesthesia.

In one study at Good Samaritan Hospital in San Jose, California, one group of surgical patients received a scopolamine skin disk the night before surgery; the second group got an empty skin disk and an injection of scopolamine; the third group did not receive scopolamine.

Patients receiving the scopolamine-impregnated disk experienced a mild degree of sedation and decreased saliva production an hour before surgery, both desirable effects for presurgery patients. More important, the impregnated disk reduced the amount of nausea and vomiting following surgery and even increased appetites, while producing none of the side effects of injectable scopolamine.

Transdermal delivery now is being used for nitroglycerin as well. Nitroglycerin is a valuable drug for relieving the chest pain of angina pectoris, which is associated with the restriction of oxygen flow to the heart muscle. Nitroglycerin tablets have long been used—taken only after pain has begun. Now a transdermal patch can be applied to the chest to provide a controlled amount of nitroglycerin for twenty-four hours to prevent and treat angina.

Tests are under way to incorporate other drugs in transdermal patches—among them clonidine, a drug used for high blood pressure.

Eye Wafer.

Patients with glaucoma often have had to instill eyedrops four times a day, each time experiencing blurring of vision and discomfort. Now, instead, many are using a tiny oval wafer (about ¼ " × ½ " " ⅒") that can be tipped into the eye. It releases pilocarpine, a valuable anti-glaucoma medication, for as long as a week at a uniform rate, usually without blurring or other unpleasant effects. And with round-the-clock release, pressure within the eye is often kept under better control.

Contraception.

Progestasert is a new type of intrauterine device (IUD) designed to retain the best features and eliminate some of the drawbacks of the conventional-type IUD and the Pill. It is smaller and less bulky than the old IUD, and is therefore reported to be less given to side effects —even if it is somewhat less effective in itself for contraception.

Combined with it, however, is a core containing progesterone, the hormone used in the Pill. The progesterone is released in tiny amounts directly into the uterus, where it protects against conception without effects outside the uterus.

Insulin Pumps.

The discovery in the 1920s that diabetes can be controlled by insulin was a major medical achievement. Yet more than half a century later, control remains far from perfect. Diabetics now seldom die of the disease itself—that is, from diabetic coma—but are more likely to be eventually affected, possibly incapacitated, and quite possibly killed by one or more of the complications of the disease: neuropathy (nervous-system complications), deterioration of the retina of the eye and deterioration of the kidneys, and atherosclerotic (artery-blocking) disease of the limbs or heart.

Now there are efforts to change insulin delivery in order to achieve better control of diabetes and thus minimize or even possibly avoid the complications.

Portable insulin-infusion pumps have been developed. Current models consist of a syringe connected by a catheter (tube) to a needle implanted under the skin. The needle is usually implanted on the abdominal wall for two or three days, after which the patient moves it to a new site. A battery-powered device maintains a steady pressure on the plunger of the syringe to produce a steady infusion of an insulin dosage needed to maintain normal blood-sugar levels. When extra insulin is needed—as at mealtimes—the patient can press a button for an additional dose.

Patients seem to find the pump acceptable to wear. It makes for a more normal pattern of blood insulin and a more flexible life-style as well because the extra insulin required at mealtimes can be administered simply by pressing a button and an occasional late or missed meal will seldom lead to the problems that can occur with a fixed schedule of injections. A disadvantage of the pump is its bulk and cost: Present models are about the size of a camera and not inexpensive. But engineering improvements to reduce the size to about that of a pack of cigarettes are on the way, possibly with a reduction in cost.

Meanwhile, a remotely programmable insulin pump has been developed for implantation. The first patient to receive it, a forty-one-year-old man with diabetes since the age of five, was doing well with it, at last report, after more than a year.

The pump consists of a silicone rubber insulin reservoir, implanted in the abdomen just below the skin so it can be refilled by injection, and the sealed pump itself, which is controlled by a palm-size push-button unit permitting the wearer to program and measure the rate and quantity of insulin delivered by the pump. The insulin is continuously pumped into the abdomen and absorbed into the bloodstream.

The advantage of an implanted pump over one that is worn outside the body may be largely cosmetic. The risks, which include reservoir leakage and pump malfunction, have yet to be fully assessed.

A Pump for Infertility.

Women who are unable to ovulate due to a deficiency of an ovulation-controlling brain hormone now may be able in some cases to conceive and bear children when given the hormone in small doses via a special timed system, which releases the hormone much as the brain normally releases it.

Through a pump carried in a purse or on a belt, the hormone—called "gonadotropin-releasing hormone"—is injected automatically into an arm vein every 96 to 120 minutes starting on the first day of menstruation and continuing until ovulation, an average of two weeks.

Of the first eight women treated by Dr. David S. Miller and other physicians of the University of California School of Medicine-San Diego, all ovulated after treatment, and seven became pregnant. Three miscarried within ten weeks of conception, but four delivered full-term, normal infants.

Pump Infusion for Cancer.

More and more hospital-weary cancer patients can expect to spend more time at home, thanks to a portable infusion pump that allows selected patients to receive their chemotherapy (anticancer drugs) at home.

The portable infusion pump is connected through intravenous tubing to a soft, silicone catheter inserted in the patient's arm or just below the collarbone. Anticancer drugs are administered through the catheter and an attached line to the central vein near the heart.

The six-by-two-inch pump weighs slightly more than a pound and may be tucked into a purse, carried in a pouch around the shoulder, or clipped to a belt. Operation is simple. A drug fills a balloon on the pump and is pumped out through a narrow opening. Its constant flow, requiring no adjustment, is predetermined by the pressure, the diameter of the opening, and drug thickness. An alarm sounds when the drug supply is almost gone, and a gauge allows the patient to check the amount left.

At the University of Texas M. D. Anderson Hospital in Houston, experience with hundreds of patients over a five-year period indicates that the pump allows a patient to avoid four to seven hospital days a month that would otherwise be needed for treatment. Being able to spend more time at home provides major cost savings and emotional benefits.

Another kind of pumping system is being used at Duke University's Comprehensive Cancer Center and at several other medical centers around the country to treat liver cancer by delivering cancer drugs directly to the tumor.

Not only may cancer arise in the liver itself; it may spread there from other sites in the body. Some 60 percent of patients with cancer of the colon will have problems with their livers during the course of their disease.

The liver-cancer pump, which is about the size of a hockey puck, is implanted in the abdomen and a catheter leading from it is usually placed in a branch of the main liver artery so the medication can be carried by the blood directly to the liver without affecting other organs.

The pump has a chamber filled with freon, a liquid that vaporizes with pressure and heat. An adjacent chamber holds about one and a half ounces of 5-FUDR (fluorodeoxyuridine), a drug used for treating liver cancer. The normal temperature of the body vaporizes the freon, which puts pressure on a collapsible metal diaphragm that then eases the 5-FUDR fluid out of the inner chamber into the catheter at a constant rate. Patients can do whatever they want—swim or play golf. They just have to return to the center every two weeks to have the device refilled with a needle.

Preliminary results from several centers indicate a median survival of over two years, compared to previous survival rates of six months to one year. In a number of patients, liver tumors have been controlled but death has occurred from spread of the tumors to other parts of the body. Doctors are hopeful that the spread can be decreased and survival improved by varying the timing of drug delivery.

Meanwhile, a new variation of the pump treatment is under study at the University of Michigan Hospitals and Medical School. Microscopic particles of starch in a saltwater solution are injected into the liver's blood supply along with the chemotherapeutic drug. The microspheres—tiny balls, each about the size of five red blood cells—are expected to retard circulation through the liver long enough to let the drug be more effective.

Tumors characteristically have very rich blood supplies, and the microspheres tend to lodge more in the tumor than in the healthy part of the liver. The microspheres temporarily clog the tumor's blood supply, holding the drug there instead of letting it wash on through the bloodstream. The starch particles are broken down by the body in about twenty minutes. The use of microspheres may further increase the life expectancy of patients.

Cancer Pain Relief at Home.

A new method of delivering drugs promises to offer cancer patients effective, long-acting pain relief at home. It makes use of a catheter so small it can be threaded through a needle and implanted, without surgery, in the epidural area—the space around the spinal cord. After the implantation is carried out in a hospital, the patient can go home.

The medication, such as morphine, is delivered from the catheter in a steady, low-dosage, uninterrupted flow. According to Dr. Terence M. Murphy of the University of Washington Hospital in Seattle, because such minuscule amounts of narcotics are used, the patient is more alert than with large, frequent amounts of painkillers given by injection, and side effects are reduced. The patient may move about normally, take showers, go outdoors. Access to the catheter is through a self-sealing port on the skin near the spine. A family member or visiting nurse can replenish supplies of the narcotic through the catheter.

Aerosol Antivirals.

Drugs effective against viruses have a long way to go before they begin to equal the huge list of antibacterials. But their numbers are growing, and presently available drugs—acyclovir, amantadine, vidarabine, and trifluridine—almost certainly will be joined by others. Meanwhile, more effective ways of delivering them are being sought, and one means —by aerosol—looks promising for acute respiratory diseases.

One study by investigators at Baylor College of Medicine in Houston suggests that flu patients may be able to swap several days of misery for one day in bed, breathing the antiviral drug ribavirin through a mask and enjoying a quick recovery. The delivery system consists of a nebulizer that disperses small particles of the drug into air delivered to the patient via a breathing tube and face mask. In this way the drug can penetrate the smallest air passages. However, because of the amount of drug needed, the patient must remain masked for at least eight hours.

In the study, the new drug and delivery system was tested on a group of flu-stricken college students. Their body temperatures returned to normal in about twenty-three hours, compared to thirty-eight hours for other students with flu who, for comparison, were treated with saline-saturated air. Only the drug-treated students showed marked improvement of symptoms at twenty-four hours. And among the drug-treated, shedding of viruses in respiratory secretions was greatly decreased in eighteen hours.

Those who will benefit most from the treatment, the investigators believe, may be those patients at greatest risk for severe disease: the elderly and the chronically ill.

The antiviral drug, ribavirin, also has proved effective in studies at the University of Rochester Medical Center when administered as a continuous aerosol spray to infants with acute respiratory disease caused by respiratory syncytial virus.

Iontophoresis.

Iontophoresis is from the Greek word meaning "to carry ions or electrically charged atoms." When the ions are impelled by an electrical charge to move through tissue, they can carry a drug with them.

More and more dentists are now using the technique on patients with supersensitive teeth and gums. In a procedure developed by Dr. Louis P. Gangarosa at the Medical College of Georgia, a local anesthetic such as novocaine, instead of being injected, is applied with a cotton swab to the outside of a tooth to be numbed. A flexible electrode is then placed against the medicated area, a minute electrical current is turned on, and the charged ions carry the medication in, without pain and with the current barely felt.

In addition to a local anesthetic, iontophoresis can be used to apply fluoride for the desensitization of teeth, antiviral drugs for infections of the mouth, and steroid drugs to treat mouth ulcers. With iontophoresis, according to Dr. Gangarosa, placement of anesthetic or medication is more accurate and less medication is required.

On the Horizon.

A whole series of new developments in the delivery of drugs are now under study, and many may be available before long.

At the University of California-San Francisco, researchers have developed a new drug-carrier system that promises to overcome a primary problem of cancer chemotherapy: how to make the cure less disturbing than the disease. The new system uses liposomes—microscopic hollow bubbles of fat—to deliver toxic drugs directly to cancer cells without harming nearby healthy cells. Each liposome is filled with a drug and attached to a monoclonal antibody designed to seek out tumor cells (see ANTIBODIES, MONOCLONAL). Sealed inside its protective liposome, the drug slips past healthy cells without damaging them and is zeroed in on a diseased cell. The system has been used successfully against animal tumor cells in test tubes.

At the Massachusetts Institute of Technology, researchers are working to perfect a method by which a magnetic signal is used to release drugs from a plastic implant under the skin. Tests with diabetic rats have shown that powdered insulin released from an implant the size of a pea with the top shaved off can decrease blood-sugar levels significantly for months. Theoretically, an implant should continue to work for years, and the technique may be useful for many other drugs as well as insulin, including agents used for inflammatory bowel disease and various heart conditions.

Along with medication, the implant contains magnetic beads. The medication is released by a magnetic signal, the source of which could be a device worn on a belt or watchband.

Also at the Massachusetts Institute of Technology, work is under way to develop bioerodable implants—drug delivery systems that self-destruct and are absorbed or expelled by the body, eliminating need for surgical removal. One test system uses a polymer originally employed in the textile industry. When slabs of drug-containing polymer were implanted in animals, they released the drug as desired, and after 153 days, less than 1 percent of the polymer remained, having dissolved away.

Still other studies may make transdermal delivery possible for drugs not readily absorbed through the skin. The tough outer layer of skin, the stratum corneum with its mass of dead cells, acts as a natural protective barrier against substances from the outside. Beneath this layer is another, the stratum granulosum, that may welcome incoming drugs, but getting a drug through the tough outer layer is much like trying to force a substance through a wall. The smaller the size of the drug molecule, the easier; and the larger, the more difficult. Quite large molecules—like those of growth hormones, insulin, and interferon—require a driving force.

Such a force may soon be available in the form of electricity stored in a tiny wafer battery in the skin patch. That would allow iontophoresis, the use of current from the battery, to push charged ions of the drug through the stratum corneum.

Another ingenious delivery system under study is a drug-carrying film designed to keep oral medications from passing too quickly through the gastrointestinal tract. The polymer film system consists of a drug-carrying matrix covered on either side by a bubble-containing barrier film. The barrier layer causes the film to float; the carrier layer releases the drug in the stomach. In one experiment, the film was cut into strips that were packed into hard gelatin capsules. When administered to dogs, the film strips unfolded after the capsules dissolved, and the unfolded strips floated around in the stomach, remaining there for about 6.5 hours—much longer than the 2.5-hour average of nonfilm systems.

Ear Resonator
New answer for mild hearing loss

A novel nonelectronic hearing aid, which provides as much improvement as listening to speech or music with a hand cupped behind an ear, is designed to fill a niche and answer the need of more than a million Americans. Developed at Stanford University School of Medicine, the device, called the Earesonator, is for people who don't feel they need a conventional electronic aid, because their hearing difficulty is limited, occurring only at certain times, such as when background noise is present or the speaker's voice is soft or high-pitched. Such difficulty, while bothersome, leaves them uninclined to bother with, or spend as much as $300 for, a conventional aid.

The Helpful Shift.

The new plastic device, worn within the ear, is ingeniously designed to give the external ear a new, extended role in hearing.

The average external ear resonates (vibrates in sympathy) only with incoming sounds of relatively high frequency, between 2,800 and 4,000 hertz. In that range, it can provide ten to fifteen decibels of sound amplification. But it provides no amplification for the middle frequencies of 1,000 to 2,500 hertz, which comprise an important speech range.

When the Earesonator is inserted in the ear, it changes the opening size and volume of the ear cavity, shifting the resonance frequency downward and providing a sound boost of ten to fifteen decibels in the 1,000–2,500-hertz speech-frequency range. By adjusting the size of its opening, the Earesonator can be fine-tuned to provide maximum amplification at the frequencies most needed by the individual patient.

Trials.

In Stanford trials, the first thirty patients with mild loss fitted with the $80 unit and studied with pure-tone audiometry have shown improvement of ten to 20 decibels at key speech frequencies.

According to one of its developers, Dr. Richard L. Goode, Stanford professor of surgery, potential users can get some idea of the improvement to be expected by simply listening to speech or music, first without and then with the hand cupped behind the ear (something many people do regularly). If the difference is significant, the Earesonator could be helpful.

The device, Dr. Goode reports, should work for anyone with mild loss in one or both ears. Most people would require two, one for each ear.

Echocardiography
And new transesophageal two-dimensional echocardiography

A valuable aid in diagnosing heart problems, echocardiography is a technique for recording echoes of ultrasonic waves—very-high-frequency sound waves beyond hearing range—when these waves are directed at areas of the heart. The principle is similar to that used in sonar detection of submarines and depth and location of other underwater objects.

In this simple, painless procedure, the patient lies on a table while a small instrument—a high-frequency generator—is moved across his chest. The instrument projects ultrasonic waves and receives the returning echoes.

As the waves pass through the heart, their behavior differs, depending on whether or not any calcification is present, whether there is a blood clot or any other mass in the cavity of the heart, whether certain heart chambers are enlarged, whether the valves within the heart open and close properly, and whether any part of the heart is thicker than it should be.

Uses.

Echocardiography often allows visualizing features of the heart that might otherwise escape detection. It can, for example, reveal an abnormal thickness of the cardiac septum, the inner wall of the heart, which may produce chest pain similar to that of angina. The technique can also detect the presence of various types of congenital heart defects.

The procedure, considered harmless even for a pregnant patient and her fetus, may allow decisive diagnosis, eliminating the need for other, more-complex tests and sometimes completely changing the course of treatment and making it more effective.

A Newer Technique.

Researchers at the University of California-San Francisco Medical Center have developed a new ultrasound technique to monitor heart function during surgery as a means of reducing the risk of heart attack during or immediately after the operation—one of the most common causes of death in the postoperative period.

The technique—called "transesophageal two-dimensional echocardiography"—makes use of the finding that a small sound transmitter swallowed by a patient produces a clear image of the beating heart without risk to the patient.

The device is located at the tip of a thin, flexible probe inserted through the mouth into the esophagus (food tube) of the anesthetized patient. It is directed in the esophagus to a position behind the nearby heart. By manipulating the angle and placement of the probe, physicians can accurately direct ultrasound waves at a particular portion of the heart and generate an image of that section of the beating muscle on a video screen.

Uses.

In one study at the medical center, investigators used the technique to assess changes in heart-wall motion. Based on these assessments, they predicted which patients might suffer heart attacks during or after surgery. Of seven patients predicted to be at high risk, five had heart attacks. Thirty-six patients predicted to be at low risk had no evidence of heart attack.

In a related study, investigators found that transesophageal echocardiography was more sensitive to a shortage of blood in the heart than conventional monitoring techniques. The ultrasound procedure identified changes in 92 percent of one group of patients studied, while techniques like electrocardiography—which measures the heart's signals with electrodes placed on the chest—detected insufficient blood supply in only 24 percent.

Changes in heart-wall motion are the earliest signs of myocardial ischemia—a shortage in the heart's blood supply that, if untreated, leads to heart attack. By using transesophageal echocardiography to measure heart-wall motion, physicians can better determine a patient's need for intensive care during and after surgery, according to the researchers, Drs. Michael Cahalan, Nelson Schiller, and Michael Roizen, thus reducing heart-attack risk. In a report late in 1983 to the American Society of Anesthesiology, Dr. Roizen observed that "as the population gets older and sicker, this technique may allow necessary surgery to be performed with even less risk than it is today on younger, healthier patients." (See also ULTRASOUND.)

Electrical Stimulation
For pain, muscle reeducation, scoliosis

Two thousand years ago, the electrical shock from a torpedo fish was used to treat headaches and gout. The crude procedure may have had some limited success.

It has taken a long time, but in recent years much more sophisticated forms of electrical stimulation have come into use for a number of important purposes, including the treatment of children with spinal curvature, the strengthening and reeducation of muscles weakened by disease or injury, and the relief of otherwise unyielding severe pain.

Scoliosis.

Until not very long ago, a child with progressive scoliosis (abnormal spinal curvature) had to face either major corrective surgery or years of treatment with a brace. But at the Hospital for Sick Children in Toronto, an eight-year-old girl had implanted under the skin in her back a small, batteryless receiver with leads impinging on muscles on the convex part of her curve. At home every night, while she slept, a bedside radio transmitter activated the internal device. Six months later, most of the curvature was gone.

It was Dr. Walter P. Bobechko, chief of orthopedic surgery at the Toronto hospital, who first thought of using electrical muscle stimulation for scoliosis. As a young resident, Bobechko had observed children with cerebral palsy and had noted that half of those with muscular imbalance developed abnormal spinal curvatures. If muscle imbalance could create scoliosis, he thought, why couldn't scoliosis be corrected by inducing another kind of muscle imbalance?

In animal studies, Bobechko and his co-workers found they could induce and then correct scoliosis in young pigs and rabbits by stimulating muscles on alternate sides of the spine with an implanted "spinal pacemaker" that induced muscle contractions every second. Later, they found that in human patients a contraction every ten seconds is enough to control curvature progression.

The receiver is inserted during a simple, forty-five-minute operation under general anesthesia. The patient is up and about the same day, returns home two days later, and resumes full activity shortly thereafter.

During the day, the patient's activity is unrestricted. At night, while preparing for bed, the patient simply tapes a little antenna over the implanted receiver and connects the antenna to the transmitter. The treatment does not interfere with sleep; the stimulation sensation is pleasant—indeed, most patients considering it relaxing—and no specific sleeping position is needed.

Not long ago, Bobechko and his colleagues reported using the technique over a six-year period to treat seventy-seven patients with scoliosis of up to 35°. Progression of the curve was arrested or partly corrected in 87 percent of the patients—an improvement considered significant because all the youngsters either had a history of progressively increasing curvature or were at very high risk for progression. The remaining 13 percent showed some progression, but in many cases it was only slight and the treatment was considered successful. Only three of the seventy-seven patients had significant progression requiring surgical intervention.

In another electrical-stimulation approach to scoliosis, a research team at Rancho Los Amigos Rehabilitation Engineering Center in Downey, California, is using external stimulation. In this technique, two electrode disks connected to a portable, battery-operated stimulator are placed on the convex side of the spinal curve before the child goes to sleep and are removed on waking.

At the Rancho Los Amigos Hospital, a team headed by Dr. John C. Brown has used the external stimulation treatment in ninety-two patients and has succeeded in arresting or reversing progression of curvature in 88 percent.

Electrical stimulation of one kind or another, replacing surgery and the encumbrance of bracing, is currently being used in more than two dozen medical centers in Canada, the United States, and Europe.

Muscle Reeducation.

Physical therapists in many hospitals now are using electrical stimulation as a safe, effective, and relatively painless way to rehabilitate muscles weakened by disease or injury. The stimulation is used to strengthen muscles, prevent contraction, reeducate muscles, manage spasticity, and even serve as a substitute for the conventional brace.

The procedure is simple. The physical therapist attaches electrodes to the patient's skin where the nerve controlling a muscle is closest to the surface. By applying an electrical charge of 40 to 100 milliamperes, the therapist can stimulate the muscle to move in desired fashion.

The electrical impulses not only stimulate muscles but facilitate motion. A stroke patient, for example, can be shown through stimulation what a motion should be; the amount of sensation felt is increased; and muscle reeducation to perform a particular function is aided.

In a patient who has been immobilized by arthritis, muscles often are weak and getting the patient to use them properly is difficult. A physical therapist can explain a desired motion to the patient, but making the muscles actually perform through electrical stimulation is frequently more effective.

For some stroke patients who have trouble walking because of weakened ankle muscles, electrical stimulation can be used as a substitute for a brace. The patient is fitted with an electrical stimulation device triggered by a switch worn in the shoe. The muscles are stimulated to work properly whenever the patient puts weight on the foot.

Electrical stimulation is hardly a cure-all for every type of physical ailment; it is best employed with other types of treatment in a total therapy plan. The stimulation, as used for muscle rehabilitations, gives a tingly, sometimes disturbing feeling, but most patients get used to it. The most serious side effect is skin irritation, but this is easy to detect and can be prevented.

TENS for Pain.

In many cases now, transcutaneous electrical nerve stimulators (TENS) are blocking pain where other methods have failed. The equipment consists of a battery-powered impulse generator (the stimulator) with wires leading to two or more electrodes that can be placed on various parts of the body. When the stimulator is turned on, pulsating current passes through the painful area.

The typical stimulator is about the size of a pack of cigarettes and can be carried in a pocket or worn on a belt clip or in a brassiere. One type attaches to arm or wrist.

In one study at Hadassah University Hospital in Jerusalem, Israel, TENS equipment was tried in 284 patients with various kinds of neuralgia, peripheral-nerve injuries, postoperative pain, shingles, cancer, and low back pain. Results were reported to be good for 153 patients, moderate for 75, poor for 56.

In a study in Sweden in which TENS was tried in 147 women during childbirth, 130 benefited, with half of them reporting good to very good relief.

At the University of Colorado Medical Center, 83 percent of 120 patients with various pain problems had fair to excellent relief.

TENS is used with and without drugs; in some patients it greatly lessens the need for pain-killing medications and helps to prevent or end narcotic addiction.

According to Dr. Richard D. Gordon of Hahnemann Medical College and Hospital in Philadelphia, TENS can lessen both chronic and acute arthritic pain but is particularly useful for patients disabled by chronic arthritis, because it reduces discomfort and enables them to resume daily lives. A substantial proportion of the more than 30 million Americans who suffer from arthritis can be helped by TENS treatments, Gordon believes.

One new miniature TENS unit designed for arthritis as well as other chronic and acute pains is matchbook-size and as thin as a chocolate bar.

Exactly how electrical stimulation affects pain is not yet well understood, but there are two commonly held theories. One, the "gate-control theory" involving nerve receptors, holds that mild electronic treatments from TENS confuse the nerve signals along the spinal cord with competing electrical signals to prevent pain messages from traveling through the spinal "gate" to the brain.

The other theory is based on the recent discovery of body chemicals known as "endorphins"—the brain's naturally produced opiates, released in response to pain or injury, or as a result of carefully produced electronic stimulation.

The Deep Brain Stimulator.

For patients with severe and constant pain unrelieved by other measures, a new electronic device called the "deep brain stimulator" now may provide relief. Electrodes planted deep in the brain allow patients to control pain via a pocket-size transmitter.

The stimulator consists of the transmitter; a receiver; and four tiny electrodes strung on a hair-thin wire. The electrodes are implanted in a brain area rich in endorphins. When pain is felt, a simple adjustment of the transmitter sends an electronic signal through the receiver to the electrodes, stimulating the release of endorphins and often relieving the pain in minutes.

At the University of Chicago Hospitals and Clinics, Dr. Frederick Brown of the Department of Neurosurgery reports that many patients seek help after undergoing several back operations. "Scar tissue which builds up along the spinal nerves leaves them in constant pain. Another operation will only result in additional scars.

"If other, less invasive forms of treatment, such as physical therapy or steroids injected into the spine, offer no relief, a deep brain stimulator could help." The device may also aid those whose pain is caused by slow-growing cancers, such as cancer of the breast or prostate.

Regardless of the pain source, all patients seen at the Chicago institution must undergo at least six months of traditional treatment to be certain the pain will not respond to other types of therapy or diminish of its own accord.

Implantation takes place in two steps. In the first, the four electrodes are precisely inserted in a predetermined portion of the brain and the wires and receiver are temporarily placed outside the body. The operation is done under a local anesthetic since the brain, which registers pain felt elsewhere in the body, is not pain-sensitive itself.

Over a period of about five days, the temporary stimulator is tested by stimulating different pairs of electrodes to determine which combination produces the best results.

If the patient has significant pain relief, a second procedure permanently installs the device entirely under the skin, usually under general anesthesia. The wires are passed down through the neck and the receiver is implanted just below the collarbone, with only a tiny scar identifying the receiver's location.

To use the device, the patient places a disk housing an antenna over the implanted receiver and adjusts the controls on the attached transmitter. The antenna needs to be in place only to activate the deep brain stimulator, typically three or four times a day for fifteen minutes at a time. When the antenna is not in use, the device is invisible and places no restrictions on activity; the patient can even shower and swim.

One example of the value of deep brain stimulation is a twenty-six-year-old woman seen at New York's Presbyterian Hospital. She was suffering from debilitating pain after surgery at another hospital for a ruptured disk. The disk area had become infected, with probable injury to a nerve. She had been hospitalized for a year, during which, she recalls, "on a scale of one to ten, the pain in my hips and knees was nine. I had started hoping I had a terminal condition."

In a first procedure performed at Presbyterian Hospital, electrodes were placed in her spinal cord with the hope of scrambling pain messages going to the brain. For several months the pain was successfully controlled, but when it returned and no medication helped, the deep brain implant was used.

Since then, she has had gratifying relief. Reports the patient: "I used to take narcotics to the point of almost being asleep. Now I'm alert. The electrode systems don't seem to have any side effects."

Much as morphine is not effective for all types of pain, neither are brain endorphins. Stroke victims and patients with pain from injuries of the spinal cord or other diseases of the central nervous system do not respond to endorphin release, but they can be helped to some extent by a deep brain stimulator. In such cases, the electrodes are placed in the thalamus, a section of the brain that registers pain. Instead of triggering the release of endorphins, the electronic signal in the thalamus alters the perception of pain. The pain relief, however, is not as great as with endorphin release. (See also BONE HEALING WITH ELECTRICITY.)

Electrocardiography
Assessing the heart . . .
continuous monitoring . . . stress testing

The electrocardiogram (known as an EKG or ECG) is the most commonly used noninvasive test of heart function.

When any muscle in the body moves, it produces small electrical currents. The heart, one of the most powerful body muscles, gives rise to a rhythmic output of currents. An electrocardiogram is a graphic recording from the body surface of the heart's electrical activity. It is produced by a machine, the electrocardiograph, which detects and amplifies the action of the heart 3,000 times or more and activates a sensitively balanced lever in contact with moving paper, tracing on the paper the pattern of heart waves that indicates heart rhythm and other action. The heart's currents are transmitted to the machine through wires from a dozen electrodes, half-dollar-size disks, which are moistened with a conductive paste and attached to the arms, legs, and chest.

The entirely painless test, which requires less than fifteen minutes, can provide valuable information.

The Waves.

The normal electrocardiogram is made up of a P wave; Q, R, and S waves known as the QRS wave; and a T wave. The P wave occurs at the beginning of each contraction of the atria, the heart's receiving chambers on top. The QRS wave occurs at the beginning of each contraction of the ventricles, the pumping chambers below. The T wave occurs as the ventricles recover electrically and prepare for the next pumping contraction.

Thus, electrocardiograms of normal hearts are reasonably characteristic. If there is a heart abnormality, the electrocardiogram may reveal abnormal wave tracings.

Actually, abnormal tracings don't always indicate a heart abnormality since anxiety, heavy breathing, use of some drugs, and other influences may make tracings deviate from normal. Taking any such factors into account, however, an experienced physician often can get a useful picture of what is going on in the heart from the electrocardiogram.

The Values.

The electrocardiogram can help diagnose any damage to the heart muscle that may have been inflicted by a heart attack. It can reveal the presence of abnormal heart rhythms, inadequate supply of oxygen reaching the heart muscle, excesses or shortages of certain elements in the blood such as calcium and potassium, and congenital or acquired heart disturbances.

In addition to its diagnostic value, the electrocardiogram can be of vital importance in a coronary-care unit when a patient has had a heart attack or may be experiencing one. When the heart stops or goes into fibrillation and quivers uselessly, the EKG reveals this, allowing resuscitation to be started immediately. In a coronary-care unit, nurses monitor heart rhythms on a televisionlike screen connected to the electrocardiograph.

Portable (Holter) Monitoring.

Because an abnormal heart rhythm is not always continuous but may come and go, a regular EKG may miss it. When there is any reason to suspect such an intermittent disturbance, a Holter EKG may be used for detection.

The Holter monitor is a special small instrument that resembles a tape recorder and uses standard EKG electrodes taped to the chest. It can be carried unobtrusively by an over-the-shoulder strap during the patient's usual activities at home, work, or even play. Instead of being recorded on paper, the heart's electrical impulses are recorded on magnetic tape in the instrument. The patient may wear the unit for as long as twenty-four hours, during which electrical impulses from the heart are continuously recorded. Afterward, a special scanner unit can be used by the physician to play back the twenty-four-hour tape recording in about forty-five minutes.

The Holter monitor's value lies in its ability to monitor heart activity over an extended period and under varying conditions of rest, exercise, sleep, mental calm, and emotional stress.

Stress Testing.

How the heart tolerates an extra work load can provide important information about its state. In a stress test (an exercise-tolerance test), an EKG is taken with the patient under controlled stress.

With electrodes on the chest, the patient exercises—perhaps climbing three stairs for three minutes, pedaling a stationary bicycle, or walking a treadmill. The bicycle activity can gradually be made more strenuous by increasing the resistance to pedaling, and the treadmill activity can be made more strenuous by gradually increasing the tread-mill's speed, angle of incline, or both.

A stress test may sometimes detect abnormalities that would not be revealed by a conventional EKG. With exercise, the heart requires more oxygen, and stress testing can determine whether required amounts are getting to the heart muscle as the exercise level increases. By observing the heart's response to measured energy expenditures, the physician can also estimate how much activity a patient can safely tolerate.

Electrode-Catheter Ablation
For a heart short circuit

When it happened the first time, he was twenty-nine. Awakened suddenly in the middle of the night by a barking dog, he found that his heart, startled into rapid beating, wouldn't slow down. He was exhausted by morning. A physician found his heart beating 250 times a minute, more than three and a half times normal. His heart had to be shocked electrically to restore normal rhythm.

When the same thing happened three years later, he sought help at the University of California-San Francisco Medical Center, where he was to become one of the very first to undergo a new treatment designed to avoid the open heart surgery that would otherwise have been necessary.

The Problem.

The diagnosis was clear enough: Wolff-Parkinson-White syndrome, a condition resulting from a kind of electrical short circuit in the heart —an extra, abnormal current pathway that made the heart unstable to the point where an extra beat, not uncommon in even healthy people, could set off sudden, uncontrolled tachycardia (rapid beating).

Sometimes Wolff-Parkinson-White syndrome can be controlled with medication, but in cases like this one, where the heartbeat is so rapid that there is a potential for sudden death, open heart surgery to sever the abnormal pathway is usually needed.

Instead, however, a then-experimental procedure—electrode-catheter ablation—was used to destroy the short circuit without surgery.

The Procedure.

In three years of research on dogs, Dr. Melvin Scheinman, a University of California-San Francisco cardiologist, had sought a way to avoid open heart surgery for uncontrollable heart arrhythmias.

In the open heart surgery for patients whose abnormal heart rhythms cannot be controlled with drugs, the normal current-conducting pathway, called His' bundle, is cut and a pacemaker is installed to provide the proper heart rhythm artificially.

In his early work with dogs, Scheinman had found that by inserting a catheter (tube) through a vein in the groin and threading it carefully up into the heart, he could sever His' bundle with a strong shock delivered through the catheter. In a third of the cases, His' bundle refused to stay cut—it healed—but in the remainder, the cut was permanent.

After the animal work, Scheinman had made two attempts to use the technique in human patients. Both were unsuccessful. The present patient was informed of this but opted for the technique.

It required a team of cardiologists, anesthesiologists, cardiovascular nurses, and skilled catheterization lab technicians to thread a catheter with an electrode at the tip into the patient's heart (see CARDIAC CATHERIZATION). The team shocked the heart twice, each time for a fraction of a second, with 400 watt-seconds of electricity. The abnormal rhythm disappeared. Several weeks of observation confirmed that the electrical ablation had been successful to the point of curing the problem.

The patient now is leading a normal life—as are an increasing number of other patients as the procedure's use is being extended worldwide.

Electrophysiological Testing (EPS)

To guide abnormal-heart-rhythm correction

Each year in the United States, 50,000 sudden deaths occur because of heartbeat abnormalities. The victims usually have a lethal combination of an abnormal beating pattern known as "nonsustained ventricular tachycardia" and an abnormal contraction of part of the heart muscle, called "chronic ventricular dysfunction."

Now clinicians from the Likoff Cardiovascular Institute in Philadelphia report that therapy involving electrophysiological testing (EPS) to guide the choice of the most effective antiarrhythmic drug has resulted in markedly fewer deaths among a high-risk patient group, compared to patients with the same problems who received conventional therapy.

The Testing.

In EPS, physicians electrically stimulate a patient's heart under carefully controlled hospital conditions to determine whether an abnormal heart rhythm can be triggered. If so, a drug is administered and the patient is stimulated again to see if the medication keeps the irregular beats from recurring. Alternate drugs are tried, as necessary, and the process repeated until the abnormal rhythm is prevented.

The patient is hospitalized an average of one to two weeks while correct drug therapy is selected from among antiarrhythmic agents such as quinidine, Dilantin, norpace, amiodarone, procainamide, and mexilitine. Once the proper drug is chosen, the patient remains on it indefinitely.

Comparative Study.

In a report to the American Heart Association, Dr. Scott R. Spielman of the institute presented findings of a study of sixty-nine patients diagnosed as having the two cardiac disorders. Of the sixty-nine, forty-one had undergone EPS to select appropriate medication. The remaining twenty-eight received medication chosen randomly by their own physicians. The two groups were followed for an average of 8.9 months.

Among the forty-one patients whose therapy was aggressively guided by EPS, nine (22 percent) died, and four of these (10 percent) died suddenly. Among the matched group of twenty-eight whose drug treatment had been chosen without EPS guidelines, sixteen (57 percent) died, and ten of these (36 percent) died suddenly.

Thus, the results of the investigation demonstrate that the incidence of sudden cardiac death can be reduced by EPS-guided therapy.

A Need for Early Detection.

Underscoring the need for prompt treatment is the study's finding that twelve of the fourteen sudden deaths occurred within six months of the patients' entry into the investigation. The problem is, however, that high-risk individuals—mostly men in the prime of life—have few warning signs of their potentially deadly disorder. Because of the lack of symptoms, the condition often goes undetected, according to Dr. Spielman, and even when it is discovered, physicians are not always "tuned in" to the level of risk involved.

Diagnoses can be made; and once made, physicians should be concerned—more so than many presently are—and should push for proper drug treatment to reduce mortality.

Electroretinography

Much as an electrocardiogram can provide valuable diagnostic information about the heart by recording electrical impulses from the heart muscle, so now can an electroretinogram provide information of potential sight-saving value by charting electrical impulses of the eye.

For electroretinography, a special contact lens fitted with an electrode is used to record impulses produced by the retina of the eye. The system allows an ophthalmologist to determine whether a retinal malfunction is responsible for causing blindness or impaired vision. Furthermore, says Dr. Peter Gouras of the Presbyterian Hospital in New York City, "We can determine if the problem involves the whole retina or just a portion of it."

Two Eyes in One.

The human eye can be thought of as really two eyes in one. The retina contains two types of light-sensitive cells (photoreceptors), making it both a daytime eye and a nighttime eye. Daylight is detected by about 7.5 million cones, while 120 million rods are used for night vision.

When stimulated by light, the rods or cones produce an electrical impulse, which is transformed in the brain into a perceived image. It is the electrical impulses produced by the rods and cones that electroretinography records. Moreover, with the aid of a computer, even very minute responses can be detected.

A Case of Retinitis Pigmentosa.

One example of the value of electroretinography is the case of a man with retinitis pigmentosa, a condition that can lead to total blindness if left untreated. It is caused by the degeneration of the light-sensitive photoreceptor cells.

The electroretinogram detected no responses from the patient's light-sensitive rods. But when a computer was used to sum up and average sixty-four of his responses, minute activity of cones sensitive to certain colors could be detected. All vision had not yet been lost.

The patient, as it turned out, had a form of retinitis pigmentosa in which degeneration was due to a genetic disease called "hypobetalipoproteinemia," which impaired his body's ability to absorb fats even if they were plentiful in his diet. Because fat is needed for the body's handling of vitamins A and E, the degeneration of this patient's photoreceptors was the direct result of huge vitamin deficiencies.

Using the electroretinogram to test photoreceptor response before and then with and after treatment, Dr. Gouras has been able to show that patients with this type of retinitis pigmentosa respond to treatment with the vitamins.

Looking Beyond Cataracts.

The electroretinogram also is useful for evaluating retinal function in cataract patients and in patients with hemorrhages in the eye. Cataracts or hemorrhages often make it impossible for a physician to look into the eye and see the retina. With the electroretinogram, the physician can determine whether the retina is working without having to see it.

"It gives us an idea of the condition of the retina and helps determine if surgery to remove a cataract, for example, is worthwhile," reports Dr. Gouras.

Endoscopy
For diagnosis and, increasingly, for treatment

Endoscopy—viewing internal organs of the body with an instrument—has in recent years markedly changed the approach to gastrointestinal disease.

With flexible fiberoptic instruments no wider than a pencil, whose hair-thin glass fibers provide light and allow visualization, it has become possible to directly inspect the esophagus, stomach, duodenum, colon, and abdominal cavity, as well as the pancreatic and bile ducts —without surgery. Moreover, the latest generation of endoscopes have extra channels that allow smaller instruments to be passed through in order to take samples of tissue (biopsies) for microscopic examination or perform polyp removal (polypectomy). Swallowed objects may be removed, and closed or narrowed ducts may be opened.

Beyond Diagnosis.

The first flexible fiberoptic endoscope was introduced into clinical practice by the Japanese in 1962. Currently, there are endoscopes in every major hospital throughout the world. In many community hospitals, endoscopy can be performed as an outpatient procedure, and some physicians who specialize in endoscopy perform the procedure in specially equipped office suites.

In the beginning, endoscopy was concerned mainly with diagnosis. More recently, it has been applied increasingly to therapy. One important therapeutic use is the removal of colon polyps, which are generally

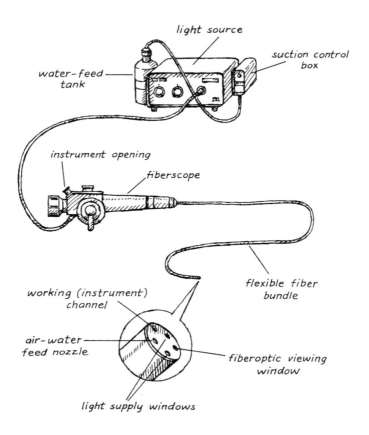

considered precursors of colon cancer. With the introduction of new electric thermoprobes and bipolar electrodes, upper gastrointestinal bleeding now can be treated by delivering electrical energy to a bleeding site. It has also become possible to probe the bile ducts to remove stones and to open a dysfunctioning sphincter muscle without performing major abdominal surgery.

The Many "-scopies."

Endoscopy is a generic term. Sigmoidoscopy—concerned with the lower end of the colon and rectum—is endoscopy. So are bronchoscopy (directed at the air passages to the lungs), cystoscopy (the bladder), gastroscopy (the stomach), and colonoscopy (virtually the entire length of the colon or large bowel). There is also EGD (esophagogastroduodenoscopy), in which a long, flexible tube, thinner than most swallowed food, is passed through the mouth into the upper digestive tract, allowing examination of the lining of the esophagus, stomach, and duodenum (the first portion of the small intestine).

Endoscopy includes, as well, ERCP (endoscopic retrograde cholangiopancreatography). For this, a long tube is passed through the mouth and into the duodenum. The opening from the bile duct and pancreatic duct into the duodenum is identified, and a cannula (a small plastic tube) is passed through the endoscope into this opening and directed into one or both of these ducts. Contrast material (dye) is then injected and X-rays are taken to study the ducts. A papillotome (a specially designed hot wire) can be passed through the cannula to open the lower end of the bile duct to remove stones.

There may be some discomfort during endoscopy, but it is usually mild. Intravenous medication to produce relaxation may be used—for example, in colonoscopy, EGD, and ERCP. In EGD, the throat is sprayed with a local anesthetic to prevent gagging.

Foreign-Body Removal.

The extraction of many kinds of foreign objects from the stomach and esophagus—toothpicks, broken chicken bones, pins, and nails, for example—is greatly facilitated by fiberoptic endoscopy. Grasping devices and snares designed for foreign-body removal are available, and it is even possible to turn objects around, when necessary, to permit safer removal—as in the case of a prisoner who had swallowed the handle of a metal spoon. X-ray showed that the jagged end of the handle in the stomach was pointing upward toward the esophagus, so that any attempt to pull the handle upward might have torn the esophagus. Once the handle was turned around so the smooth, unbroken end was near the esophagus, removal was simple.

To remove sharp objects such as razor blades, a protective sleeve can be placed over the end of the endoscope; once the object is grasped, it can be pulled up into the sleeve for safe removal.

Bezoars are masses formed in the stomach by compaction of material that does not pass into the intestine. Most commonly, they are formed of the fibers of citrus fruits, persimmons, or stringy vegetables such as celery; occasionally, they may be mixed with hair. Bezoars may cause ulcers by pressing against the stomach wall. If large enough, they may interfere with normal stomach emptying.

Enzyme preparations have been used to disintegrate bezoars, but the preparations can act only on the outer surface of the concretions and destruction is a slow process. An expedient way now to handle the bezoar problem is to direct a water jet through the endoscope. Its forceful pulses usually break up the mass and the pieces can then pass on into the intestine and be eliminated.

Endoscopic Polypectomy.

The removal of growths called "polyps" from the colon—and in some cases from the esophagus, stomach, or duodenum—is another endoscopic procedure that often avoids need for major surgery.

Through the endoscope, a technique can be used to slice through the polyp and at the same time stanch bleeding. The equipment consists of an electrocautery wire that is looped at the end. Pedunculated polyps —those with fairly long stalks—can be lassoed and the stalk then burned through with the electrocautery wire. Sessile polyps—those without well-defined stalks—can be snared several times until they are, in effect, shaved down so their base is level with the surrounding intestinal wall, and the base then can be coagulated.

Endoscopic polypectomy can be performed as an outpatient procedure and is successful in more than 95 percent of cases. In 1 to 3 percent of cases, there may be some bleeding from the polypectomy site, but this usually can be controlled by electrocoagulation (forming a clot with an electric current).

Polyp removal, particularly in the colon, is considered of major importance in cancer prevention. Colorectal cancer—cancer of the colon and the rectum (the lower end of the bowel)—affects at least

100,000 Americans a year and kills 50,000. It is our most common internal malignancy, more prevalent than cancer of the lung, breast, prostate, or uterus.

Before the availability of today's fiberoptic colonoscope—which is almost six feet long and able to view the entire colon—only the last ten inches of the colon could be examined, with a rigid instrument called a "proctosigmoidoscope." Although about 45 percent of all colon cancers are beyond the range of the procto instrument, the removal of polyps found in the limited area reachable by the procto has nevertheless proved of great importance. In a twenty-five-year study at the University of Minnesota Cancer Detection Clinic where some 18,000 patients underwent periodic proctosigmoidoscopy and prompt removal of any polyps found, the anticipated incidence of rectosigmoid cancer has been reduced by 85 percent.

Many physicians now consider it advisable to perform proctos routinely during general physical examinations of all people over forty-five, to remove any polyps found in the lower colon or rectum, and then to follow this with colonoscopy to detect and remove any polyps higher up in the colon. Although polyps of the esophagus, stomach, and duodenum are less likely than colonic polyps to become malignant, it is now considered essential to remove any that may be found during a diagnostic endoscopy procedure. Apart from risk of cancer, upper GI (gastrointestinal) polyps may ulcerate and bleed, and their removal is an even simpler procedure than colonic polypectomy because the endoscope can be manipulated more easily.

Esophageal Stricture Dilatation.

Esophageal strictures (abnormal narrowings of the esophagus) may be congenital, or may result from inflammation produced by abnormal return of stomach contents into the esophagus, or may stem from accidental swallowing of caustic materials. Whatever their cause, endoscopic techniques are now making surgical treatment of many strictures unnecessary. Over a fine guide wire inserted through the endoscope, metal "olives" of increasing diameter can be passed to gradually dilate the stricture.

Endoscopic Hemostasis.

Despite advances in critical care, the death rate from acute upper gastrointestinal bleeding—hemorrhage from ulcers or erosions—has remained at 10 percent over the past forty years. Now, however, endoscopic techniques—using special electrocautery probes inserted through the scope or in some cases using photocoagulation from a laser —are achieving immediate control of hemorrhage in more than 80 percent of patients.

Esophageal Varices.

Esophageal varices (varicose veins of the esophagus) can be dangerous because they tend to rupture easily and may result in serious hemorrhage. The death rate associated with bleeding varices is in the range of 40 to 50 percent. Most cases result from advanced cirrhosis of the liver; an occasional case may be caused by the parasitic infection schistosomiasis, or by a blood clot in the portal vein.

Now there is an endoscopic technique in which a sclerosing (hardening) agent, such as ethanolamine or morrhuate sodium, can be injected into or around each enlarged vein through a short needle pushed out of a protective sheath inserted in the scope. A major advantage is that bleeding can be stopped almost instantly and the enlarged veins are destroyed without adverse effects on liver function. A disadvantage is that the sclerosing solution is an irritant that may cause severe inflammation and sometimes ulceration. Both of these, however, eventually heal.

Therapeutic ERCP.

Endoscopic retrograde cholangiopancreatography, which, as noted on p. 186, allows injection of a dye into the bile and pancreatic ducts so that clear X-ray pictures can be taken, has greatly helped accurate diagnosis of diseases in these areas.

One of the first therapeutic uses of ERCP was for removal of stones left in the common bile duct after removal of the gallbladder, a condition that used to require a second surgical procedure. More recently, ERCP has been used for the same purpose in some patients with intact gallbladders and impacted stones but who are considered at unacceptably high risk for surgery.

In the procedure, a papillotome (a specially designed hot wire) is inserted through the endoscope and used to form a slitlike opening of about half an inch toward the end of the common bile duct. This is often enough to allow stones to pass spontaneously from the duct into the duodenum. If a stone fails to pass, a catheter with a small balloon at its tip (see BALLOON THERAPY) can be introduced into the bile duct to a point beyond the stone and then inflated. Often the stone is dislodged as the balloon is withdrawn.

Endoscopic removal of stones larger than about two centimeters (almost an inch) in diameter may be difficult, but an experimental technique now under study may solve the problem. It involves using a catheter positioned endoscopically to infuse a chemical, mono-octanoin, above the large stone in the duct. The chemical acts to dissolve the stone and may reduce it enough in size so it can pass out spontaneously or be removed with a balloon-tipped catheter or other means.

Evoked Potential
An emerging, versatile medical tool

Infants who may have hearing or visual problems, victims of head injuries, and patients with multiple sclerosis, spinal tumors, or low back pain are among the many who can be helped by a sensitive, noninvasive diagnostic procedure called "evoked potential" (EP) testing.

Like electroencephalography, EP testing measures brain waves by means of electrodes. The difference is that while EEGs measure spontaneously occurring brain waves (see p. 66), the EPs are brain waves that arise in response to specific stimuli—light patterns, clicks, or shocks, for example.

The technique works like this. A part of the body where there may be a problem is stimulated by suitable means: for a hearing loss, a series of sounds; for a vision disorder, changing visual patterns. Through electrodes attached to the patient's head and connected to an amplifier, signals traveling through the nervous system to the brain are picked up and fed into a computer. The length of time the signals take to reach the brain and their wave-form configurations are used to distinguish normal from abnormal.

An Objectivity Benefit.

Because there is no need for a voluntary response from the patient, EP testing is useful with nonverbal subjects, especially young children. For example, one common use is in testing infants suspected of having poor hearing, so they can be fitted with corrective devices as soon as possible before learning to speak.

Because of the objectivity, too, EP testing can be used in neurological evaluations to determine whether a complaint is organic or psychogenic—for example, in compensation lawsuits. Rather than having to depend totally on a patient's subjective, possibly misguided, or even profit-motivated report, stimuli can be applied to different parts of the skin to see whether or not there is a response in the brain.

Sensitivity to MS, Tumors.

Multiple sclerosis is a notoriously difficult disease to diagnose. Its onset is insidious, with variable symptoms that often come and go and may include any or many such manifestations as double vision or loss of part of the visual field, weakness, fatigue, tremor, slowing of speech, impaired balance, and still others. There is a risk of diagnosing MS on the basis of such likely symptoms alone—a risk that they may in fact be due to another disorder, a curable one, which may be overlooked.

With visual EPs (VEPs), 90 percent of MS patients show distinguishing abnormalities.

Because of their sensitivity, EPs have also been used to help point to tumors at early stages. One example: A twenty-four-year-old medical student had first experienced walking difficulties and great pain around the chest and back, all of which had disappeared after a month. When the symptoms returned a second time and routine X-ray and CAT scan (see CAT SCANS) of the spine were normal, the patient was told that his symptoms might be psychogenic. Another physician suspected multiple sclerosis, but an EP test was normal, so it wasn't MS. Further testing revealed what it was: a small, benign spinal-cord tumor that could be successfully removed.

Avoiding a Hole in the Head.

One of the most gruesome-sounding medical procedures, drilling a hole through the skull in order to measure pressure on the brain, is no longer necessary in many cases, thanks to visual evoked potentials. Determining intracranial pressure is important in treating head injuries and brain abnormalities, such as those in children with hydrocephalus ("water on the brain").

This new and important application of EP came about because of a suspicion of investigators at the University of Missouri-Columbia. Dr. Clark Watts, a neurosurgeon, had wondered for some time if unusual visual EPs often found in children who were victims of hydrocephalus (an enlargement of the skull with increased fluid volume), might be due to increased pressures within the head rather than abnormalities in vision pathways. This interested Donald York, a professor of physiology, who had noted changes in VEPs when intracranial pressure was experimentally raised in laboratory animals.

Over a four-year period, the two measured VEPs in a group of hydrocephalic children having trouble with their shunts—devices placed in their heads to drain off excess fluid. In addition, patients with suspected edema (accumulation of fluid) due to head injuries were measured. Patients' intracranial pressures were then determined by the usual methods, including boring a hole in the skull in the case of accident victims.

With the finding that VEPs correlated consistently with direct measurements, the far less traumatic VEP technique has come into use at the University of Missouri-Columbia Hospitals and Clinics and is now beginning to be used at other hospitals.

VEPs are especially helpful in "uncertain" cases. "Sometimes," notes Watts, "you suspect the pressure may be elevated, but you are not sure and you are worried. In the past, patients have had holes put in their skulls and it turned out their pressures were normal."

VEP testing can be done quickly, with little discomfort, and works even if the patient's eyes are closed, as when an accident victim is unconscious. Exactly why increased pressure in the brain causes an abnormal VEP is still unknown, but one hypothesis is that stretching of the fibers along the visual pathway alters their ability to conduct electrical impulses.

Diagnosing Slipped Disks.

An estimated 7 million Americans suffer from some form of back trouble. Of that number, some 200,000 each year are diagnosed as having "slipped disks" and are operated on.

Although a number of tests are used to determine whether a back patient has a disk problem, the accuracy is not as precise as it could be. According to Dr. Timothy B. Scarff, associate professor of surgery and chief of pediatric neurosurgery at Loyola University Medical Center in Maywood, Illinois, of the 70,000 persons operated on for slipped disks who fail to get good results, approximately 80 percent were misdiagnosed and should not have had the surgery.

As the result of research beginning in 1978, Scarff has developed a more sensitive test called "dermatomal somatosensory evoked potentials" (DSSEP). A dermatome is an area of skin served by one nerve root. Each nerve is made up of a number of different roots.

For the test, which is noninvasive and not painful, skin electrodes are placed over the root dermatome in the patient's leg and on the scalp. After electrical stimulation of the skin over the root, the time required for the signal to reach the brain is measured. In patients with slipped disks, the response is abnormal and the diagnostic accuracy rate is 93 percent.

At the Medical College of Wisconsin, when sixty-two patients with leg and low back pain were EP-tested, the recordings were abnormal in forty-seven. Of this group, 90 percent did well after surgery; of the remaining fifteen patients with normal EPs, only 20 percent benefited from surgery.

Safer Surgery.

Recently, EP monitoring has been introduced into the operating rooms of Columbia-Presbyterian Medical Center in New York and a few other medical centers around the country to protect patients from injury to the brain and spinal cord during a number of complex surgical procedures. The technique is proving especially useful in increasing the margin of safety during operations to correct major disorders of the spinal column, such as in scoliosis, and during intricate neurosurgical procedures, such as removal of spinal-cord tumors.

In the past, surgeons might not have known until after the operation whether any healthy nerve tissue had been injured inadvertently during surgery. In some cases where the risk of injury was high, patients actually had to be brought out of anesthesia during an operation so surgeons could test the integrity of the nervous system by asking them to move fingers or toes, for example.

Now, EP readings are taken before surgery starts and are repeated frequently as the operation proceeds. A significant interruption or variation in signals compared to the preoperative recordings makes injury to the brainstem or spinal cord obvious immediately, and corrective measures can be instituted at once.

Potential Uses.

Many other possible applications for EP testing are now under investigation. They were the subject of preliminary reports by many researchers at an international conference on EP held under the auspices of

Northwestern University Medical School and the Illinois Institute for Developmental Disabilities.

One potential area is in the diagnosis and monitoring of childhood learning disabilities and mental disorders, including Down's syndrome, autism, hyperactivity, dyslexia, and emotional problems. To measure behavioral function, specific components of EPs—those occurring within a time period such as fifty- to sixty-thousandths of a second after the signal—are being explored. Such components appear to be useful in measuring the contributions of a patient's attitude, interest, and stability to a problem.

Autistic children's responses to sound, as measured by auditory EPs, have been found to be different from those of other children. Some studies suggest that EPs also may provide early indications of adult mental disorders, including alcoholic brain damage.

EPs also seem promising as a means of providing an index of recovery from stroke and determining when the patient's brain cortex has reached a point where it can facilitate learning and rehabilitation.

The use of EP testing with other diagnostic tools—such as electro-encephalograms, PET scanning, and CAT scanning—is expected to increase its value. For example, a PET scan—which shows localized activity in the brain—may help to establish specific sources of some abnormalities shown in EP recordings. (See CAT SCANS and PET SCANS.)

Fat Suctioning
(Suction Lipectomy)
Removing unwanted bulges of fat

Early in 1983, a twenty-nine-year-old North Carolina woman underwent a newly imported procedure for removing unsightly bulges of fat in her abdomen and thighs after two years of exercise had failed to get rid of them. The fat was literally sucked out in a procedure known by several names—"fat suction," "suction curettage," "lipolysis," and "suction lipectomy."

"It smoothed out the lumps," she remarks. "It was more contouring than changing sizes, but now my clothes fit better. I didn't have much pain at all and I was back playing sports a week and a half later. And I was real surprised at how small the scars were."

The procedure has attracted considerable public attention. It has also become the focus of investigation and debate among plastic surgeons, some of whom have reservations, particularly about its being regarded as a miracle cure for fat, which it is not, and its performance by unqualified opportunists.

The Origins.

The dream of being able to get rid of unwanted fat bulges is, of course, an ancient one. As far back as the 1920s, removal of localized fat deposits by scraping them out with a curette was tried a few times but got nowhere. In the 1960s, Dr. Josef Schrudde, a Cologne, West Germany, plastic surgeon, developed a technique of scraping out fat through small incisions. In the 1970s, Dr. Ulrick Kesselring of Lausanne, Switzerland, added suction to the process.

In the mid-1970s in Paris, Dr. Yves-Gérard Illouz began to inject a hypotonic saline solution and an enzyme, hyaluronidase, into the fat to be removed, believing this breaks down fat cells and simplifies removal. Many other surgeons, however, believe that results are just as good without the injections.

Early in 1983, the American Society of Plastic and Reconstructive Surgery sent a panel of fourteen American specialists and cosmetic surgeons to France and Switzerland to study the operation. Upon their return, the American doctors reported that the procedure, in expert hands, could be effective.

How It Is Done.

Through a half-inch incision, which may be hidden in the navel or in a buttock crease, the surgeon inserts a long, hollow rod attached to a suction machine. As the rod is manipulated, the fatty deposits are drawn through it. The manipulation involves making a series of radiating tunnels, and the amount of fat removed depends on the number of thrusts of the rod in each tunnel.

Immediately after completion of suctioning, tight elastic dressings are applied to compress the treated areas and support the skin until it contracts to the new shape. This is continued for at least a week, and the patient must wear a girdle or other support for another month or two.

Small areas often can be done under local anesthesia on an outpatient basis. More extensive lipectomies require general anesthesia with one to three days of hospitalization afterward.

Some patients, however, experience burning, tearing pain in the treated area that may persist for months.

Surgical fees may range from $750 for a small procedure up to $4,000 for a more extensive one.

Although lipectomy can remove as much as three kilograms (about six and a half pounds) of fat with little or no scarring, contraction of the tunnels afterward may sometimes leave a slightly wavy body surface. Most women, however, reportedly feel that a little rippling is of no great concern as long as they can "get into jeans and not have these bulges sticking out."

Suitable Candidates.

In its report, the expert panel that investigated suction lipectomy in Europe emphasizes that the procedure is not a cure for obesity and should be used only for localized fat deposits that do not respond to dieting and exercise.

The panel members emphasize, too, that the procedure will not improve sagging skin or surface dimpling due to cellulite—and good results require the contractility of young skin, so patients usually should not be over forty years of age. The panel has suggested that young women with localized fat deposits on the lower torso and on the thighs make the best candidates, especially when they are of reasonable weight, but it has also indicated that candidates may include slightly to moderately overweight women who are willing to accept some postoperative surface irregularities for a better silhouette in clothes.

Going beyond the panel's criteria, some surgeons have used lipectomy on moderately obese women with large fat accumulations on lower torso and thighs resistant to diet and exercise. Early results appear promising. Promising results have also been reported in men with gynecomastia (breast overdevelopment). Up to 200 cubic centimeters of fat have been removed from each breast.

Permanence.

How long the benefits of suction lipectomy can be expected to last is not definitively known. Theoretically, because adults are believed to have a set number of fat cells, removal of many of the cells from areas that have tended to accumulate undue amounts of fat should lessen the disproportionate buildup of fat in those areas even with weight gain.

Experience thus far suggests that this may hold. But recent research with animals indicates that under some circumstances new fat cells can be produced—at least in animals. Whether this applies to humans is not known. Some researchers believe that complete replacement of removed fat cells is unlikely in humans (when replacement occurs in animals, it usually is not complete), and that if in fact a quarter or half of the cells were replaced, the lipectomized patient would still have gained something.

Not all plastic surgeons are enthusiastic about suction lipectomy. One who isn't, Dr. Dicran Goulian, Jr., chief of plastic surgery at New York Hospital–Cornell Medical School, is quoted in a report in the professional magazine *Medical World News* as contending: "We shouldn't operate on fat people. I just don't think this is a proper way for my colleagues to approach the problem. It's not medically sound. I'm one man who won't do it."

On the other hand, the same report notes that Dr. Jerome A.

Adamson, professor of plastic surgery at Eastern Virginia Medical School in Norfolk, is convinced the technique is a good tool here to stay. "I'm certain there are lots of applications no one has thought of yet."

CAUTION.   Suction lipectomy sounds easier than it actually is. Considerable skill is needed to carry it out effectively and safely. Poor handling of the rod, for example, could perforate the abdominal wall. Also, excessive fat removal can lead to shock. Even experienced plastic surgeons need special training to use the procedure properly, and many are taking such training.

Yet, as Dr. Simon Frederics of St. Luke's Episcopal Hospital, Houston, chairman of the fourteen-man panel that investigated the procedure in France and Switzerland, has reported, beauty salons and health spas are advertising the procedure and some surgeons without special training or experience are seeking to buy the suction machine.

Anyone considering the procedure would do well to consult a certified plastic surgeon and to determine that he or she has had special training in suction lipectomy.

Fertilization in Vitro ("Test-Tube Babies")
Help for the infertile

The first child resulting from fertilization of a human egg outside its mother's body was born in England on July 25, 1978. Since then, there has been a remarkable proliferation of programs to carry out the technique known as *"in vitro* fertilization."

It took more than a decade of unsuccessful attempts before Drs. Patrick Steptoe and Robert Edwards of Cambridge, England, had their first success with the birth of Louise Brown in 1978. Two years later, Eastern Virginia Medical School in Norfolk became the first center in this country to offer *in vitro* fertilization. By 1983, there were well-established programs at several other institutions—among them, Presbyterian Hospital in New York City, George Washington University School of Medicine in Washington, D.C., and the University of Texas Health Sciences Center in Houston. In addition, an estimated 100 to 200 other centers were doing or planning to do *in vitro* fertilization.

Couples Who May Be Helped.

Among those for whom the technique may be applicable are couples whose female partners have tubal disease that is surgically irreparable or cervixes that do not allow sperm penetration, or couples for whom intrauterine insemination has not been successful.

It may also be applicable for some couples with male partners who have inadequate sperm. Why this is so is not understood and is under study, but it is already clear that some patients can be helped.

There are also some couples in whom even the most sophisticated diagnostic tests do not identify a cause for infertility. Such couples have been labeled "normal infertile couples." Some women in this category have become pregnant through *in vitro* fertilization.

The Technique.

Although each step in the process is simple, *in vitro* fertilization as a whole is not.

"The fertilization and embryo transfer," says Dr. Raymond L. Vande Wiele, director of the Obstetrics/Gynecology Service at Presbyterian Hospital, "are based on separate tests and steps. We know how to do each step, but they're difficult to coordinate."

A patient accepted for the procedure at Presbyterian is instructed to let the staff know when her menstrual period begins. For a period of time—usually between the third and twelfth days of her cycle—hormones are administered to stimulate the ovarian follicles so that a greater number of eggs will be brought to maturity, thus improving the chance of fertilization. During the period of hormonal stimulation, an ultrasound specialist observes the daily development of eggs within the follicles.

When the follicles are mature, another hormone is administered to bring about ovulation (release of the eggs from the follicles). Once the eggs are ready for release, a small instrument, a laparoscope, is inserted into the patient's abdomen to retrieve them. Through the instrument's optical system, the physician can identify the ovaries; and with the aid of a tiny suction device on the laparoscope, he can remove the eggs from the follicles.

After their removal, the eggs are fertilized by the husband's sperm in a laboratory dish (*vitro* is from the Latin for "glass"). The fertilization process, whether it occurs naturally or *in vitro,* takes six to twelve hours.

As in the natural situation, so in the laboratory: Growth of the fertilized egg may stop after it begins, or the egg may go on to develop into an embryo.

After a brief incubation period to confirm that normal development of the egg into embryo is occurring, the embryo is transferred back to the uterus through a small catheter (tube). Because only a fraction of transferred embryos are likely to "take," whenever possible more than one embryo is transplanted to increase the likelihood of pregnancy.

At Presbyterian Hospital, a twenty-member team is involved with *in vitro* fertilization. It includes physicians who carry out screening of patients, ovulation monitoring, harvesting of the eggs, and implantation of the embryos. Other members include an egg-preparation specialist, a nurse practitioner, hormonal and ultrasound specialists and technicians. The team has to be available on a round-the-clock basis, ready whenever the eggs are ready for harvesting.

Success Rates.

The first two births reported by the original British pioneers in the field of *in vitro* fertilization resulted from a series of 109 embryo transfers —a success rate of just below 2 percent. More recently, the same group in England reported a series of cases involving 330 laparoscopies that resulted in 195 embryo transfers yielding forty-six pregnancies. At the time of the report, two babies had been delivered and there were twenty-nine stable pregnancies—an anticipated success rate of about 9 percent (births per laparoscopy).

Other teams have reported similar rising success rates with increasing experience. Those with greatest experience (in England, Virginia, and at two centers in Melbourne, Australia) have most recently reported success rates approaching 20 percent for pregnancies per laparoscopy.

Such rates are encouraging, considering nature's own success rates. At Presbyterian, Dr. Elynne B. Margulis points out that "nature itself isn't very efficient. A fertile couple is not assured of becoming pregnant on the first try. It takes an average couple about three months to conceive, which is about a 31-percent success rate. With the *in vitro* success rate at 20 percent, we're not far from nature."

Costs.

Patients today usually are charged $3,000 to $4,000 for each *in vitro* fertilization attempt—and at the well-established medical centers, each attempt has a 15 to 20 percent chance of success. Thus, it takes three attempts and $9,000 to $12,000 for less than a 50 percent chance of becoming pregnant.

Yet there is no shortage of people eager—and waiting—to pay for the procedure. At Eastern Virginia Medical School in Norfolk, which schedules patients six months ahead of time, more than 3,000 patients are waiting to get on the six-month list. Since Eastern Virginia can handle only about 270 patients a year, this represents a backlog of more than ten years. Fortunately, however, many of these patients may be handled by new centers springing up around the country.

Although the cost is considerable, it does not appear to be an overwhelming obstacle. Remarks Dr. Howard Jones, who with his wife, Dr. Georgeanna, established the Eastern Virginia center, "A lot of people consider having a child a high-priority item when it comes to doling out their budget."

Risks.

Originally, there were concerns about possible harm to the mother and/or the child with *in vitro* fertilization.

Two possible risks for the mother are identifiable: from the surgical procedures and from ectopic (outside the uterus) pregnancy. But among more than 2,000 laparoscopies for egg retrieval, only a single untoward event occurred. So the risk for this is minimal, like that of laparoscopy used for other purposes.

As for ectopic pregnancies, published reports show only 2 in 184 *in vitro*–induced pregnancies—a rate well within the range of up to 3 percent for natural pregnancies.

There have been two possible concerns about risk to the embryo: excessive death rates of early embryos and induced congenital abnormality in children born. As yet there is no clear-cut evaluation of the excess of embryo deaths—for one thing, because there is still a question about the percentage of embryo deaths that would have occurred anyhow because of genetic or other defects. It is generally assumed, however, that there is some cost, perhaps only relatively small, in a higher rate of early embryonic death.

As for congenital abnormalities, no certain conclusions are yet possible. According to one report of 125 births after *in vitro* fertilization, only one abnormality occurred—a heart malformation corrected by surgery. But until a sizable number of children reach older ages, subtle effects, such as nervous-system impairments that might be reflected in impaired intelligence, may not be apparent.

Extensions of the Basic Procedure.

There are a number of possible variations of the basic *in vitro* fertilization procedure.

Some success has been reported in using it with women who are normally fertile but whose husbands have low sperm counts, low sperm motility, or are infertile due to other causes. In such cases, conception may not be possible with normal coitus but sometimes is when the husband's sperm are united with the wife's ova in a laboratory dish.

Another possible variation is embryo adoption—the transfer of "surplus" embryos from a treated couple to another sterile couple. Some interest in this possibility has been reported from the Queen Victoria Medical Centre in Melbourne, Australia.

Freezing of embryos for storage is also a possibility. At Monash University Centre in Melbourne, a small number of embryos have been frozen and later transferred to a uterus. A first successful pregnancy has been reported.

Writing about freezing in the journal *Science,* Oct. 14, 1983, Drs. Clifford Grobstein, Michael Flower, and John Mendeloff of the University of California-San Diego observe:

Freezing becomes an option because hormonal stimulation before laparoscopy yields multiple eggs that can be recovered in a single operation. This is advantageous because transfer of more than one embryo gives a higher pregnancy rate, but also a higher twinning rate than normal, and because embryos not used in a first transfer attempt can be, if frozen and stored, used in a second transfer attempt without repetition of egg recovery.

However, if stored for longer periods, the embryos might constitute an embryo bank. It might, for example, be judged desirable to store embryos early in a marriage (not necessarily involving infertility) for use at some later times. This would provide the ultimate in family planning, as well as possibly allowing later childbearing without added risk of genetic defect (for example, Down's syndrome). Success in identifying sex type in cattle embryos has been reported and selection of sex of human offspring may not be far behind. Finally, embryo banks also make possible embryo adoption, if the genetic parents are willing to release the frozen embryos for transfer to other sterile couples or to any woman unable to bear her own child by the natural process.

These are all technical possibilities—but not without uncertainties. There are questions still to be answered about the safety and efficacy of embryo freezing, for example. There is little information about possible damage to offspring.

And there are, of course, important ethical, legal, and social implications that are going to need careful consideration, a process already begun in Australia and England, though not yet to any significant degree in the United States. (See also ADOPTIVE PREGNANCY and SURROGATE EMBRYO TRANSFER.)

Fetal Medicine
Tests and treatments in the womb

For expectant parents, no news can be more devastating than to be told that their unborn baby has a serious defect. Until recently, choices were limited: therapeutic abortion, or birth of a child doomed to early death or severe lifelong handicaps.

Now it appears likely that many fetuses with treatable birth defects are on the threshold of becoming patients while in the womb, and a promising start has been made in treating several—with dramatic success.

- Four months after doctors at the Medical College of Virginia reached in and drained fluid from a kidney cyst, a boy in Charlottesville, Virginia, was born healthy.
- Just five days before she was born, Medical College of Virginia doctors removed fluid from the lungs of a female fetus.
- At the University of Colorado, fluid was removed from the brain of a male fetus with hydrocephalus two and a half months before birth.
- In New Haven, Connecticut, Yale University physicians successfully drained fluid from an unborn child's chest and abdomen.

Moreover, short of actual treatment of the fetus in the womb, there are now other therapeutic alternatives becoming available for use when a fetal malformation is diagnosed: changing the timing of delivery, changing the mode of delivery, and sometimes treating the mother to help her unborn baby. The new developments in therapy give new importance to the rapidly developing field of prenatal diagnosis.

Prenatal Diagnosis.

Most pregnancies require no more than simple periodic monitoring by the physician of the progress of mother and fetus. There are, however, some situations in which something more may be required because there is increased likelihood of a problem. Such situations may arise, for example, when the mother's uterus is too small or too large for the stage of the pregnancy; when an earlier pregnancy has led to birth of a child with a defect; when there is a genetic history that gives concern; or when the mother's age increases chances of abnormalities.

Several important prenatal diagnostic tools are now available. One is amniocentesis, in which, through a needle inserted into the uterus through the mother's abdomen, a small sample of amniotic fluid containing cells cast off by the fetus can be withdrawn for study. Amniocentesis allows detection of chromosomal defects (such as the defect responsible for Down's syndrome, once called "mongolism") and inherited metabolic abnormalities. It also permits evaluation of fetal lung maturity.

Another major tool is sonography—the use of an ultrasound or very high-frequency sound-wave machine with probe placed on the mother's abdomen to see within. Ultrasound can determine the age, size, and position of the fetus, and can yield important information on fetal breathing, fetal movements, and fetal vital functions. (See ULTRASOUND.)

Fetoscopy can be used to actually see the fetus in the uterus and spot certain physical defects. For the procedure, sound waves are used to locate the fetus, the umbilical cord, and the placenta. Through a small incision in the mother's abdomen, a pencil-lead-thin tube is inserted into the uterus and the amniotic sac. The tube contains an endoscope with fiberoptic bundles that transmit light. Through the scope, the physician can see small areas of the fetus as it floats by, discern eyes, ears, mouth, fingers, genitals.

Through the tube, too, the physician can insert a needle to puncture one of the fetal blood vessels on the surface of the placenta and draw a sample of blood—and by inserting a biopsy forceps into the tube, the physician can take a one-millimeter (.04-inch) skin sample from the fetus. From these samples, the physician can diagnose skin disease and such blood disorders as hemophilia and thalassemia, plus any sickle-cell cases that may have been missed by amniocentesis (see GENE THERAPY).

The delicate fetoscopy procedure, done under local anesthesia, must be carried out with great care and skill.

Fetal Medicine.

Only a beginning has been made in the medical treatment of the fetus *in utero*—but it is a promising beginning.

One of the first developments was *in utero* transfusions for unborn children suffering from a life-threatening anemia caused by an Rh incompatability between their own blood and that of their mothers.

In 1964, when Dr. Vincent Freda, an obstetrician at Columbia-Presbyterian Medical Center in New York City, performed some of the first transfusions, it was done by making an abdominal incision through the uterus, exposing the foot of the fetus, making an incision in the fetus's femoral artery, and inserting a polyethylene catheter. The procedure was effective but very complex and subjected the mother to major surgery.

Now Freda uses a less invasive technique—a needle approach. It begins with the injection of a dye into the amniotic fluid twenty-four hours before the transfusion. Because the fetus is constantly swallowing amniotic fluid, the dye enters its intestine and, using a fluoroscope, the doctor can see the intestinal tract of the fetus and avoid it as he guides a needle into the lower abdomen. A catheter is threaded through the needle and the needle is removed. Blood is then injected into the fetus.

Freda and his colleagues have treated more than 400 babies *in utero,* performing the transfusion technique as early as twenty-two weeks into pregnancy and transfusing the same fetus as many as five times before delivery with successful results.

Recently, too, injections of thyroid hormone into the amniotic fluid have been used to treat congenital hypothyroidism (low thyroid-gland functioning) and goiter and to help mature the fetal lungs.

The instillation of nutrients such as amino acids, the basic constituents of proteins, into the amniotic fluid has been used to feed intrauterine growth-retarded fetuses orally.

Severe fetal hydrops (dropsy) has been treated *in utero* by administration of digitalis and diuretics, and digitalis and propranolol have been used to stabilize irregular fetal heartbeats.

Treating the Fetus Indirectly, Through the Mother.

In 1981, for the first time anywhere, physicians at the University of California-San Francisco were able to successfully diagnose a fetus's potentially fatal dependence on the vitamin biotin—and also for the first time they were able to intervene *in utero* and treat the condition.

Biotin plays a key role in the chemical reactions that provide nourishment and eliminate cellular waste products. The reactions are stimulated by enzymes, and at least five of these enzymes must have biotin attached to them in order to function. If the biotin pathways from the intestine to body cells are blocked, the enzymes fail to work properly and metabolic reactions slow down. This itself can kill a child, or it can interfere with the immune system, leaving the child susceptible to deadly infections.

Nicole, as the child in San Francisco was to be named at birth, was the second in the family to inherit a genetic disorder that disrupts the process by which biotin is used in the body. When her mother became pregnant with her, doctors suspected there was a one-in-four chance this child would have the same problem.

Using a sample of amniotic fluid obtained through amniocentesis, doctors discovered that biotin-dependent enzyme activities were not normal unless biotin was added. This indicated that the unborn child was biotin-dependent, requiring more than normal amounts of biotin to thrive.

The decision was to give the mother large quantities of the vitamin with the hope it would be absorbed by the fetus. To minimize risk of injury to the fetus, treatment was delayed until midway in the twenty-third week of pregnancy, when the major organs of the fetus are already formed.

It worked. Nicole was born a healthy child and remains so, while requiring a daily dose of biotin.

Other fetal deficiencies are being overcome by treatment of the mother before birth.

In respiratory-distress syndrome, glucocorticoids—cortisone and similar hormones—given to the mother increase deficient fetal lung surfactant (a substance that helps keep the lung's air sacs expanded) and alleviate the disease.

At least one fetus with methylmalonic acidemia—an enzyme problem that can lead to lethargy, coma, and mental and physical retardation—has been treated successfully *in utero* by giving the mother massive doses of vitamin B_{12}.

Fetal Surgery.

Because the term infant is a better surgical risk than the preterm infant, most correctable malformations that can be diagnosed *in utero* are best managed by medical and surgical treatment after delivery. Such malformations include atresia (absence of the normal opening) of the esophagus, small intestine, or rectum; deformities of the face and head, extremities, or chest wall; ovarian and intestinal cysts; a multicystic kidney; a small intact omphalocele (protrusion of part of the intestine through a defect in the abdominal wall); a small intact meningocele (protrusion of a covering membrane of the brain or spinal cord through a defect in the skull or spinal column). When any such anomaly is detected *in utero,* delivery can be planned so that appropriate specialists are available.

For some fetal anomalies, early delivery may be indicated. In each case, the risk of premature delivery has to be weighed against the risk of continued pregnancy. In ruptured omphalocele, for example, early delivery can minimize damage. Early delivery can also be valuable for correcting malrotation of the intestine when it threatens to cause intestinal gangrene, perforation, and peritonitis. It can be useful, too, in some cases of intrauterine growth retardation, fetal hydrops, and hydrocephalus. When hydrocephalus is severe, the high pressure from the excess fluid can compress the brain and early delivery for treatment to eliminate the excess fluid and bring down the pressure can maximize the opportunity for normal brain development and may avoid the difficult problem of delivering a baby with an abnormally large head.

Elective cesarean delivery may be indicated for fetal malformations that may make for difficult vaginal delivery, such as giant omphalocele or large hydrocephalus. Cesarean delivery may also be used when there is a malformation requiring immediate surgical correction best performed in a sterile environment. One example is a ruptured omphalocele. In this situation, the baby can be resuscitated in a nearby sterile operating room and undero immediate surgical correction.

There are, however, fetal disorders for which surgery *in utero* now may be tried—as it was not long ago when Dr. Michael Harrison, codirector of the Fetal Treatment Program at the University of California-San Francisco, performed kidney surgery on a fetus, believed to be the first operation of its kind.

The mother was pregnant with twins, one of whom had a bladder obstruction and was unable to urinate. There were several problems. If untreated, the sick twin's kidney would have deteriorated. But if the surgery was performed, there was risk of initiating premature labor and both babies could have been lost. To add to the difficulty, the mother was only two months pregnant at the time.

For a time, surgery was held off. But when it became apparent that the buildup of urine in the sick twin's bladder had reached dangerous proportions, the surgical team operated. Guided by ultrasonography (see ULTRASOUND), the surgeons inserted a tiny plastic tube through the mother's abdomen and uterus into the fetal bladder, where it remained to drain urine into the amniotic fluid. After birth, the drain was removed and the baby's urinary tract was reconstructed.

Draining procedures are also being used for fetuses afflicted with hydrocephalus. In this condition, a blockage in the central nervous system causes fluid to accumulate in the hollow ventricles of the brain, eventually causing brain damage. At Harvard, a team treated a fetus with hydrocephalus, starting at the twenty-fifth week of pregnancy, by periodically inserting a needle into the fetus's head to withdraw excess fluid.

A procedure used at the University of Colorado to combat hydrocephalus involves inserting a catheter through the soft bone of the fetal skull to drain fluid from the enlarged ventricle into the amniotic sac. About 80 percent have survived such surgery, but how well these children fare in the long run will not be known until they reach school. After birth, the catheter is removed and another tube is substituted to divert fluid from the brain into the abdomen.

At Yale and the Medical College of Virginia, a number of successful *in utero* operations have involved inserting a drain to extract excess fluid from kidney cysts, fluid-filled and collapsed lungs, and the abdomen.

Fortunately, such defects are relatively rare. But many doctors expect that fetal surgery will be applied before long to more-common congenital problems, including diaphragmatic hernia. In this condition, an opening in the diaphragm that separates chest and abdomen allows the intestines to squeeze into the chest and press against the lungs. Although this is easily correctable after birth by placing the intestines in normal position and closing the defect in the diaphragm, more than half of these infants die of pulmonary insufficiency because the lung compressed by the herniated intestines fails to develop properly. To allow the lung to grow and develop enough to support life at birth, the lung compression must be relieved before birth.

At the University of California-San Francisco, Dr. Harrison and his colleagues, Drs. Mitchell S. Golbus and Roy A. Filly, have demonstrated in fetal lambs that compression of the fetal lung during the last three months results in fatal lung underdevelopment and that eliminating the compression allows the lung to grow and develop sufficiently to reverse the underdevelopment and allow survival at birth.

For correction of the problem in humans, the California team hopes to actually remove the fetus from the mother's uterus, close the hole in the diaphragm, and return the fetus to the womb. The operation has been performed successfully on fetal lambs.

Risks.

The risks involved in fetal diagnosis and treatment are generally greater for the fetus than for the mother and vary greatly, depending on the invasiveness and magnitude of the procedure.

Sonography carries no known risk. Puncture of the amniotic cavity involves a small risk of fetal injury or loss. Fetoscopy, fetal blood sampling, and puncture of the fetal abdomen for transfusion carry some risk, but the risk is quite acceptable in terms of the benefits to be obtained.

The greatest known risk of fetal manipulation is the triggering of premature labor and delivery. Fortunately, drug control of uterine contractions is improving with the advent of compounds such as ritodrine and prostaglandin synthetase inhibitors.

Fetal therapy, as Drs. Harrison, Golbus, and Filly have pointed out, raises complex medical and ethical issues. For the fetus, the risk of a procedure is weighed against the possibility of, and benefit to be derived from, correction. For the mother, risk and benefit assessment is more difficult. Most fetal abnormalities do not directly threaten maternal health, yet there is some risk for the mother in a corrective procedure. She may consider the risk worth it in terms of helping her unborn baby, increasing his or her chances for normal life, and relieving her own burden of raising a child with a severe malformation.

In concluding a report in the *Journal of the American Medical Association,* Aug. 14, 1981, the three California doctors remark: "Our ability to diagnose fetal birth defects has achieved considerable sophistication. Treatment of several fetal diseases has proved feasible, and treatment of more complicated lesions will undoubtedly expand as techniques for fetal intervention improve. It seems likely that the fetus with a treatable birth defect is on the threshold of becoming a patient." (See also AMNIOCENTESIS and ULTRASOUND.)

Fever: New Insights
It may often be good, not bad

Unlike man, a lizard has no internal temperature-raising mechanism. But inject the reptile with disease bacteria and it will go bask in the sun until its body temperature shoots up to fever levels. Prevent the basking and it dies of infection.

At the University of Michigan, Dr. Matthew J. Kluger has shown the need for fever in reptiles and in many other organisms. Sick fish, too, raise their internal temperatures by seeking out warmer areas of water. Watch an ailing one in a home tank and you see it migrate toward the tank's heater and stay there, between heater and tank wall, to keep body temperature at fever level.

In mice, dogs, and pigs exposed to viruses, modest body-temperature elevations have been shown to be beneficial. In a study with infected rabbits, every animal given drugs to prevent fever died promptly, while 71 percent of those not receiving treatment to keep temperature down remained alive.

At the Veterans Administration Hospital in Dallas, Dr. Philip A. Mackowiak and other investigators have shown that even antibiotics are more effective—able to kill bacteria more rapidly—when there is fever than at normal body temperature.

Other recent research reports have noted that some people, usually elderly, seem unable to respond to infection with fever, and that helping them to produce fever—with such measures as warm clothing, warm blankets, warm room air, and warm drinks—dramatically increases survival rates.

Mounting evidence from these and many other recent investigations indicates that fever, far from being the enemy it is commonly thought to be, often may be a friend: It may strengthen the body's defense system, aid significantly in fighting infections, even help in the battle against cancer (see HYPERTHERMIA).

Behind the Bad Reputation.

In a sense, recent discoveries should not be totally surprising. Modern measurement capabilities have shown that the human body must expend 7 percent more energy for each 1°C rise in body temperature. That's a costly process, hardly likely to have been retained for hundreds of millions of years of evolution, and in so many species, unless it had some advantage.

Actually, the ancient Greeks respected and celebrated fever, even if for the wrong reason (they believed it caused excess harmful "humor" to be cooked and eliminated from the body). And three centuries ago, before there were effective fever-reducing drugs (antipyretics), Thomas Sydenham, a great English physician, observed that "fever is Nature's engine which she brings into the field to remove her enemy."

But by the mid–eighteenth century, as antipyretic agents became available, the idea that fever could be helpful began to change. Before very long, elevated temperature came to be looked upon as invariably harmful, and treatment to bring it down was considered essential. Only now are physicians beginning to respect fever as a potential ally.

Fever and Body Defense.

When infection strikes, the body mobilizes its defense system. Protective white cells in the blood increase in numbers. The white cells have the job of engulfing and destroying invading organisms. As they do that, they also produce a material—endogenous pyrogen—that travels via the bloodstream to the brain. There it stimulates production of prostaglandins, hormonelike chemicals, which act on the brain's temperature-regulating center, a kind of thermostat, resetting it to call for higher body temperature. Fever follows.

The effects on the body's immune (defense) system are many.

At fever temperatures, it has been found, the ability of white cells to move about, to rush to an infected area from other sites, is increased, and their ability to engulf and digest disease microorganisms is enhanced.

At the same time, antibodies in the blood increase. These molecules, another part of the immune system, also can act against microorganisms, locking onto and inactivating them.

Interferon, a body protective substance much publicized in recent years as a potential antitumor and antiviral agent, has been found to be more effective at fever temperatures.

With fever, too, blood levels of iron drop. At Tufts University School of Medicine in Boston, Drs. Charles A. Dinarello and Sheldon M. Wolff have determined that when pyrogen, the fever stimulator, is added to human cells, the cells release a substance that removes iron from the blood, making it unavailable for use by disease organisms that require it. Lowered iron concentration appears to be an important defense mechanism—a kind of "nutritional immunity." There are data now indicating that many bacterial species grow poorly in an iron-poor medium, and that the combination of fever and low iron results in virtually no growth.

Interestingly, too, after exercise a fever-producing agent appears in the blood plasma of human subjects. And when animals are injected with just one milliliter of plasma taken from human subjects after exercise, the animals develop fever and their plasma iron is reduced. No such effects occur when plasma taken from subjects prior to exercise is injected.

As Dr. Kluger points out, "The coupling of a defense reaction with physical exertion makes sense from an evolutionary standpoint. Exercise in lower species generally involves fleeing or fighting off attackers, both involving high risk of injury and infection. Gearing up host defenses in anticipation of injury would be beneficial in terms of survival."

Treatment for Fever.

Despite the evidence that fever is a defense mechanism, there can be times when it is advisable to use an antipyretic agent such as aspirin or acetaminophen, or to bring down a fever by other means, such as sponge bathing.

"Although moderate fever appears to enhance host defenses while inhibiting pathogenic microorganisms, extreme fever in some circumstances may have a detrimental effect on the host as well as the pathogen," according to Dr. Mackowiak.

Among patients for whom the risks of fever might possibly outweigh the benefits are young children predisposed to fever convulsion; pregnant women because of possible effects of fever on the fetus; and elderly or debilitated people because of possible effects on the cardiovascular system.

But otherwise, should there be a rush to bring down fever anytime it occurs?

There are as yet no definitive answers—more research is needed. But medical attitudes are changing and many physicians now are making an effort to reassure parents in particular about the usefulness of fever, particularly when it is moderate.

To be sure, temperature elevation can have unpleasant effects. It can lead to dehydration through loss of moisture unless that is compensated for by increased fluid intake. Headache, appetite loss, nausea, and vomiting may sometimes occur. There may be chills and shivering (the shivering, in fact, helps to raise the temperature to the level at which the thermostat in the brain has been reset). But discomfort usually does not begin until temperature reaches 103° or 104°F. "Every physician," says Dr. Barton D. Schmitt of the University of Colorado Medical Center, Denver, "has seen children who are happy and playful and who to everyone's surprise are found to have a temperature of this level."

When fever does produce discomfort, including physical weakness and mental dullness, that may be all to the good, many physicians now believe. Weakness helps to ensure physical inactivity, while dullness keeps the mind at rest, both allowing body resources to focus more completely on fighting illness.

Some physicians now advise parents to use aspirin or acetaminophen only if the rectal temperature is over 102° and the child is uncomfortable. A low-grade fever doesn't require any treatment except light clothing and added fluids, Dr. Schmitt advises, and emphasizes that the main reason for treating fever is to help the patient feel comfortable, not to prevent harm.

Fibrinolytic Therapy

To dissolve dangerous blood clots

Although blood clotting is a natural body defense, essential to prevent fatal hemorrhage from even a slight cut, clotting can also provoke problems, including heart attacks.

It was a clot that precipitated a heart attack in a sixty-two-year-old man as he waited at Long Island Jewish-Hillside Medical Center in New Hyde Park, New York, for news of his injured son. When he began to experience chest pains, he was rushed from the waiting room into a nearby laboratory. On the way, his heart stopped twice and the beating had to be restored by electric shock.

In the laboratory, a thin catheter (tube) was threaded through a vessel in the groin area up into his heart for the procedure known as "angiography" (see ANGIOGRAPHY) in which a dye is injected and X-ray films of blood vessels are made. The films revealed a blood clot blocking a major coronary artery feeding the heart muscle.

It was then an hour after symptoms had first appeared. Now, through the catheter, a chemical, streptokinase, was injected into the clot area. Fifty-five minutes later, repeated films showed the clot beginning to disintegrate and blood flow starting to resume to the heart muscle. Twenty-five minutes later, pain had subsided, and half an hour later—an hour and fifty minutes after start of the streptokinase injection—the infusion could be stopped and the patient transferred to a coronary-care unit.

The use of clot-dissolving drugs—known as "fibrinolytic therapy" or "thrombolytic therapy"—appears to be helpful in some cases in limiting the damage to heart muscle during early stages of a heart attack. It also provides a new weapon against dangerous blood clots of the legs and lungs.

The Threats.

Clots play a major role in the majority of heart attacks. Although an attack is a sudden event, it is the long-term result of a slowly developing disease process, atherosclerosis, in which fatty deposits are laid down on the inner wall of a coronary artery. At the same time, some scarlike tissue forms and projects into the artery channel and bloodstream. Such projections may encourage clotting of blood. Tiny clots may cause no problems, but if a large clot should form in a narrow artery, it may block the blood flow, resulting in a heart attack.

Sometimes a fatty deposit on an artery wall may rupture, and the ruptured material may then move through the bloodstream to a site in a smaller coronary vessel or branch where it may lead to a blockage. Expert estimates are that 85 to 90 percent of heart-attack victims have a clot blocking a major heart-feeding artery, while the remaining 15 percent or so have blockage without a clot.

Other clot-related conditions can develop. A common one is venous thrombosis (thrombophlebitis), in which a clot forms in a vein, usually a leg vein, producing aching pain and swelling. It may develop soon after childbirth; after accidental injury; when inflammation occurs; and when blood accumulates, or "pools," in the legs because of inactivity, bed rest, heart disease, obesity, varicose veins, fractures, and after surgery.

In a deep vein of the leg, a clot can be especially serious. Part or all of it may break loose and be carried to a lung vessel. There, known as a "pulmonary embolism," it can cause chest pain, labored breathing, cough, spitting of blood. Pulmonary embolisms are responsible for more than 100,000 American deaths a year.

Filling a Gap.

Prior to 1977, drug treatment for leg and lung clots was limited to a defensive approach employing anticoagulants—drugs such as heparin and warfarin, which often can prevent or slow further clot formation but have no effect on existing clots or their painful symptoms. What was needed, in addition to anticoagulant therapy, was a means of eliminating existing clots in order to restore circulation and normal vein anatomy. Surgical therapy has had some limited success. Fibrinolytic therapy—chemical clot dissolution with streptokinase or another agent, urokinase—appears to be a major advance.

The two agents are enzymes—chemicals that initiate and accelerate chemical reactions. (The body makes use of enzymes for many purposes. For example, digestive enzymes split starches, fats, and proteins.) Streptokinase is produced by strep bacteria in a culture medium and is then purified. Urokinase comes from human kidney cells grown in culture. Neither actually dissolves a clot itself; instead, each stimulates the body's own ability to liquefy and dissolve clotted blood.

In multicenter hospital trials sponsored by the National Institutes of Health, both streptokinase and urokinase proved highly effective in the treatment of pulmonary embolism. In a period of twenty-four hours, 66 percent of the patients had complete or significant clot dissolution. Only 11 percent of patients treated with traditional anticoagulants had similar benefits. Trials in patients with deep-vein thromboses have shown similar results.

Often, use of a clot-dissolving agent may be followed by use of an anticoagulant—a treatment with a double purpose: The fibrinolytic agent eliminates the existing clot, restores circulation, relieves painful symptoms, and may prevent permanent damage to a vein; the anticoagulant helps to prevent future clots.

In 1980, a consensus report of experts emerging from a National Institutes of Health conference held that "when properly used, in tandem with anticoagulation, thrombolytic therapy as currently practiced represents a significant advance in the management of acute deep-vein thrombosis and the more severe forms of pulmonary embolism."

In some cases, the treatment may produce complications, most often minor. There may be minor bleeding at a catheter site, mild allergic reactions, sometimes fever, local skin flushing, hives, muscular pains. These are usually readily controllable.

For Heart Attacks.

The usefulness of fibrinolytic therapy in heart-attack victims was discovered in the late 1970s by two West German physicians, Peter Rentrop (now at Mount Sinai Medical Center, New York City) and Karl Karsch of the University of Göttingen. The two men were in the midst of using angiography to examine a patient with a narrowed coronary artery when suddenly the patient had a heart attack. Desperately, they inserted a thin wire through the catheter and pushed it through the blockage in the artery, then withdrew the wire. Within two minutes the heart-attack signs were gone.

There was some possibility, then, of stopping an attack in its tracks. But the method used was hardly ideal. When blockage has persisted in a vessel for as little as thirty minutes, its sudden removal can be dangerous, triggering potentially lethal heart-rhythm abnormalities.

Eventually, Rentrop and Karsch thought of the possibility of using streptokinase to achieve gradual dissolution. It worked. In an early study, the two physicians succeeded in dissolving coronary-artery clots in twenty-eight of thirty-seven patients.

In the U.S., after successfully trying the technique in dogs, Dr. William Ganz and his associates at the UCLA School of Medicine and Cedars-Sinai Medical Center, Los Angeles, were able to report using fibrinolysis in twenty human patients within one and a half to three and a quarter hours after a heart attack and successfully opening the clot-blocked arteries in nineteen of the twenty. Since then, many successes have been reported elsewhere.

Timing is a critical factor. If fibrinolysis is to be useful, a blockage must be dissolved before the shutoff of blood to the affected area of the heart muscle leads to irreversible damage. Most physicians using the technique now believe that it is best done within three to eight hours after heart-attack symptoms first appear.

When used for heart attack, the clot-dissolving agent is introduced into a coronary artery via a catheter through the cardiac catheterization technique (see CARDIAC CATHETERIZATION). The catheter is threaded up through an arm or leg artery and the drug is infused through the catheter directly into the coronary artery to the site of the clot, dissolving it in many cases within an hour. The effectiveness has been shown in dozens of reports worldwide. For example, in one study of 337 patients (105 Americans and 232 West Germans), an 81 percent success rate of blood-flow reestablishment was achieved.

Toward Overcoming a Drawback.

A problem with fibrinolytic therapy administered through a catheter is that it requires a catheterization laboratory, a facility found in only about one in seven U.S. hospitals, with need, too, for an angiographer and other specially trained personnel, many of whom must often be located and called in after normal hours.

To overcome the problem, Dr. William Ganz at Cedars-Sinai

Medical Center has begun a trial of administering streptokinase by vein instead of catheter. He has reported excellent results in the first group of patients treated intravenously. Clot dissolution occurred in seventy-five of the seventy-eight patients (96 percent).

Dr. Ganz and his associates suggest that the intravenous approach may be just as effective as the catheterization method, and are urging large-scale trials.

The Frankel Appliance
For correcting buckteeth

At fourteen, an Atlanta girl's overbite had become so severe that even with mouth firmly closed, she could run her thumb up between her upper and lower teeth. Like 85 percent of all people with extremely protruding front teeth, her teeth were not the problem and braces not the answer. She suffered from an underdeveloped, markedly receding jaw. Eighteen months after receiving treatment developed in East Germany and now being incorporated into American dentistry, her mouth is no longer misaligned, her appearance is normal.

The Frankel appliance, a formidable-looking device worn inside the mouth, forces facial muscles to hold the lower jaw forward. If its use is begun early enough—preferably when a child is seven or eight —it can cause the lower jawbone to grow more forward over a longer period. When muscle function is altered, there is much less chance that the jaw will revert to its original position, as is often the case with teeth whose position has been changed by braces.

The appliance—called the "Frankel function regulator" in Europe —was developed by Dr. Rolf Frankel in East Germany in the 1950s. According to Dr. Michael Dierkes, head of Emory University School of Dentistry's Department of Orthodontics in Atlanta, who studied the technique in Zwickau, East Germany, and is encouraging its use in this country, the appliance will be as significant a development in altering function and appearance of misaligned mouths as was the invention of braces, those tangles of cemented bands and wires at which American dentistry already excels. Emory has established a center for treatment, training, and research associated with the appliance.

Unusual Case.

Among the growing number of successful cases treated at Emory, the fourteen-year-old girl's is considered a special triumph. At this age, especially for girls, the jaw is often fully developed. The effect of the Frankel appliance on a jaw whose growth potential already has been realized is simply unknown.

The girl had decided she could not go through life being called "gopher" and was willing to undergo the traditional treatment for adults: having the jawbone broken and a section of upper jawbone removed so the jaws could heal in a different direction. But her Emory orthodontist, Dr. Gerald Samson, believed she might still have a growth spurt coming, during which her unbroken jawbone might be coached to grow into a more symmetrical position.

The girl had fairly tall parents, but she was only 4′10″ and weighed only seventy pounds. Samson began a series of low-dosage X-rays of her wrists to measure the development of her bones. From these, it appeared that her skeletal development was two years behind her chronological age.

When the specially molded Frankel appliance was first placed in her mouth, the change in appearance was immediate: Her lower jaw was pulled forward, her cheeks filled out. However, she was barely able to move her mouth. Although only a front wire showed, looking much like the retainers worn by many of her peers, the effect of the appliance was much more akin to having the jaws wired together. (This effect is very much milder for younger patients with more growth potential.)

She wore the appliance around the clock, except during meals. At first, even with the device out, it was difficult to eat; her jaws were too exhausted to chew. Despite the discomfort, fatigue, and limited movement, however, the girl was highly motivated, especially as the improvement in her looks became increasingly apparent.

After eighteen months, she no longer needed the appliance. Her jaw had grown forward into a position that functions well and is aesthetically pleasing.

According to Emory orthodontists, the Frankel appliance can correct many misalignments of the lower jaw, both congenital and caused by trauma. They are currently investigating its use to correct *protruding* lower jaws in children, and are studying whether or not changes in muscle function brought about by the appliance might also benefit adults whose jawbones are fully developed.

The "G" Suit
For internal hemorrhaging and shock

One of the most effective means of controlling shock and internal hemorrhaging is the "G" suit. Also known as the "gravity suit" and the "antishock suit," it consists of three inflatable chambers—one for each leg and one for the abdomen.

The Shock State.

Medical shock can be a potentially grave emergency, capable of leading to death from injuries or illnesses that in themselves would not be lethal.

Shock is a state resulting from disturbance of the mechanisms that keep blood circulating properly throughout the body. Because of the circulation failure, the brain and other vital organs may be deprived of blood.

Shock may follow severe injury, severe burns, infection, bleeding, stroke, heart attack, poisoning, or exposure. Among its manifestations are a sharp drop in blood pressure, increased breathing rate, weak and rapid pulse, paling of the face, cold and clammy skin, restlessness, confusion, trembling, or unconsciousness.

The Effects of the Suit.

Inflation of the three chambers of the G suit to a pressure of ten to twenty millimeters of mercury compresses blood vessels in the abdomen and legs. This has two effects. First, it causes blood to be shunted away from the legs and abdomen to the vital structures of the head and chest, almost like a transfusion of as much as a liter of blood precisely where it is immediately most vital. The second effect is hemostatic—that is, it stanches the escape of blood. By reducing the radius and tension of vessel walls, the inflated suit encourages clot formation.

To and in the Hospital.

The G suit can be used not only in the hospital but also by paramedics when transporting a patient in shock to the hospital.

There are many dramatic applications.

For a woman in shock from a ruptured fallopian tube due to an ectopic pregnancy (pregnancy in which the fertilized ovum has become implanted outside the uterus, almost always in one of the fallopian tubes), application of the suit leads to a rise in blood pressure and slowing of the pulse rate, allowing time to restore blood volume and get the patient to surgery.

Postoperative bleeding, when uncontrollable by packing, can be effectively controlled with the suit. Such bleeding may sometimes occur, for example, after cesarean section or after hysterectomy in patients with adhesions due to chronic pelvic inflammatory disease or endometriosis. Use of the G suit in such cases often can avoid need for second operations.

Patients in shock without blood loss also respond to the use of the G suit.

The G suit's benefits, as noted in a recent report in the *Western Journal of Medicine,* "can be lifesaving as well as reducing the amount of blood products needed and their associated complications."

Gene Mapping

A new science now is beginning to shed light on a variety of major medical problems, ranging from mental retardation and life-threatening childhood blood diseases to heart attacks and senile dementia in later life.

Consider the twenty-three pairs of chromosomes in human cells as a cluster of large and small islands. The genes—the discrete bits of DNA, the units of heredity—can be viewed as hills, valleys, ponds, streams, and towns on the islands.

Gene mapping is based on the fact that, like most geographic features, most genes tend to keep their places relative to one another for millennia. Although certain genes, like towns, can relocate abruptly, such moves do not render the overall map obsolete.

How Maps Are Made.

Gene mapping had its relatively unsophisticated beginnings early in this century when it was recognized that some traits and disorders—color blindness, for example—are passed down by unaffected women and almost exclusively affect male offspring. This suggested that the normal genes that provide for color vision—and their mutant forms that fail to do so—must lie somewhere on the chromosome designated "X," one of the two chromosomes (the other being the "Y" chromosome) that determine sex.

But if it was relatively easy to trace sex-linked traits to a sex-determining chromosome, finding the precise location of the responsible genes within the chromosome did not become possible until very recently.

Before 1970, in still-early stages of gene mapping, researchers did family studies to establish which traits are inherited together with each other—a help in determining how close the governing genes are to one another.

Then, in the 1970s, came two major advances that speeded up the pace of gene mapping. One was the finding that a human cell could be fused with a rodent cell, and that the resulting hybrid cell, while multiplying, would tend to lose its human chromosomes, one or a few at a time, while keeping its natural rodent chromosomes. With good luck, a mass of such cells would end up with only a single human chromosome remaining in each cell, or even just a fragment of one human chromosome. Any human characteristic then found in such cells—for example, a specific human blood protein—would obviously be governed by a gene in whatever bit of human chromosomal material remained in the hybrid cell.

The second major advance was the finding that certain chemical stains could produce consistent patterns of uneven light and dark bands on chromosomes. Under the microscope, after staining, each human chromosome or fragment of one has its own "fingerprint," and the individual light and dark bands serve as landmarks for the position of specific genes.

By 1980, about 300 genes had been mapped, nearly all of them during the 1970s.

The Latest Revolution.

Explosive progress in mapping has come even more recently as the result of the newest methods of locating and dissecting individual genes. These methods stem from the discovery that various bacteria produce a versatile array of enzymes that can cut genes apart from each other and even cut genes into pieces in predictable fashion.

When cut up with enzymes, a specific strip of genetic material—DNA—ends up as a specific pattern of differing lengths. In this way, a segment of genetic material—containing perhaps a gene or two, plus some gene-activating material, plus some other DNA without function or with function still to be determined—can be distinguished from other bits of genetic material.

Geneticists now can even distinguish between normal and abnormal variants of the same gene, or between two entirely normal variants.

Human genes can be mapped in terms of the patterns of fragments produced by enzymes, and such a map can be integrated with gene maps made by studying human families or rodent-human hybrid cells —just as, for example, a political map of Europe can be superimposed on a map of the rivers and mountains of Europe.

Aiding Diagnosis.

Even within the space of a single year (1983), several important developments have stemmed from the new gene-mapping techniques.

In May, working under a March of Dimes Birth Defects Foundation grant, Dr. Haig Kazazian and colleagues at The Johns Hopkins University showed that sickle-cell disease and certain other severe hereditary anemias can be diagnosed or ruled out before birth by amniocentesis in the great majority of pregnancies at risk. Diagnosing these blood diseases in non-blood cells from the amniotic fluid surrounding the fetus is possible because scientists now have a detailed map of the genetic region responsible for the diseases. The landmarks used for this purpose are fragments carved out by enzymes.

Only a few months later, Dr. Susan L. Naylor of Roswell Park Memorial Institute in Buffalo and other scientists reported finding that a certain segment of genetic material of unknown function, called "G8," lies very close to the gene whose mutant version causes Huntington's disease (HD). HD is among the most tragic of human diseases. It is a slowly progressive deterioration of brain cells that causes movement disorders, depression, dementia, and death. It usually begins only in the third to fifth decade of life, and any child of an affected person has a 50 percent risk of developing the disease someday.

The finding that G8 variants can serve as markers for the HD gene means that in at least some families with histories of HD, it will almost certainly become possible for individuals to learn—if they choose to— whether they are destined to develop HD, to make informed decisions about childbearing, and to obtain prenatal diagnosis in pregnancies at risk. Intensive mapping of genes in the neighborhood of G8 should ensure that if G8 proves to be an unreliable marker, better markers, or even the HD gene itself, will be identified.

Genetic abnormalities in the way the body handles fats are emerging as risk factors for heart attacks. These late-manifested birth defects are under study by, among others, Dr. Vassilis Zannis and his colleagues at Children's Hospital Medical Center in Boston.

In a series of recent reports, Zannis and his co-workers have described genetic abnormalities in the amounts of two related blood proteins whose functions include transporting and disposing of fats. They have mapped the two causative genes to the same neighborhood and have mapped an introducing stretch of genetic material that may account for the two genes' substandard behavior.

Abnormalities of the two genes may be very important in the life of the coronary arteries, which feed the heart muscle. One of the genes codes for the main protein component of HDL (high-density lipo-protein), known as the "good cholesterol" because high levels of it appear to lower the risk for heart attacks. Patients with the genetic abnormality described by Zannis have low levels of HDL and early, severe coronary artery disease.

In 1983, too, Dr. Lowell R. Weitkamp of the University of Rochester reported that as yet unidentified genes within specific parts of two chromosomes, #6 and #14, may contribute to the risk of developing Alzheimer's disease (AD). AD is the most common form of progressive mental deterioration or dementia.

Weitkamp's evidence for genetic factors in AD comes from a study of a very large Canadian family plagued by the disorder for at least five generations and from previously published data on some smaller families. He found that AD tends to occur in family members in a pattern that reflects inheritance of certain testable traits known to be governed by genes in the two chromosomes. It may be significant that genes in the implicated areas of both chromosomes # 6 and #14 play major roles in the body's immune system, suggesting the involvement of the immune system, and possibly an infectious agent, in AD.

Another group of genes on chromosome #6 have come in for intensive study. They influence the configuration of the HLA (human leukocyte antigen) system, a kind of chemical fingerprint on the outside of all body cells that allows the body's immune system to distinguish the body's own material from foreign material.

The HLA system has been of importance to transplant surgeons in matching organ donors and recipients. More recently, genes in the system have been matched with certain diseases. For example, gene B-27 of the HLA system has been found in 95 percent of patients with ankylosing spondylitis, a chronic lower-spine arthritis common in men. Another HLA gene, D-7, is found in almost three of every four multiple-sclerosis victims. HLA genes have also been connected to hay fever, juvenile-onset diabetes, and more than seventy other disorders.

All told, the forty-six human chromosomes contain an estimated

100,000 genes. Scientists now are mapping these genes at the rate of about 200 a year, and some researchers—among them, Dr. Frank Ruddle, professor of biology and human genetics at Yale University—believe this rate will accelerate so rapidly over the next few years that "by the turn of the century, the major outline of the human gene map should be known."

From Diagnosis to Therapy.

The science of genetics is now at a stage that is mainly diagnostic. Its current thrust is to define genetic mechanisms in health and disease. Applications to individual cases are mainly diagnosis and prediction. But throughout medical history, ability to accurately diagnose and predict has tended to be followed by new insights into prevention and treatment.

In a recent statement, the March of Dimes Birth Defects Foundation, which has been a major supporter of gene-mapping research, declared that "mapping the fine details of human genes has immediate clinical application to diagnosis, but only the most pessimistic or unimaginative student of this new branch of biology can seriously doubt that its applications will lead to new means of preventing and treating human diseases."

Mapping a gene to a small area of a chromosome, the foundation observed, can lead to snipping it out with enzymes, cloning it, analyzing its structure in normal and abnormal versions, analyzing neighboring genetic material that may govern its activity, and identifying the protein for which the particular gene is a blueprint. Such bits of information may lead to preventing or treating an abnormal gene's ill effects by a variety of routes. One possibility is direct gene therapy to activate an inactive gene or replace a harmful one in specific tissues or cells. Another is to provide a substance that is deficient—a reality, for example, in the treatment of inherited growth-hormone deficiency with growth-hormone supplements from cadaver pituitary glands or from mass production by genetically programmed bacteria.

Spotting Cancer Genes (Oncogenes).

One of the most remarkable new genetic developments is the discovery of cancer genes. It is expected to shorten by many years the job of finding the underlying cause of cancer and could lead to better methods of detecting and treating malignancy. "The discovery of oncogenes," says Dr. Frank J. Rauscher, Jr., senior vice-president for research of the American Cancer Society, "is unquestionably the single greatest breakthrough in all our years of cancer research."

How does cancer arise? The disease is known to be promoted by some chemicals, excessive radiation, and perhaps viruses. But whatever the promoter, or trigger, when a single previously healthy body cell is transformed into repeated generations of rapidly growing malignant cells, genes that control cell function and reproduction have to be involved.

Recently, scientists have been able to identify specific genes, oncogenes, that are involved in cancer.

The discovery came about when researchers exposed mouse cells to a cancer-producing chemical, methylcholanthrene. When they then extracted DNA from the malignant cells and inserted the DNA into normal mouse cells cultured in the laboratory, the normal cells became malignant. Evidently, the DNA from the cancer cells contained oncogenes.

When similar experiments were done with DNA from human cancers, the results were similar.

Soon investigators at three institutions—the Massachusetts Institute of Technology, the Cold Spring Harbor New York Laboratory, and the Sidney Farber Cancer Institute in Boston—were able to identify oncogenes in human cancers of the breast, bladder, colon, and lung, and some forms of leukemia. In a few cases, they have been able to isolate the tiny DNA segment that makes up the oncogene and produce it in quantity for study. Such studies now suggest that oncogenes can be found not only in cells that have become malignant but in normal cells as well.

Clearly, according to Dr. Robert A. Weinberg of MIT, the cancer genes are altered forms of normal genes. Weinberg believes that normally the genes control production of proteins needed for cell growth of the embryo. Later, with maturity, the genes no longer function. But still later—because of exposure to carcinogens or viruses—oncogenes may be switched back on, leading to the appearance of what is characteristic of cancer: uncontrolled growth of rapidly dividing "embryonal" cells.

The importance of the oncogenes' discovery is expected to be tremendous. They can be made in the laboratory, and as Dr. Weinberg remarks, "Never before have we had an experimental handle to learn just how a normal cell is converted to a tumor cell."

Oncogenes can help explain why there is a high incidence of certain cancers—breast and bowel, for example—in some families. More-over, once researchers, who are now busy looking for them, can identify the proteins whose production is controlled by cancer genes, drugs may well be found or synthesized to counter the action of the proteins and bring the malignant process under control. Tests developed to uncover these proteins in the body could enable physicians to diagnose cancer earlier and treat it in the very earliest stages, when it is most readily controllable.

Gene Therapy

It has been a dream of many scientists for years to be able to help people suffering from hereditary diseases by overcoming their problems at the source—fixing their genes. The ability to do so would make a tremendous difference in the lives of an estimated 20 million Americans with inherited afflictions.

In reality, doctors are a long way from being able to accomplish such feats to any significant extent. But progress is being made.

A First Attempt.

In the summer of 1980, Dr. Martin Cline of UCLA undertook to try to help two victims of an often-fatal blood disorder, beta thalassemia, by replacing their defective genes. Beta thalassemia, also known as "Cooley's anemia," is most often seen in Italians, Greeks, and other Mediterranean peoples. It involves defective hemoglobin, the blood protein that transports oxygen.

Red blood cells are manufactured in bone marrow, and Cline's idea was to remove bone marrow from the patients' thighbones and incubate the marrow cells with quantities of the normal hemoglobin gene they lacked. The hope was that the cells would incorporate the genes and function normally when injected back into the patients.

The results were inconclusive: The patients did not seem to be helped to any significant extent. However, Cline's approach does illustrate one strategy for gene therapy that many scientists believe could yet be refined and be of some use.

Another Strategy.

Just two years after the Cline effort, scientists at the National Heart, Lung and Blood Institute and at the University of Illinois took another approach with three victims of beta thalassemia and two others with sickle-cell anemia, another blood disorder involving defective hemoglobin. In sickle-cell anemia, because of the defective hemoglobin, red cells, normally saucer-shaped, assume a sicklelike shape and, unable to pass through tiny blood vessels, clog them.

The attempt to treat was based on knowledge that only a few of the thousands of genes in every human cell are active at any one time. Each gene controls production of a specific protein, and since the cell and the body may require a particular protein at one time but not another, genes turn on and off. Some proteins are needed only in fetal life and their controlling genes may be turned off completely later in life.

In fetal life, two genes control hemoglobin production. In infancy, one of these is turned off and a new gene, the beta gene, is turned on to work with the still active remaining fetal gene to turn out adult hemoglobin. Both Cooley's anemia and sickle-cell anemia result from beta-gene defects. Perhaps, the scientists reasoned, both anemias could be corrected if the turned-off fetal gene could be switched back on.

Recent genetic research has suggested that a drug, 5-azacytidine, might switch on the long-dormant gene because of the drug's ability to free DNA of chemical substances that attach to the genetic material and render it inactive.

The first patient to be treated with 5-azacytidine, a forty-two-year-old man with severe thalassemia, had a long history of anemia and serious heart problems because of defective hemoglobin production and had required a blood transfusion every two weeks. For seven days, he received a continuous infusion of the drug through a vein in his arm. At the end of the week, the concentration of healthy red cells in his blood had increased dramatically, and the improvement persisted for a month.

Similar beneficial effects were experienced by the four other patients in the experimental trial—two with beta thalassemia and two with sickle-cell anemia. And at Johns Hopkins, a medical team achieved similar results in another sickle-cell patient. An editorial in the *New England Journal of Medicine* late in 1982 called the trials "the first encouraging attempts" to manipulate genes in humans.

Investigators are cautious. For one thing, 5-azacytidine is highly toxic and probably cannot be used for a prolonged period. There is a question, too, that must be answered: Does it turn on other genes as well as the fetal hemoglobin gene—and if so, what are the effects?

But even if the drug is not the way to treat the two diseases other than on an experimental basis, it is important for demonstrating the potential of genetic manipulation for treating disease.

A Third Strategy.

Still more recently, a genetic defect responsible for a severe human brain disorder has been corrected on an experimental basis in the laboratory by infecting defective human cells with a virus that inserts a new gene into them, thereby restoring normal function.

The brain disorder, known as Lesch-Nyhan syndrome, causes mental retardation and strange behavior patterns, including a tendency to self-mutilation and compulsive aggressive behavior. The cause of the disorder lies with a defective single gene that normally controls production of an enzyme known as "HPRT." When the gene is defective, HPRT is not produced and cells in certain brain areas malfunction.

The new technique—developed by Dr. Inder Verma of the Salk Institute in San Diego and Dr. Theodore Friedmann of the University of California-San Diego—involves using genetic-engineering techniques (see GENETIC ENGINEERING) to insert the normal human HPRT gene into a mouse leukemia virus, one of a class called "retroviruses." At the same time, the virus is modified in such a way that it does not cause cancer. Human cells with a defective HPRT gene are then exposed to the virus, which enters the cells. Thereafter, the cells begin to produce HPRT.

Dr. Friedmann says, "I tend to think this kind of manipulation will find its place in therapy." It will not, he emphasizes, cure everything, but among likely candidates for this type of treatment could be blood disorders and immune-system-deficiency diseases. Dr. Howard Temin, a Nobel laureate at the University of Wisconsin, considers the research to be "a very important development" that "potentially opens the way" to the use of viruses in human gene therapy.

Problems To Be Overcome.

Although serious investigators are optimistic about gene therapy, they are realistic about the problems that remain to be faced.

Curing a cell in a laboratory dish with a functional gene is not the same as curing cells in a living organism. There are two major obstacles. For one thing, the gene must be inserted into the right cells. Bone-marrow cells are easy to remove, treat, and reinsert—and they multiply frequently. But as Dr. W. French Anderson of the National Heart, Lung and Blood Institute points out, what about brain cells or liver cells or pancreatic cells? Some genetic diseases may be untreatable because of an inability to get the gene into enough of the affected cells.

A second obstacle lies in the fact that in a laboratory dish, growth conditions can be manipulated to kill any cell that loses the healthy gene, thus allowing only cells retaining the gene to be selected under a kind of positive pressure. But no such pressure exists inside a living organism. Critical information that remains to be acquired is how to stabilize a gene once it is in the proper target cell.

And as Dr. Anderson notes, still more remains to be learned about risk. Every procedure has some potential for harm. Whether or not inserting a gene into a human cell would prove detrimental to the cell over time is not known. Although cells cured in the laboratory appear to grow and divide normally, such criteria are relatively crude. Is there any possiblity that changing the genetic makeup of a cell may eventually make the cell malignant?

Such questions remain to be answered by studies in experimental animals.

The Potential and the Limitations.

Writing in the *Journal of the American Medical Association,* Dr. Anderson makes these informed comments:

Gene therapy is a procedure with enormous potential. It should, in the future, provide a cure for hereditary diseases caused by a single gene. It is even possible that the germ line might be corrected so that the children of a patient will also be free from disease. This is, indeed, a powerful therapeutic weapon.

But some claims made about the potential of genetic engineering in humans are farfetched. Patients with multigenic diseases [due to more than a single gene defect], where the genes as well as the intracellular products involved are unknown, are not candidates for gene therapy.

Likewise, characteristics such as personality and intelligence are probably outside the realm of this technique's potential. Only traits produced by identifiable single genes can be approached. . . .

The power to cure a genetic defect is an awesome one. But . . . "the goal of biomedical research is, and has always been, to alleviate human suffering. Gene therapy is a proper and logical part of that effort."

Genetic Engineering
Gene splicing—recombinant DNA

Time magazine has called it "the most powerful and awesome skill acquired by man since the splitting of the atom."

A panel of U.S. scientists has ranked it as "one of the four major scientific revolutions of this century, on a par with unlocking the atom, escaping the Earth's gravity, and the computer revolution."

Genetic engineering—also referred to as "gene splicing" and "recombinant DNA"—already is capable of modifying the hereditary mechanisms of bacteria so the microorganisms become manufacturing plants turning out human insulin for diabetics, human growth hormone for dwarfs, and the antiviral-anticancer drug interferon. It is showing promise for producing a blood substance needed by thousands of hemophiliacs to curb excessive bleeding, and for producing important new vaccines and even safer older vaccines. It is opening the way to introducing disease-resistant genes into agricultural crops. And it has still further promise.

The Mechanism.

Although DNA (deoxyribonucleic acid) has long been known to be present in living cells, proof that DNA contains genetic information—is the storehouse for it—didn't come until it was provided in the mid-1940s by a group of American scientists.

Then, in 1953, Drs. James Watson of the U.S. and Francis Crick of England discovered the actual structure of the DNA molecule. They found it composed of two long strands hooked together at intervals, much like a microscopic, twisted rope ladder—a double helix.

The steps of the ladder are called "nucleotides." On them are paired chemical bases: A, adenine; T, thymine; G, guanine; and C, cytosine. On the steps, A on one side is always paired with T on the other side, and C is always paired with G. The sequence in which the A-T and C-G steps appear codes for the hereditary instructions needed to produce proteins, the essential material of living organisms.

The era of genetic engineering began about a decade ago with the discovery of restriction nuclease enzymes, called "biological scissors" because they are able to recognize and chemically cut apart specific sites along a DNA molecule. It turned out, too, that the same restriction enzymes that snip a gene from one organism's DNA can cut similar sites in the DNA of an unrelated organism.

Another significant finding was that another enzyme, ligase, allowed a gene snipped from one DNA molecule to be "glued" into a similar site in the DNA of an unrelated organism, even another species. The hybrid thus formed is called "recombinant DNA."

Thus a human gene, such as the one responsible for insulin production, can be spliced into a bacterium, which then can produce human insulin.

More than 200 restriction enzymes have been discovered to date, giving genetic engineers a great variety of scissors for snipping out desired genes and installing them in new homes. But moving DNA from one organism to another is not simply a cut-and-paste job; a gene to be transferred must be attached to a special carrier, a vector.

One useful group of vectors are plasmids—small DNA loops that exist in bacteria outside the bacterial chromosome. A plasmid can be removed from a bacterium, a gene can be inserted in it, and the plasmid can then be returned to the bacterium. Thereafter, every time the bacterium divides to form two bacterial offspring, so does the recombinant plasmid. Thus, the recombinant DNA continuously makes clones of itself.

Bacteriophages (viruses that attack bacteria) make up another group of vectors. A bacteriophage multiplies many scores of times within its bacterial host before the bacterium bursts and releases the many copies of the phage.

It is in the process of cloning—the reproduction of large numbers of identical genes, proteins, or organisms—that the potential of genetic engineering lies. With its new spliced-in DNA, an individual bacterium produces scores of identical daughter bacteria, all with the same inherited ability to turn out the engineered product.

Results.

The first genetically engineered drug to be marketed was human insulin, introduced in 1983. Others are on the way.

Genetically engineered microorganisms have been put to work producing human growth hormone. Other microorganisms are manufacturing interferon for use as an antiviral and anticancer agent. Still others are making a blood-clotting factor for the treatment of hemophilia.

Engineered bacteria are also producing the enzyme urokinase, which is used to dissolve dangerous blood clots; the hormone thymosin alpha-1, which appears to hold promise as a treatment for brain and lung cancer; and beta-endorphin, one of the brain's natural pain-relieving chemicals.

Much more may be in store. For one thing, the human body makes scores of thousands of proteins, of which fewer than 2 percent have been identified. As more are identified, many may merit testing for medical purposes, and production in quantity by genetic engineering would make that feasible.

A Whole New Vista for Vaccines.

In what may be among the most important medical payoffs from genetic engineering, researchers now are applying the technique to the production of disease-preventing vaccines. The possibilities include not only protection against diseases for which no protection now exists but also a single vaccine that would be effective against a dozen or more different diseases.

THE NEW CONCEPT.   Since the late eighteenth century when the English surgeon Edward Jenner prepared the first one to ward off smallpox, the nature of vaccines has changed very little. Jenner used the cowpox virus to stimulate body defenses against the smallpox virus. Ever since, the production of vaccines has relied on nature for the basic ingredient. Vaccination has been a matter of injecting viruses, bacteria, or other microorganisms—either killed or weakened to the point of not being able to cause disease yet still able to stimulate the body's immune system to build up specific defenses. Polio vaccine, for example, uses a weakened polio virus that causes the body to produce a defense against the strong, disease-causing polio virus.

Growing microorganisms weakened to just the right point—not so weak as to be nonstimulating to the body, but not so inadequately weakened as to remain capable of causing disease—is not a simple matter. It can take years of effort. Moreover, inability to achieve successful growth has prevented development of vaccines against many diseases, including malaria, gonorrhea, and infant diarrhea.

Genetic engineering can avoid such problems. Each disease-producing microorganism carries on its surface an antigen—a distinctive protein that identifies it and alerts the body to produce defensive antibodies against the invader. The fact that antigens alone might make virtually ideal vaccines—safe, effective, with few or no undesirable effects—has been known. Much, too, has been learned recently about how to identify antigens.

Now, with genetic engineering, it has become possible to isolate the gene responsible for producing an organism's antigen. The gene then can be inserted into harmless bacteria, which begin to produce the antigen.

That technique has been used to produce a whole series of new vaccines, including some against diseases for which there has been no protection. Some are in early development stages; others are being tested.

A genetically engineered herpes vaccine—against the herpes virus that causes cold sores and the herpes virus that causes genital herpes —is in advanced stages of development and is being tested in animals.

A genetically engineered gonorrhea vaccine is under development.

A genetically engineered hepatitis B vaccine is being developed in several laboratories. Although a conventionally produced hepatitis B vaccine became available recently, it costs about $150 a treatment and its use has been limited. It's expected that a new gene-spliced vaccine will be far less expensive, costing perhaps as little as $10 a treatment.

A malaria vaccine, for the first time, is finally in sight. The malaria parasite has resisted all efforts to grow it in the laboratory, but the gene that produces the parasite's antigen has been identified and a vaccine is in early development stages.

TOWARD A MULTIPURPOSE VACCINE.   One of the latest feats of genetic engineering is what researchers call a brand-new concept in vaccines: a technique for manipulating vaccinia, the virus used in smallpox vaccine, so it may provide immunity against other infections as well.

Late in 1983, researchers at the New York State Department of Health announced that they had succeeded in turning ordinary smallpox vaccine into vaccines that may be able to prevent herpes, hepatitis, and influenza. So far they have been tested in animals only, but the researchers are confident they will work in humans as well. Furthermore, Dr. Enzo Paoletti, a senior scientist and virologist at the department, says: "We see no reason why our approach won't work with virtually any infectious disease, whether it is viral, bacterial, or even parasitic in nature."

The researchers decided to try their idea with vaccinia because it is a quite large virus and has long been familiar to scientists. What they did was attach pieces of vaccinia DNA to antigen-producing genes isolated from herpes, hepatitis, and influenza viruses. The recombinant segments then were introduced into cells infected with vaccinia. As the vaccinia reproduced in the cell, some incorporated the recombinant segments. The altered vaccinia viruses then could be grown in culture for use in vaccines.

When tested in animals, the new, genetically engineered vaccines led to the production of large quantities of defensive antibodies against hepatitis, herpes, and flu. However, the new vaccines must go through years of testing before they can be tried on humans, and it will be several more years before they can be made generally available.

The advantages of the new approach are many. For one thing, it eliminates any risk of getting herpes, hepatitis, or influenza from an injection since the viruses are not present. Second, the vaccines are expected to be very inexpensive—perhaps as little as 30 cents a shot. Third, they can be freeze-dried for easy storage.

Perhaps the biggest advantage of the new approach, however, is that it may lend itself to the creation of a single vaccine effective against many different diseases. The cowpox virus is large. "There is enough room," observes Dr. Paoletti, "to insert twelve to fifteen different foreign genes. We could perhaps develop a polyvaccine that would render a person immune to herpes, hepatitis, malaria and other diseases, all in one shot."

There are, however, safety aspects of the new vaccines that must be considered. Side effects with vaccinia—such as encephalitis—are rare but do occur. Paoletti believes that it may well be possible, using the techniques of genetic engineering, to delete the genes responsible for the undesirable effects of vaccinia, making the vaccines safer.

Other Genetic-Engineering Applications.

Actually, animals have been the first to benefit from the new genetic-engineering approach to vaccine production. It takes much less time—

only about two years—to obtain approval of a new vaccine for animal use, as against the five to seven years needed in the case of a human vaccine.

The first genetically engineered vaccine to be marketed is one for a potentially deadly diarrhea in piglets. Others are being developed. One of the most important is a safe, effective vaccine that has been developed for foot-and-mouth disease. This devastating, highly contagious, and incurable disease affects cattle, sheep, pigs, goats, and deer, blistering the feet, tongues, and mouths of animals and producing lameness and weight loss. Often farmers have had to slaughter entire herds when only one animal has been stricken, in order to prevent disease spread.

Genetic engineering holds out many other possibilities for agriculture. Among other things, it may allow introduction of disease-resistant genes into crop plants; the development of plants capable of producing their own insecticides; and grains able to make their own nitrogen fertilizer. New farm products may be possible; already at Kansas State University, a "pomato"—a cross between a potato and tomato—has been developed.

Much genetic-engineering research is going on in industry. Efforts are being made to engineer algae able to increase the yield of hydrogen from water, and microorganisms that will breed in brine and could be pumped into oil wells to bring up more oil. There are efforts to get bacteria to produce rennin, an enzyme from the stomachs of calves, used in the cheese industry. Another possibility: creating bacteria that can dissolve scarce metals directly out of the earth.

Hyperbaric Oxygen Therapy (HBO)

It is credited with helping to save the heart of a four-week-old girl at Duke University Medical Center after she suffered a massive heart attack from a strange disease first uncovered in Japan and responsible for several outbreaks in the U.S.

At the VA Medical Center in Los Angeles and the UCLA School of Medicine, it healed eighteen of twenty-seven chronic, previously unyielding leg ulcers within six to twenty-one days, and more than halved the size of seven others.

Hyperbaric oxygen therapy—the delivery of oxygen under pressure—is making a comeback after long being on medicine's back burner.

It began as—and remains—an effective treatment for the "bends" of divers. During the 1950s and 1960s, however, it was overenthusiastically hailed as almost a panacea for many ailments, with little real basis for the claims, and, after disappointments, was largely forgotten as a therapeutic measure.

But research in the last ten years has been opening up a number of important areas for HBO—in the treatment of carbon-monoxide and some other poisonings, resistant infections, gas gangrene, and more. Over the decade, the number of HBO facilities in the U.S. has grown from less than three dozen to more than 200. The federal government has taken an increased interest in HBO therapy, and the Food and Drug Administration is now involved in ensuring its safety.

The Treatment.

A patient undergoing HBO therapy inhales pure oxygen while inside a pressurized chamber. The chamber may be either an individual vessel for a single patient or a multiplace unit in which several patients can be treated simultaneously. The pressure in the chamber is gradually increased to two to three atmospheres—the equivalent of the pressure at thirty to seventy feet below the surface of water. At the end of the treatment, the chamber is decompressed to normal pressure.

Several mechanisms of HBO action are now recognized. The procedure increases oxygen delivery to body tissues where oxygen may be in short supply because of low blood flow, anemia, or edema (waterlogged tissues). It enhances the healing of compromised wounds and has antibiotic effects as well, acting to combat disease microorganisms. In no case does HBO supply basic medical and, when necessary, surgical treatment. It is always adjunctive.

HBO treatments are usually for sixty to ninety minutes; the frequency and total number of sessions vary with the disorder and the response of the patient.

Saving a Heart.

When the four-week-old girl was brought to the Duke University Medical Center, it was clear that there was going to have to be a hard fight for her life.

She had Kawasaki disease, first identified by Japanese physicians in that country in 1967 and subsequently diagnosed in 20,000 cases in Japan over a fifteen-year period. Less common by far in the U.S., it has nonetheless turned up in about 150 cases a year here. It strikes mainly children under five, producing fever, rash, lymph-gland swellings, and sometimes also pneumonia, arthritis, and jaundice. Its most feared complication affects the heart.

Upon entering the medical center, the little North Carolina girl's right foot was already blue from lack of blood flow, and a week later she had a massive heart attack. The disease had caused the child's blood vessels to go into spasm, severely impairing the blood flow to her heart, hands, and feet. Eventually, she required amputation of the toes on her right foot, several of the toes on her left foot, and half of her right hand. She was the most severe Kawasaki case ever seen at Duke.

There is no known cause of the disease and no specific treatment.

Large doses of aspirin may be used to bring down the fever, which can go as high as 106°. In the hope that HBO treatment might save at least some of her damaged tissue, the infant was given three such treatments. The supersaturated oxygen is credited with the significant improvement in her heart function that followed. A few months after being released from the medical center with tests showing her heart functioning normally, she celebrated her first birthday and began to take her first steps.

Carbon-Monoxide Poisoning.

When the patient, an eighteen-year-old woman, was found unconscious in her home, along with two other family members who were dead, the estimate was that the family had been exposed to carbon monoxide from a faulty heating system for some thirty-six hours prior to discovery. When treatment in a local hospital with 100 percent oxygen by face mask produced only a slight response, she was transferred to the Maryland Institute for Emergency Medical Services Systems in Baltimore for HBO therapy.

After forty-six minutes of 100 percent oxygen at three atmospheres, she was sufficiently alert to give her name. Six hours later she underwent a second HBO treatment, during which she became fully responsive to commands and was able to talk coherently. Five days after admission, she showed no residual effects.

Other Uses for HBO.

Carbon-monoxide poisoning is a clear example of a condition for which HBO can be lifesaving and can reduce the complications resulting from brain damage. Cyanide poisoning is another.

The treatment can also be of great value for a gas embolism, particularly in the brain, which can result from diving, diagnostic procedures, kidney dialysis, or any circumstance in which air or another gas is introduced into the heart and blood-vessel system. In gas-gangrene infection, HBO has been found to greatly reduce the death rate, lessen the amount of tissue loss, and even save limbs. It has also proved very useful in aiding the "take" of doubtful skin grafts and in cases where previous skin grafts have failed.

A major force in establishing a scientific basis for HBO and in investigating situations in which it is or may become clinically useful is the Undersea Medical Society in Bethesda, Maryland. The society recently issued a report that groups conditions that have been treated with HBO into four categories according to the apparent efficacy of such treatment, as follows:

CATEGORY I.   Category I disorders are those for which HBO is the primary method of treatment (such as decompression sickness and diving air embolism) or for which the value of adjunctive HBO therapy has been amply shown by research and clinical experience. Among Category I disorders are carbon-monoxide and cyanide poisoning; smoke inhalation with possible carbon-monoxide or cyanide poisoning; air embolism; gas gangrene; infections causing tissue loss; and cases of exceptional blood loss or life-threatening anemia when blood transfusion is impossible or delayed.

CATEGORY II.   These are conditions for which animal studies and clinical experience indicate a beneficial role for adjunctive HBO but for which data are still limited. They include acute artery blood-flow insufficiency in the arms or legs; crush injuries; head and spinal-cord trauma; retinal artery insufficiency in the eye; thermal burns; acute cerebral edema (brain waterlogging); intestinal obstruction; unyielding bone infections; and some ulcers. Some investigators have also found HBO a useful adjunct in reimplantation operations, heart and blood-vessel procedures, and some surgical procedures in severely ill patients.

CATEGORY III.   For these, clinical data are very limited or only theoretical reasons suggest a possible useful role for HBO. Considered as investigational only, Category III disorders include frostbite, stroke, migraine headache, nonhealing bone fractures, abdominal and brain abscesses, meningitis, and sickle-cell crisis.

CATEGORY IV.   These are conditions for which the usefulness of HBO therapy is considered remote, for which there is only hearsay evidence that HBO is of any benefit, or for which no theoretical basis for treatment exists but which nonetheless are listed in the interest of objectivity and fairness. They include arthritis; breast firming and enlargement; loss of normal hair color; high blood pressure; skin wrinkles; loss of sexual vitality; and multiple sclerosis.

Multiple sclerosis has come under repeated study in terms of HBO. In a number of investigations, benefits have been claimed but not proved and could have been due to factors other than HBO. Because of this, Dr. Boguslav H. Fischer and co-workers at New York University Medical Center undertook a scientifically controlled study of forty patients with advanced MS.

Four patients at a time received treatment in a multiplace chamber. Twenty of the forty patients actually got 100 percent oxygen while the other half, serving as a comparison group, received 10 percent oxygen and 90 percent nitrogen. Twenty ninety-minute treatments were given in all, five days a week for four weeks. For various reasons, three of the patients receiving 100 percent oxygen dropped out of the study.

Twelve of the remaining seventeen patients on oxygen and one of the twenty controls showed clinical improvement—mainly reduced fatigability and increased mobility and coordination—after an average of twelve treatments. The HBO benefits were long-lasting (more than a year) for five patients and transient for seven. Improvement was greater and longer-lasting among those with less severe disease. Both the researchers and the National Multiple Sclerosis Society emphasized after the study that HBO cannot yet be recommended as a treatment for MS.

A tremendous amount of reliable research is needed to determine how valuable, in fact, many proposed uses of HBO may be. For example, as Dr. Fischer of New York University pointed out at a recent symposium on HBO, animal studies strongly suggest that early HBO treatment can lessen loss of function after spinal injury. But testing this application in humans is very difficult. In a study in Baltimore with fifty cord-injury patients, there was little evidence of benefit. It appears that if the treatment is to do any good, it must be started within six hours after injury; therefore, plans are now under way to resume the Baltimore trial with patients admitted early enough.

Fortunately, the renewed interest in HBO is likely to intensify research. And whereas the therapy was once an exotic one confined to a very few centers, the development of less expensive and less complicated single-place hyperbaric chambers, the increasing evidence of its benefits in specific situations, and to some extent the increase in both recreational and commercial diving recently have led to a marked increase in the number of HBO facilities.

Plastic-Bag HBO.

A simple and inexpensive new method of administering HBO was devised very recently for treating chronic leg ulcers. It uses a heavy-gauge plastic bag as the chamber.

The treatment is carried out by placing a patient's leg in a four-by-two-foot polyethylene bag and delivering oxygen through plastic tubing inserted in one end of the bag. Three sides of the bag are sealed and the open end is taped around the upper thigh. Oxygen is administered at a rate of fifteen liters a minute.

Developed at the Veterans Administration Center and University of California-Los Angeles School of Medicine, this innovative technique has been used to treat chronic arterial leg ulcers in half a dozen men with a total of twenty-seven ulcers that had resisted previous treatment. Each treatment lasted four to six hours, four times a week. Eighteen of the twenty-seven ulcers healed within six to twenty-one days, and seven of the nine unhealed ulcers decreased in size by 50 to 90 percent after three weeks of therapy.

Such efforts to simplify HBO treatment and make it less expensive can be expected to continue.

Hyperthermia
Heat treatment for cancer

Thanks to major advances in technology—notably, electronic methods of delivering this form of treatment—hyperthermia (heat treatment) is producing encouraging results in managing cancer at many medical centers across the country.

In 1982 at Washington University School of Medicine in St. Louis, for example, hyperthermia used together with radiation therapy caused some degree of tumor regression in 80 percent of 101 patients for whom other forms of therapy—such as chemotherapy or radiation therapy alone—had proved ineffective. In several of these cases, treated tumors disappeared and at last checkup had not returned.

"These tumors were of many different types and sizes and all were still relatively close to the surface of the skin," says Dr. Carlos Perez, director of radiation oncology at Washington University. "We are advanced now to the point that the combination of heat and radiation therapy can be used with optimism in the treatment of breast cancer, cancer of the head and neck, and skin cancer. In some cases it can be used in tumors that have spread to the lymph nodes."

An Ancient Therapy Revived.

As early as 2000 B.C., healers reported suspicions that heat could cause tumors to shrink. One Greek physician described a temporary toe-to-neck burial in hot, sunbaked sand as a treatment. In 400 B.C., Hippocrates, often called the "father of medicine," told of the shrinkage or disappearance of tumors heated with red-hot irons.

In the modern era, the use of hyperthermia for cancer was first mentioned in 1866 by a German physician, W. Busch. He reported that a patient's facial tumor disappeared after two attacks of high fever caused by a bacterial infection, and he suggested that temperatures above normal might be useful in preferentially killing cancer cells. The problem was that although healthy tissues might not be quite as sensitive as tumors to the lethal effects of heat, they could still be damaged, causing unacceptable complications.

At the turn of the century, a faddish interest in hyperthermia arose, and resulted in some quackery. Some cancer patients were treated by being exposed to bacterial agents in the hope that a high fever would develop. Others were subjected to various methods of heating the body from the outside. Says Dr. Bahman Emami, a Washington University cancer specialist, "I have seen reports written by one therapist who asked his cancer patients to rest beneath infrared lights like the ones now used to keep hamburgers warm at McDonald's. Several other ineffective methods of heating were also used."

Interest in hyperthermia waned among legitimate physicians both because of the existing quackery and because new cancer treatments, particularly radiation, were becoming successful. It wasn't until the 1970s that advances in two technological areas—thermometry and heat generation—and new understanding of the role of heat treatment in cancer led to a marked, and now very rapidly growing, revival of interest.

The Right Temperature Range.

The specific goal today, based on findings from many studies, is to elevate the temperature of a tumor to 110°–114°F while keeping the patient's core temperature, or fever, below 104°. Temperatures of about 110° have been found to take a high toll on cancer cells.

Another finding, according to Dr. Perez, is that tumors that have been treated with radiation are more susceptible to heat than are normal tissues. "Heat and radiation work very well together." Radiation heavily damages those tumor cells that are rich in oxygen and reproducing rapidly—cells at the periphery or outer areas of a tumor. On the other hand, heat treatment seems to damage a tumor's core cells, which are poorly oxygenated, malnourished, slow to grow.

A tumor grows its own network of tiny vessels, capillaries, to siphon oxygen and nutrients from the bloodstream. In animal experiments, Washington University workers have been able to show that hyperthermia has a direct effect on these capillaries, substantially and permanently reducing circulation through them. "It's like destroying the railroad tracks that move cargo in and out of the tumor," says Dr. Emami.

The Techniques.

In one procedure, used by Dr. Michael R. Manning of the University of Arizona Health Sciences Center, Tucson, the patient is placed under general anesthesia and two parallel or concentric rows of hollow stainless-steel needle guides are inserted into the tumor tissue. The guides are connected together and then to a radio-frequency generator, and heating is begun. The needles are loaded with radioactive sources such as iridium 192 seeds for radiotherapy. The tumor is heated for thirty minutes, and five or six thermistors placed in and around the tumor provide measurements of heat intensity at various sites. Radiation is given over a three-hour period.

In one study, the combined technique was used for forty-seven patients with tumors of the head and neck, tongue, pharynx, breast, pelvis, cervix, colon, and the extremities. In all cases, previous treatments—including combinations of surgery, chemotherapy, and radiation therapy—had been exhausted.

In twenty-four of the patients (52 percent), the tumor completely disappeared; in nineteen (40 percent), there was at least a 50 percent tumor reduction; and in four (8 percent), there was no response. Duration of response ranged from two to twenty-four months. Although many patients ultimately succumbed to disease at other sites, twelve who had complete disappearance of tumor remain alive and free of cancer.

In another technique, external heat from a microwave or radio-frequency source is applied along with external radiation therapy. At Washington University, the first heat treatments were given with a diathermy microwave generator borrowed from the physical-therapy department. Although not designed to treat cancer patients, it was modified somewhat and found useful. First results were encouraging. More recently, at Washington University, several commercial applicators have been adapted for special use in hyperthermia therapy. These resulted in tumor regression rates of 80 percent.

So far, the promising results have been achieved only with tumors close to the surface of the skin, not those buried deep within the body.

Now, newer equipment to treat deep tumors is being installed at Washington University and other centers.

The computerized device at Washington University, for example, looks something like a small CAT scanner (see CAT SCANS). It surrounds the patient with four large microwave applicators and allows deep heating of the pelvis, abdomen, and lung. Temperatures are monitored at up to eight different locations within the body, and the computer continuously samples and displays these temperatures throughout treatment.

Lack of Toxicity.

One of the encouraging findings from the various clinical trials of hyperthermia is the relative lack of significant toxicity and morbidity. In the Arizona trials, for example, complications were confined to a few cases of second-degree burns and minor blistering. In the first sixty-seven patients treated at Washington University, four showed thermal burns, twenty showed only reddening of the skin, and forty-seven showed some shedding of skin cells.

Remaining Problems.

Much research remains to be done. As some investigators point out, tumor-temperature differences of only a few tenths of a degree can lead to significant differences in results. As of now, however, it is difficult to deliver heat with absolute uniformity. Heating the center of a tumor to the right temperature may be of no ultimate value if the tumor regrows from cells elsewhere in the tumor where the temperature may have varied from the optimum. In short, making tumors disappear may be easier than making them stay away—and for the latter, much more research and refinement appear to be essential.

Another question under study is which is best: heat before radiation or after, or heat combined with radiation?

Observes Dr. Emami: "I am an optimist. Yet there is still so much we have to learn. In the end, it's going to come down to whether or not we can fool Mother Nature and successfully circumvent the systems of temperature regulation that thousands of years of evolution have built into the human body." (See also FEVER: NEW INSIGHTS.)

Hypervolemic Hemodilution
To speed recovery from stroke

Every year, nearly 600,000 Americans become stroke victims. At least two-thirds of those who survive the event have some degree of permanent disability. However, a promising new treatment that rapidly increases blood flow to parts of the brain deprived of oxygen during a stroke appears to minimize the destruction of brain cells and speed recovery from loss of movement, speech, or memory.

The treatment was first employed at Woodruff Medical Center of Emory University in Atlanta, for seven men and two women within ten minutes to four days after an acute stroke that produced loss of speech or loss of motor function and strength. Eight of the nine patients improved dramatically within twenty-four hours, regaining some or all of their ability to move limbs, talk, and think clearly. One patient responded within less than two hours. The ninth patient, unconscious at the time treatment efforts began, continued to deteriorate.

The response is considered excellent inasmuch as an editorial in the *Journal of the American Medical Association* has pointed out that usually, in a group of nine consecutive stroke patients, three to four could be expected to improve, three to five to remain unchanged or to deteriorate, and one to three to die.

The Treatment.

The stroke victims in the Emory study received intravenous infusions every four to six hours of either human serum albumin (a simple protein found in blood) or of low-molecular-weight dextran, which is sometimes used as a substitute for plasma (the fluid portion of blood). The infusions increased the patients' total blood volume (hypervolemia) but decreased both the relative number of red blood cells and the thickness of the blood (hemodilution).

Hypervolemic hemodilution has a basic purpose. Most strokes occur when the middle cerebral or carotid artery—the main route by which blood travels from the heart to the brain—is blocked by a clot or by narrowing of the vessel through the gradual accumulation of atherosclerotic deposits. Diluted blood has a lower viscosity (thickness), which allows it to flow more freely to the oxygen-deprived areas of the brain through the smaller secondary collateral arteries, bypassing the blocked carotid artery.

Since using the technique for the first group of nine patients, Dr. James Wood, assistant professor of neurosurgery at Emory University School of Medicine, has employed it for others. In a second group of thirty recent stroke patients, more than half showed rapid recovery from impaired speech, intellectual, or motor functions. The improvements were associated with increases in the amount of blood flow through the brain, and EEG readings showed more normal brain-wave patterns than are usually seen at the early stage of stroke.

Further Implications.

Hypervolemic hemodilution has been used only within the four or five days immediately following the first signs of stroke—commonly, weakness on one side of the body or loss of speech or motor function. For these patients, the treatment appears to have restored function more rapidly than would be expected. However, whether the treatment is capable of reversing brain damage in patients who have had previous or "completed" strokes is unknown. The success with recent stroke victims, Dr. Wood believes, may have positive implications for further understanding and future treatment of stroke.

Most physicians now believe that brain cells deprived of oxygen during the first hours or days of an evolving stroke are damaged beyond recovery. Consequently, rehabilitation customarily involves the slow process of teaching new functions to other living brain cells. However, another, less-known theory of what happens in stroke—the "idling-neuron theory"—suggests that many of the brain cells in affected areas may simply be idling or nonfunctioning for varying periods of time before they ultimately die. If this is so, then increased oxygen delivery through improved blood flow may revitalize these cells and thus bring about some restoration of the functions they once controlled as well as prevent their death. But this is not yet established.

Meanwhile, for acute stroke patients, widespread use of hypervolemic hemodilution is possible since the equipment required is the same used for conventional treatment of stroke in primary hospitals, where most acute stroke patients are taken immediately.

Use for Surgery.

Another use to which Wood is now putting the treatment is for patients during the critical weeks following cerebral-artery bypass surgery (see MICROSURGERY). In such surgery, a blocked artery to the brain is bypassed by connecting a scalp artery directly to brain arteries above the blockage. This smaller vessel carries only about one-tenth of the blood that the blocked artery normally would carry to the brain, but the brain's immediate need for oxygen remains unchanged.

Hypervolemic hemodilution provides a means of increasing the amount of oxygen to the affected area during the month normally required for the bypass vessel to increase enough in size to deliver adequate amounts of oxygen for maintaining normal brain function. This helps to lessen the loss of function and risk of another stroke during the period following surgery.

Hypothermia
Suspended animation for surgery

In Baltimore, surgeons at The Johns Hopkins Medical Institutions cooled an Alexandria, Virginia, man's body to 66°F and stopped his blood circulation for forty-one minutes to remove a kidney tumor that had metastasized (seeded) to his heart. The operation was one of the first in which a kidney tumor was removed using hypothermia, which involves cooling the body to subnormal temperatures, and circulatory arrest.

Stopping the heart and the blood flow temporarily with hypothermia provides a way of handling unusual, difficult surgical problems. It has been used in some cases of heart surgery and brain surgery, and may have applications in other areas, such as surgery for cancer of the liver.

The Procedure.

Cooling the body slows bodily processes and decreases the need for oxygen, which is distributed via the blood throughout the body. In the cooled body, even the brain can survive without damage—but only for a limited time; after about sixty minutes, body tissues will become damaged. Lowering body temperature further does not help. If tissues are frozen, they will be damaged as they thaw.

In the case of the Alexandria man, the tumor had spread from a kidney into the vena cava, a major vein that collects blood from other veins bringing it back from the body and empties the blood into the heart's right atrium, a storage chamber from which the blood is pumped to the lungs for freshening with oxygen.

The situation was complex. Unless the heart and blood flow were stopped, surgery would be risky. Part of the tumor might break off into the circulation, which could be fatal. Also, there is no adequate way to control bleeding while removing a tumor that extends into the heart.

In the first part of the operation, the cancerous kidney was freed from surrounding tissue while the patient was kept alive on a heart-lung machine, which completely took over the work of his heart and lungs, freshening the blood with oxygen and circulating it throughout his body.

In preparation for the second stage of the operation, the patient's body was cooled by chilling his blood as it circulated through the heart-lung machine. When the body temperature reached 66°, 32° below normal, the heart automatically stopped beating. The machine then was turned off, the patient's blood drained into the reservoir of the machine's pump, and there was no circulation at all.

At that point, the surgical team could proceed to cut the vena cava and open the right side of the heart to extract the tumor from there. Finally, the remaining parts of the tumor were pulled out of the vena cava. Now the kidney with attached tumor was removed.

During the second part of the operation, the patient had not really been kept alive on the machine. Cooled down, he had been in a state of suspended animation. Once tumor removal was complete, the machine was turned on to warm and circulate the blood. Shortly, the patient could be removed from the machine, his heart now carrying out its normal circulation function.

Six months after the procedure, the patient was back at work full-time. Followed up after a year, he was in excellent health.

Implantable Defibrillator
To prevent cardiac arrest and sudden death

Each year in the United States about 450,000 people, including many who are young, die from cardiac arrest. Heartbeat abnormalities—extremely rapid, ineffective rhythms called "ventricular arrhythmias"—cause their hearts to stop pumping blood. Death follows in a few minutes—except in the relatively few cases where emergency help is prompt and cardiopulmonary resuscitation maintains life until appropriate treatment in a hospital can be started.

A device that could automatically restore normal heart rhythm in people with known, recurrent, serious rhythm disturbances has seemed a logical solution that could be useful for at least some patients. And indeed, such a device—an automatic implantable defibrillator—has been developed and tested with promising results: Its surgical implantation has led to a reduction of death rates by as much as one-half. The defibrillator is capable of doing what hospitals do with their personnel and equipment: It continuously monitors its wearer, instantly detects abnormal rhythm, and delivers treatment.

People who may be subject to serious heartbeat abnormalities cannot always be identified in advance. But many can be, and, once diagnosed, they generally receive preventive drug treatment. Unfortunately, not all respond to treatment, and it is for the latter, who remain at high risk, that the miniature defibrillator holds hope.

How It Works.

Invented by Dr. Michel Mirowski, associate professor of medicine at The Johns Hopkins Medical Institutions, the defibrillator has been under development for more than a dozen years. Most of the device fits inside a pocket-size package that goes under the skin of the abdomen. It contains a microcomputer and, as a power source, a lithium battery that lasts about three years and is replaceable with minor surgery. Two electrodes lead from the defibrillator unit: One covers the apex of the heart; the other is placed in the superior vena cava, a major blood vessel emptying into the heart.

The tiny computer can sense the beginning of a dangerous rhythm through one electrode and can send an electrical pulse to the heart through the second electrode to restore normal rhythm. The electrical pulse, since it can act directly on the heart without having to go through the chest as in the case of the conventional transchest defibrillation used in hospitals, has only about one-fifteenth the energy of the latter. If the first pulse fails to work, the unit delivers a second, followed by two more of slightly greater energy. Normal rhythm for thirty-five seconds resets the unit for use, if necessary, on another occasion.

Originally, implantation required thoracotomy—major surgery involving opening up of the chest wall. Now a new surgical procedure for implantation, developed by Dr. Levi Watkins, a Hopkins heart surgeon, enables patients to avoid the pain, cost, and potential complications of major chest surgery.

In the new procedure, one electrode is inserted in a vein and maneuvered up to its position in the vena cava. The second electrode is placed over the apex of the left ventricle, the heart's main pumping chamber, through an incision below the chest wall.

Results.

A review of the first 150 cases since the defibrillator was implanted in the first patient in 1980 at Johns Hopkins Hospital has shown encouraging results. The defibrillators automatically resuscitated many of the patients who were stricken as they pursued normal activities at home and work. On some occasions, the pulses were delivered to conscious patients without producing undue discomfort or pain. Although 23 percent of the patients died during the first year after implantation, Dr. Mirowski states that few of these deaths could be attributed to cardiac arrest, and that without implantation at least 48 percent would be expected to die in the first year.

Newer Models.

The defibrillator originally corrected ventricular fibrillation, a useless twitching of the heart muscle. A second-generation model, now in use, also corrects hypotensive ventricular tachycardia, a condition in which the heart beats too rapidly. A third-generation model will also contain a pacemaker, which speeds up the heart when it beats too slowly (see PACEMAKERS).

The second-generation defibrillator may be even more effective than the original. In the first twenty-five patients who received the newer model, there have been no deaths after nine to twenty-four months of observation, according to Dr. Roger A. Winkle of Stanford University Medical Center. These results have been so encouraging that the new defibrillator now is being used at several medical centers throughout the United States and France.

Originally, use of the defibrillator was limited to patients with catastrophic rhythms who had survived at least two episodes of cardiac arrest and whose malignant arrhythmias had occurred despite intensive medical treatment. More recently, even with the device still considered experimental, it has been implanted in some patients before a first cardiac arrest. Ultimately, the defibrillator is expected to attain more widespread use when more patients at high risk for sudden death can be identified—such as those who have had a heart attack and show occasional abnormal heartbeats during twenty-four-hour electrocardio-graphic monitoring (see ELECTROCARDIOGRAPHY).

Experts, however, are quick to point out that the device is an adjunct to, not a replacement for, drugs and, when indicated, surgery that may correct underlying defects.

Intraocular Lens Implants

When surgeons replace the cloudy lens of a cataract patient's eye with a tiny piece of special plastic, they are performing what has become one of the most popular operations of the 1980s.

Intraocular lens implants in the U.S. now number almost half a million annually. After the less than one-hour procedure, many patients experience clear vision for the first time in decades. According to some estimates, about 95 percent of all persons with cataracts would benefit from the implant, but the proportion receiving it is much lower—a discrepancy likely to diminish as not only the public but the medical community as well realize the excellent results currently being achieved with such surgery.

Some authorities in the field expect, too, that in a few years about 80 percent of the implants will be done on an outpatient basis. The operation currently requires a two-night hospital stay.

The Cataract Problem.

About one in every five cases of blindness is caused by cataracts, which also impair the sight of many other people, most of them elderly. Surgery is the only treatment.

The lens in a healthy eye is a capsule of transparent protein behind the iris. Its function is to change its shape—lengthen and shorten—in order to focus images on the retina at the back of the eye. A cataract forms when changes in the structure of the lens protein cause it to lose its natural transparency and gradually become opaque. This can happen at any stage of life as the result of injury, inflammation, or disease, and may even be present at birth, but it is most commonly a by-product of aging.

Surgical removal of the clouded lens is relatively safe and simple, but it merely allows previously shut-out light to pass through to the retina; a means of refracting light to help vision must still be supplied or vision will be hopelessly blurred. Until not many years ago, the patient had no option: It was glasses as thick as Coke-bottle bottoms, or nothing. Then came contact lenses, and most recently lens implants.

Glasses.

Spectacles for cataract patients have improved, but they still act as magnifying glasses, making things look 30 percent bigger, while limiting side vision. Some wearers have difficulty going up and down stairs and even performing such a simple act as reaching for a cup on the table.

Contact Lenses.

Contacts fit over the cornea, providing good vision with minimal magnification. But they have some drawbacks. Glasses are still needed for close work. Older people may have difficulty handling the lenses, and this age group generally tends to be more susceptible to eye infections that can result from contacts.

Intraocular Implants.

The idea of lens implants is centuries old, but the present operation had its origins in a chance observation by a British eye surgeon, Harold Ridley, during World War II. Ridley noticed that when fragments of plastic from fighter-plane windshields shattered by enemy gunfire lodged in the eyes of pilots, the tiny particles sometimes became embedded and remained in place for years without causing any reaction or rejection.

Clinical-quality artificial lenses became available for implantation in 1949, but Ridley's pioneering efforts to perform the first implants failed more often than not. It was not until the mid-1970s that modern microsurgical techniques and materials made possible the current implantation procedure.

The operation involves making a small incision between the cornea and the white of the eye and extracting the cataract-marred lens. This is done with an operating microscope and very small instruments while the patient is under sedation and a local anesthetic. The plastic lens—flat on one side, convex on the other—is slipped into place and precisely positioned. The incision is then sutured with thread thinner than a human hair to enchance rapid healing.

Pain following surgery is minimal. According to Dr. Michael A. Callahan, clinical associate professor at the University of Alabama in Birmingham, who does some 350 such operations annually, most people experience little more than the feeling for a couple of days that a speck of dust is in the eye. No narcotic pain medication is necessary. "After a couple of days," he reports, "when the swelling has gone down, most patients remark that they can see better than in many years. Their vision has been restored, they can see clearly, and they can see bright, spectrally accurate colors."

In his experience, Callahan notes, 95 percent of patients will have 20/20 to 20/30 vision; the others, due to other preexisting factors, will have vision of slightly less quality, but lens-implant surgery will have allowed them to recover the best possible vision. He also has found that people who undergo an implant in one eye elect, within an average of three years, to have the same procedure on their other eye.

The typical intraocular-lens-implant patient is more than fifty years old and has lost 60 to 70 percent of vision due to cataracts. Many physicians believe that because the effects of implants worn over many years are not yet known, the implants should be limited to older people and used in younger patients only as a last resort when there is urgent reason.

Keratotomy, Radial

For correcting nearsightedness

Introduced into the United States from Russia in 1978, a new surgical procedure aims at correcting nearsightedness (myopia) through a series of incisions made in the cornea, the clear, transparent front covering of the eyes. Ophthalmologists have been cautious about its safety and efficacy; their opinions about the procedure have ranged from mild endorsement to confidence about its effectiveness. Latest studies indicate that, at least for the short term (since long experience is not available), it can be helpful for many but far from all cases of nearsightedness.

The Fighting Boy.

Nearsightedness, which affects some 16 million Americans alone, is caused when light is focused in front of the retina instead of on the retina in the back of the eye because of abnormal curvature, length, or size of the eye. Glasses to correct myopia have lenses that change the focus of light back to where it should be.

Radial keratotomy, in which the outer layer of the cornea is cut with a series of tiny incisions, is designed to permit it to relax and flatten out the curvature. Its developer, Dr. Svyatoslav Fyodorov, who is professor and director, Moscow Scientific Research Laboratory of Experimental and Clinical Problems of Eye Surgery, is said to have received the inspiration for the procedure from a happy misfortune of a pugnacious Russian teen-ager. While the boy was fighting, his glasses shattered, cutting his cornea and reportedly correcting his myopia.

The Procedure.

To perform the surgery, which is done usually on an outpatient basis, the surgeon drops a topical anesthetic into the eyes. Using a diamond-blade scalpel, eight to sixteen incisions are made in the cornea, extending from the outer edge to the center in spokelike fashion. The incisions cause central flattening and some bulging at the edge of the cornea, changing the curvature.

The operation takes fifteen to thirty minutes, the eye is patched, and the patient goes home, to be seen the next day and for follow-up later. If all goes well, vision should be markedly improved and in some cases even normal in about three months.

Results.

Nearsightedness is measured in diopters—units of refracting power of a lens. In the experience of Dr. Peter Brazis, clinical associate professor of ophthalmology at Loyola University Medical Center near Chicago, who has performed the procedure on more than 100 patients, the average correction for nearsightedness to allow the patient to see the big E on the eye chart is four diopters. Patients who need between one and a half to five diopters of correction are the best candidates for the surgery. Those who need a three-diopter correction have an 85 percent or better chance for recovery of normal vision.

There have been reports of side effects in some cases. The two most common have been susceptibility to nighttime glare and diurnal fluctuations in vision, both of which have lessened over time. More serious have been some incidents—very few—of corneal perforation, ulceration, or scarring.

One of the most recent studies has been reported by Dr. Peter N. Arrowsmith and colleagues of Nashville's Parkside Surgery Center. The report notes that "although the predictability of radial keratotomy is controversial, this study has shown that radial keratotomy can be effective for reducing myopia over a range of approximately 10 diopters."

The study was conducted on 156 eyes of 101 patients. Before surgery, uncorrected distance acuity was 20/200 or worse in 96 percent of the eyes, and the mean spherical equivalent was −5.0 diopters. Six months after surgery, distance acuity was 20/20 in 43 percent and 20/40 or better in 73 percent of the eyes, and the mean change in spherical equivalent was +4.8 diopters. Visual acuity and refractive results were best for eyes in which preoperative myopia was less than 3.0 diopters. In those eyes, 92 percent achieved 20/40 or better uncorrected distance acuity six months after surgery, and 61 percent had 20/20 acuity or better.

Dr. Arrowsmith and his co-workers note that complications must be weighed against the benefits. "Although other studies have claimed alarming postoperative complications, no such complications occurred in this study," they report. "Two previously reported adverse effects, glare and fluctuating vision, were noted. In general, these adverse effects appeared to lessen with time and to be well tolerated even when persistent.

"The procedure appeared safe short-term and no evidence has appeared that suggests a long-term threat to vision or the integrity of the cornea of the eye."

Further ongoing evaluations for long-term safety and efficacy are being conducted by Arrowsmith and by many other investigators.

Laser Therapy

Imagine, if you can, partially swallowing an egg and then trying to talk. That would be much like the condition faced by a seventeen-year-old high-school student in Fond du Lac, Wisconsin.

An egg-size tumor at the back of his tongue was causing him difficulties in talking and swallowing, with the probability that soon it would also affect breathing. Conventional treatment to remove the tumor would have required major surgery and a two- to three-week hospital stay. Additionally, a tracheotomy (an opening through the throat into the windpipe) would have been needed until healing after the operation.

The boy was spared the extensive trauma when a carbon-dioxide laser was used to cut out the tumor without external surgery and with virtually no bleeding and very little swelling. The patient was out of the hospital in a couple of days and back at school soon after.

He is one of a rapidly growing number of beneficiaries as the laser comes into use for a wide variety of problems. It is allowing the correction of many physical problems once extremely difficult to manage or even considered hopeless. Among the many uses of surgical lasers, for example, are the spot-welding of detached retinas in the eye, vaporization of abnormal growths and tumors, halting of internal bleeding, and erasing of port-wine birthmarks without scarring.

The Principle.

For many years, it was a science-fiction concept. Before the turn of the century, H. G. Wells, in his *War of the Worlds,* wrote of Martians invading and nearly conquering the planet Earth with weapons that fired deadly light beams. In the 1930s, Buck Rogers of comic-book fame was using a ray gun.

Actually, in 1916, Albert Einstein had predicted that electrons in an atom, if properly stimulated, could emit light energy (photons) of a particular wavelength. But it was not until 1960 that he was proved right, when Theodore Maiman, a thirty-three-year-old engineer, built the first working laser.

Laser is an acronym for "light amplification by stimulated emission of radiation." Basically, a laser consists of a glass rod or tube filled with a gas. When the laser is "pumped" with energy in a variety of ways, electrons in the gas are excited into higher energy states. The high-energy electrons are unstable and fall back to a lower energy level —but on the way down, their extra energy is released as light. That light is amplified as it is bounced back and forth between mirrors. The light that emerges—the laser beam—is a thin line of pure color, amplified and coherent light that shines with tremendous power. An ordinary incandescent bulb gives off a collection of many colors going in many directions. The laser emits light in a single color (depending on the gas used) and in a very narrow, concentrated, powerful beam.

Since the laser's invention in 1960, many different types have been created—gas (of many kinds), solid-state, diode, and other lasers. Each shines at a different wavelength. Some pulse on and off; some operate continuously. The differences provide great versatility.

For Eye Diseases.

Ophthalmologists were among the first to make use of the laser. One of the earliest applications was in the repair of rips or tears in the retina, which can cause detachment and vision loss. A beam aimed through the front of the eye can seal down the edge of a tear, acting as a weld to prevent retinal detachment.

Diabetic retinopathy, a major cause of blindness, affects about half of those who have suffered with diabetes for ten years or more. It causes tiny eye blood vessels to deteriorate and leak, and new vessels to grow on the retina and hemorrhage into the normally clear fluid in the center of the eye. A fine laser beam coagulates weakened vessels and destroys proliferating new ones. A major National Eye Institute study of thousands of diabetics has shown a 60 percent reduction in vision loss from retinopathy, and the Institute now has another major study under way in twenty-two clinics for laser treatment of early diabetic retinopathy.

The macula, a tiny area of the retina, is responsible for detail vision. Senile macular degeneration is the leading cause of new cases of blindness in people over sixty-five. Another National Eye Institute study in twelve medical centers recently has shown that a ten-minute laser treatment, if used early in the course of the disease, can often prevent vision loss.

Patients with open-angle glaucoma—in which fluid of the inner eye fails to drain as it should, accumulating and building up potentially sight-destroying pressure—also can benefit from laser therapy. Brief pulses of laser light are beamed to make a series of tiny holes through which fluid can drain. The twenty-minute procedure can be done in a doctor's office with a local anesthetic.

In neovascular glaucoma, blood vessels grow over the drainage system that normally controls fluid and pressure in the eye. Surgery to create an artificial drainage system can be impossible since any incision may rupture the blood vessels, causing a hemorrhage. Until recently, patients with the condition would eventually lose sight in the affected eye. Now a carbon-dioxide laser has been used successfully to punch a microscopic opening in the eyeball at the site of the blood-vessel buildup, and to instantly cauterize the wound so no bleeding occurs. Excess pressure is immediately released, and the perforation made by the laser acts as a valve to release any further buildup of fluid within the eye.

In the first such procedure, a malignant melanoma of the inner eye, one of the most difficult tumors to eradicate, was successfully treated by Dr. Francis L'Esperance of Presbyterian Hospital in New York City. Three days before use of the laser, the patient, a forty-three-year-old blacksmith, received an intravenous injection of hematoporphyrin, a light-sensitive substance that locks onto tumor cells. When exposed to red laser light at a particular frequency, cancer cells attached to the hematoporphyrin were destroyed by the instantaneous release of oxygen from the hematoporphyrin. The patient, who had expected to lose his eye, now has useful vision.

Other Uses.

The port-wine birthmark may cover several square inches of skin and can be disfiguring, especially on the face. It's made up of abnormally dilated blood vessels, which is why the laser, because of its effect on such vessels, is showing promise. In one study at the Palo Alto Medical Clinic, in California, substantial lightening of color has been obtained in about two-thirds of more than 800 port-wine stains.

Laryngeal papillomas are benign tumors of the larynx, common in children. Thought to be virus-caused, they tend to reappear quickly when removed. Although no cure, the laser is superior to other surgery because it burns the growths out with minimal bleeding and scarring.

Traditional treatment for precancerous lesions of the cervix, vagina, and vulva has been by freezing (see CRYOSURGERY) or thermocautery (burning abnormal cells to coagulate tissue). Laser treatment now appears to be simpler, relatively painless, more precise, and safer.

The laser's cell-vaporizing properties have also been used to remove dangerous precancerous lesions of the mouth—for example, epithelial dysplasia, a condition in which white patches form on the tongue, gums, and inner cheeks. Believed caused by various irritants such as tobacco and alcoholic beverages, the lesions may remain benign or may undergo malignant transformation. Conventionally, the lesions have been removed surgically, resulting in extensive pain, swelling, and bleeding. Laser surgery, by contrast, is performed under local anesthetic and causes so little pain and swelling that at least one patient recently was able to enjoy a nine-course banquet just hours after the procedure.

The laser has been used recently in many other types of surgery, including removal of breast lumps, stomach removal, partial liver removal, and for cancerous lesions of the back, chest, arm, leg, shoulder, thigh, and neck.

At the University of California-San Diego Medical Center, neurosurgeons report performing brain and skull surgery with greater precision and safety than previously possible, using a carbon-dioxide laser attached to a microscope. The beam is aimed by means of a small "joy stick" that moves a red dot in the optical field of the microscope. When the dot is over the area to be cut, the beam is fired—by a pedal. This keeps the surgeon's hands and instruments from obscuring the operating field, making it easier to reach areas where there is little room to work, and also reduces the need to manipulate delicate brain tissue, which tends to swell when handled, with some risk that the swelling may cause brain damage. Because the laser is so precise, tumors can be removed more safely near delicate structures, such as around the optic nerve. Happily, too, bleeding, which can cause brain damage, is minimized, since the laser cauterizes the ends of small severed blood vessels.

For infants born with face and skull deformities, laser surgery offers better cosmetic results than possible before, according to Dr. Hector E. James, pediatric neurosurgeon at the UC-San Diego Medical Center. The laser beam can cut through the skulls of infants because young bone is thin and contains a high percentage of water. Very precise cuts at difficult angles, such as in the bone around the eyes, are possible with the laser, since the mirrors inside the device reflect the beam in any angle desired. Infants born with deformed skulls usually must have surgery in the first few weeks of life to make room for the brain to grow properly. The laser's cauterizing effect is especially important in such young patients, who cannot afford to lose much blood.

Among many other uses for the laser is its application in stopping severe and dangerous hemorrhaging in the gastrointestinal tract. By inserting through the mouth and into the stomach a flexible fiberoptic scope with an attached laser bundle (see ENDOSCOPY), the physician can see the actual hemorrhaging site through the scope and focus the laser beam on it.

There is some possibility that in the future laser power may have usefulness in blasting through atherosclerotic plaques blocking arteries. A Stanford University team has reported using a laser to restore blood flow in blocked femoral arteries in the leg. The procedure was tried in two patients with almost total blockages. One has done well, with no nightly or at-rest pain, and can walk two or three blocks before experiencing leg fatigue. In the second patient, the vessel closed up again several weeks after the treatment and required a bypass.

Currently, at least half a dozen medical teams in the U.S. are experimenting with the use of the laser to open up clogged heart-feeding coronary arteries in animals and cadavers. In a very preliminary trial in France, at the University of Toulouse Medical Center, participated in by several U.S. physicians, laser treatment was used in five patients, all scheduled for bypass surgery. Introduced via a special catheter, an argon laser was employed in one coronary artery in each patient; all subsequently required bypass surgery on at least one additional artery. The results "appeared clinically encouraging," according to one of the participating U.S. physicians, but much additional study is needed before the procedure is considered anything but highly experimental.

Mammography
Breast imaging

Cancer of the breast, it is now known, begins as *in situ* cancer, a highly confined and tiny growth that for a time remains where it starts. It may take years before it develops into a tumor or spreads. During the *in situ* stage, it is usually not large enough to be detected by physical examination alone—yet this is the optimum time to find it.

For this purpose, mammography has been developed. A mammogram is a soft-tissue X-ray of the breast, often able to detect cancer before a lump is big enough to feel. According to some experts, mammography may detect cancer as much as two years before a lump can be felt. Very early cancers found by mammography are curable in 85 to 95 percent of cases. Cancers found in a more developed state but still confined to the breast, with no spread to the lymph nodes, are curable in better than 80 percent of cases. The earlier breast cancer is found, the smaller it is when detected, the less radical the surgery as well as the better the chance for full recovery.

Mammography has had its ups and downs. Valuable as the technique is, it cannot do what every physician would like it to do. With few exceptions, it cannot take the place of biopsy to establish whether a growth is benign or malignant. When a mass can be felt and mammography suggests the diagnosis of cancer, the probability that cancer is present is almost 100 percent. Given a mass—whether big enough to be felt or not—which meets strict radiographic criteria for benignity, the chances of a benign lesion being present are about 98 percent. But only a relatively few cancers offer sufficient radiographic findings to permit a diagnosis with such confidence. Some cancers produce no changes on the mammogram; others are missed because of geographic positioning; and even in the case of what seem to be radiographically benign lesions, 2 percent prove to be malignant.

So mammography is not a panacea. It is, however, a valuable diagnostic tool—and improvements in the technique have been making it increasingly sensitive.

Risk.

If there were no risks at all attached to mammography, it would make sense for all women to be checked once a year or even more often. But the procedure does expose breasts to radiation, and X-ray in unsafe amounts is known to cause a number of problems, cancer among them.

Exactly what dosage is safe is not known, but refinements in technique have materially reduced radiation exposure. Where some studies in the past have shown dosages as high as 47 rads, the dose level now achievable is as low as 0.03 rads per exposure.

Thus, the amount of radiation received during any single mammogram is low, not considered hazardous. But if a woman is exposed to a small dose of radiation yearly for many years, her breast tissue may react as if it had been exposed to the sum of all the small doses. That still does not necessarily mean greatly increased risk of malignancy, but it does mean that mammography should not be used indiscriminately. It does mean that a woman and her doctor should consider the possible benefit as well as possible risk.

For a woman who may be at greater-than-average risk for breast cancer—because of family history or other influences—routine mammography may be advisable, its potential benefit far outweighing any possible risk. The frequency should be determined by the physician.

For the average woman, use of mammography may be governed by age. Generally, risk is relatively low, though not entirely absent, below age thirty-five. After thirty-five, risk increases, and the older a woman gets, the greater on average is the risk.

Xeroradiography.

This is another breast-cancer detection technique that has gained some popularity. It combines X-ray imaging with the Xerox copying technique.

For a time, xeroradiography produced clearer pictures than those of mammography and the edges of lesions were more distinct. More recently, with improvements in the mammographic technique, many experts believe that the two procedures may be about comparable. And one may complement the other.

With both techniques available, a patient with a particular problem that cannot be diagnosed adequately by mammography may need an additional view with xeroradiography to clarify the problem.

Microsurgery

In New Jersey, a three-year-old girl seems certain to require amputation of a leg because of a congenital disorder, neurofibromatosis. Amputation is avoided, and for the first time in her life, she is walking.

For a fifty-year-old New York man, the prospect is for a deadly or crippling stroke. He is experiencing repeated forewarning "little strokes"—episodes of vision loss, speaking difficulty, weakness. The danger is averted.

A young housewife has the entire side of her face paralyzed, with strong muscles on the normal side pulling the weaker side, wrenching and distorting her mouth, nose, cheek, and eyelid. All of that is overcome.

All three patients—and a growing number of others—are beneficiaries of new microsurgical techniques. Those techniques—employing high-powered surgical microscopes, needle and thread thin enough to pierce and tie together two hairs, and surgical instruments developed for working with microscopic tissue segments—are greatly improving the possibilities of recovery for patients suffering from many diverse conditions.

Although successes in the last few years in reattaching severed limbs have focused considerable attention on microsurgery, the field has been a long time in development. The earliest beginnings go back to 1921 when Dr. Carl Olif-Nylen in Stockholm, Sweden, decided to try using a monocular microscope to operate in a case of chronic otitis (ear infection) and in two patients suffering severe dizziness because of inner-ear disorders. But general use of the technique was limited because the microscope was limited, its illumination poor and its field of view small.

It wasn't long, however, before Dr. Gunnar Holmgren, a Swedish surgeon, adapted a Zeiss binocular microscope to enlarge the area that could be seen and provide greater magnification. Using this microscope, Holmgren pioneered special operations to treat diseases of the temporal bone, which forms part of the side and base of the skull and contains the middle and inner ear.

Much later, over a period of many years, were to come a whole series of developments: binocular operating microscopes powerful enough to provide a three-dimensional view of the field of operation at magnifications ranging up to forty diameters; microscissors; miniature probes, hooks, blood-vessel clips, and suture-needle holders; and suture material a fifth as thick as human hair, with which, for example, a surgeon can place thirty stitches along a three-quarter-inch incision in an artery only one-tenth of an inch in diameter.

Among the first to make frequent use of microsurgery have been ear surgeons. According to some estimates, 80 percent of ear surgery now successfully performed couldn't even be attempted without microtechniques. For example, the techniques have made possible the reconstruction of the middle ear with its eardrum and three tiny bones that transmit sound vibrations to the inner ear.

Ophthalmologists also have been among the first to make frequent use of microsurgical techniques to greatly improve the success rate of delicate eye operations, including transplants of the cornea (the window of the eye).

Now microsurgery is being applied to many other kinds of problems.

Microsurgical Bone Transplanting.

It was a team of six orthopedic surgeons at Presbyterian Hospital in New York who saved the leg of the three-year-old New Jersey girl. Using microsurgery, the team removed a section of healthy bone from the child's left leg and transplanted it to the right side to replace the diseased bone tissue that had to be excised because it was soft and fractured easily—so soft that even in a cast the leg bowed 45°.

The transplanted bone, according to Dr. Harold Dick, chief of pediatric orthopedic surgery at Presbyterian, would have required six months to a year to heal had it been implanted without using microsurgery. Microsurgery involved connecting the bone to surrounding blood vessels, which greatly increases the chances of success in any kind of implantation surgery. The operation, known as a "fibular transplant," took nine and a half hours. The bone healed in six weeks. The child now walks on her own, without a cast or brace.

Stroke.

Stroke can be a devastating disorder, often disabling when not fatal. Prior to microsurgery, two developments helped cut into the toll. One was the finding that there can be advance warnings before a crippling or fatal stroke occurs—so-called little strokes, brief episodes of weakness, numbness, or heaviness on one side of the body, dizziness, vision disturbance, speaking or writing difficulty indicative of impaired blood flow to a brain area.

Another was the discovery that in up to about 35 percent of patients, the focus of the problem is obstruction in an artery running up the neck and accessible to surgery. In a procedure called "endarterectomy," the artery could be split lengthwise at the site of obstruction and the obstruction could be reamed out—or, if that was not feasible, a patch could be added to enlarge the blood pathway, or blood could be detoured around the obstruction through a vein or other graft. That, however, left many patients with obstructions of vessels deep within the brain.

Now a microsurgical procedure called "cerebral revascularization" holds promise for many of the latter. The four- to five-hour operation uses microsutures to connect a segment of the superficial temporal artery of the scalp, through an opening made in the skull, to a segment of the middle cerebral artery, which extends over the brain. The scalp has a rich blood supply and can spare the superficial temporal artery. The operation creates a bypass of the circulation around an obstruction and connects two arteries rarely affected by obstruction.

It was this procedure that was used for the New York man mentioned earlier. And according to reports at an international symposium on 400 patients followed for an average of two and a half years, strokes occurred in only three after the operation, with others experiencing marked reduction of little strokes and in most cases their almost complete elimination.

Brain Tumors and Other Critical Problems.

At the Neurological Institute of the Columbia-Presbyterian Medical Center in New York, a middle-aged man is seated in an elevated chair resembling a dentist's treatment chair. He has been totally anesthetized to prevent movement. Oxygen intake and heartbeat are controlled artificially.

The operation—called a "suboccipital craniotomy"—is required to remove a large tumor growing inside the brain. "By combining high-powered magnification and extremely fine surgical instrumentation, tumors like this, in deep and inaccessible areas, can be removed with excellent precision and with minimal damage to very sensitive surrounding tissues," according to Dr. Gennett Stein, head of neurological surgery at the medical center.

For the first time, some critical areas not only of the brain but also of the spinal cord can be entered by neurosurgeons to precisely cut away life-threatening tumors and arteriovenous malformations (abnormal tangles of blood vessels). Before, many had to be left untouched because of the grave risk of death or of serious injury to surrounding vital structures. Now, even when tiny nerves or blood vessels must be damaged to remove a tumor, they can be restitched or reconstructed because of the operating microscope and fine angled needles.

Brain arteries sometimes develop aneurysms—weak spots on their walls, which, like a weak spot on a car-tire wall, may balloon out. In such cases, there is risk that at some point the aneurysm may burst, with blood spilling into the brain substance, pressing on vital structures, and causing strokelike symptoms or coma. Now aneurysms can often be clamped off with tiny metal clips.

Microsurgical techniques are providing a greater chance of cure for tumors and arteriovenous malformations in the spinal cord that may threaten death or produce spasticity, weakness, and other serious consequences. Where before neurosurgeons rarely attempted to cut into the cord, now, with enlarged view through the microscope, they can work within the cord, cutting out a tumor or entire clump of tangled vessels from inside.

Surgery on pituitary-gland tumors has advanced. Previously, an incision had to be made at the base of the skull and often the whole gland had to be removed in order to get the tumor out, with the patient then requiring hormone treatment for the rest of his or her life to replace the vital pituitary hormones lost with gland removal. Now, using microsurgical techniques, a special instrument can be inserted under the upper lip and through the nose and the tumor alone can often be removed through the instrument, leaving the gland itself intact.

Facial Paralysis.

About 30,000 Americans a year suffer facial paralysis. Most recover spontaneously, but 15 to 20 percent face some degree of permanent distortion. For many of the latter, microsurgical techniques can help, as they did for the young housewife mentioned earlier.

Using a needle more slender than the finest baby hair, and sutures even more delicate, doctors were able to replace the damaged section of facial nerve with one of the nerves running on either side of the tongue. Since the second hypoglossal (tongue) nerve alone is capable of controlling tongue motion, its partner can be spared.

After the operation, by studying their faces in a mirror, patients exercise and strengthen the muscles on the previously paralyzed side that have weakened from inactivity, and gradually the weak side begins to look more like the normal side.

Spinal Disks.

When herniation of a spinal disk causes unyielding leg and low back pain, a laminectomy operation can be performed and has been for more than fifty years. Through a four-inch incision, part of the bony plate (the lamina) over the disk is removed so the disk can be reached. The disk is then cut and forceps are used to remove the extruded disk material, the nucleus pulposus, which has been pressing on a nerve. The disk interior is also scraped to remove as much as possible of the remaining nucleus pulposus. The operation takes about ninety minutes and the hospital stay usually is nine days.

In 1972, Dr. Robert W. Williams of the University of Nevada School of Medicine began to wonder if a better operation might not be possible. Williams was seeing patients with failed laminectomies, their pain returned. While reoperating, he began to use a microscope to study morbid anatomy—the scars, adhesions, or other disturbances that could account for operative failure. What was needed, it seemed to him, was an operative technique that could remove extruded nucleus pulposus to take pressure off the nerve with minimum damage to and alteration of normal spinal anatomy.

The procedure he developed—which uses a surgical microscope

and special miniaturized instruments he had to devise—appears to do exactly that and is coming into increasing use. Using the microscope, Williams found he needed only a one-inch instead of four-inch incision —and he could see well enough through that small incision to get to the disk without doing a laminectomy at all.

When the naked eye is used in operating, fat lying over the nerve has to be removed. With the microscope, Williams was able to just move the fat aside and proceed. The fat later fell naturally back into place, and appeared to play an important role in preventing later adhesions.

Nor did he see any need to make a sharp cut to enlarge the opening in the disk from which nucleus was protruding; instead, he turned a blunt instrument just enough to dilate the opening and get out the protruding part of the nucleus. The opening then closed spontaneously, minimizing likelihood of herniation recurrence.

Nor did he scrape out healthy nucleus within the disk. As long as it was healthy and the opening closed up to contain it, the nucleus could help the disk act as a buffer, keeping the vertebrae normally apart.

A success rate well above 90 percent in many hundreds of operations has been reported by Williams. And in more than 600 patients, a cure rate of 96 percent has been reported by one of Williams's first followers, Dr. Harold Goald, chief of neurosurgery at Jefferson Memorial Hospital in Alexandria, Virginia.

The one-inch incision causes little pain so narcotic drugs are unnecessary in the postoperative period. Patients are walking on the evening of surgery and are discharged by the third day, with substantial savings from the shortened hospitalization. Most patients are able to return to their original jobs—to desk work in four to five weeks and in some cases sooner; to heavy work in nine to ten weeks. (See also CHEMONUCLEOLYSIS.)

Reversing Sterilization.

An estimated 10 million American men and women have chosen sterilization as their means of birth control. Each year, many thousands, because of remarriage or otherwise altered circumstances, seek reversals. Not all can be helped, but now a growing number can be.

The problem in women is to reconnect the severed fallopian tubes. Through an instrument, the laparoscope, inserted in a small abdominal incision, the surgeon can see whether reconnection is possible. If the tube ends have not become heavily scarred and can be brought close enough together, reconnection may be feasible. A larger abdominal incision is made and, using a surgical microscope, the surgeon opens the tube ends and stitches them together meticulously with fine sutures —a very delicate procedure taking from three to six hours.

The same microsurgical techniques may be used when fallopian tubes are blocked by adhesions (scars) resulting from infection, damage caused by an ovarian cyst, rupture of the appendix, or endometriosis, and in cases of congenital tubal malformation. The surgeon's task is to cut away the scar tissue and create a clear passage through the tube.

In men, the surgeon opens the scrotum and, using magnification, fine-sutures together the ends of the sperm-carrying vasa deferentia, the tubes severed in the original vasectomy.

Other Uses.

Microsurgical techniques are absolutely essential for reattachment of severed limbs. They are also employed for skin-flap and muscle transplants following major injuries and in reconstructive surgery. In these cases, tissues are transferred with nerves and blood vessels from areas such as the chest, foot, or groin.

A new microsurgical procedure has been used at Duke University Medical Center in a series of patients who lost a thumb in an accident. It involves unwrapping the skin, toenail, nerves, and blood vessels from a large toe and placing these around a bone graft in the missing thumb space. The procedure requires up to three surgical teams—one to take the tissue from the toe, one to prepare the hand for the transplant, and one to take a bone graft to place on the hand. According to Dr. James Urbaniak of Duke, the procedure has been successful in every one of the first nine patients. All walk without limping and wear regular shoes. The toe is minus a toenail but otherwise looks similar to the toe on the other foot.

Nuclear Imaging

Although the word *nuclear* has unpleasant connotations for many people, nuclear imaging is a valuable medical diagnostic tool. It allows noninvasive viewing of the beating of a heart and the functioning of other organs.

Unlike CT scanning, which "sees" by means of externally produced radiation, nuclear imaging does so through radiation emitted from within the body. And while CT scans provide data about anatomy, nuclear imaging offers information about organ function instead.

Tagging for Targets.

Although it is a relatively young technique, the origins of nuclear imaging date back to 1946 when the Atomic Energy Commission released radioisotopes—now called "radionuclides"—for medical applications.

Radionuclides are unstable atoms that emit rays of energy. Some occur naturally, as in the cases of radium and uranium, and many can be created artifically by bombarding stable atoms of an element with subatomic particles in a nuclear reactor or in an atom smasher or cyclotron. When the nucleus of a stable atom is charged by bombarding particles, the atom usually becomes unstable (radioactive) and is said to be "labeled" or "tagged."

In the beginning, the use of radionuclides in medicine was directed at treating cancer. But just before World War II, investigators had been looking into the possible diagnostic usefulness of radioactive iodine for evaluating thyroid disease. It was known that iodine would travel through the body and locate in the thyroid gland, attracted there because the thyroid uses iodine to manufacture certain hormones needed by the body. There were ways to detect it there, but no means of imaging just what was happening.

Then, in 1951, the rectilinear scanner appeared, and for the next two decades became the mainstay of nuclear imaging. It was based on the finding that many substances can be tagged with tiny, trace amounts of radionuclides, and that after being taken by mouth or injection, the substances will locate in specific body organs, depending on the materials used. The scanner, much in the pattern used by a farmer in plowing a field, targets on the low-level radiation of the radionuclides and moves back and forth over the area of location, in effect "drawing a picture" of the organ.

In recent years, the scanner has been largely replaced by the scintillation or gamma camera. With its wider field of view—about as wide as the human body—the camera does not have to scan, and when coupled with a computer can provide "moving pictures" of functioning organs, such as a beating heart.

Radionuclides are chosen for their half-life and the amount of radioactivity they emit. One with a long half-life and high radioactivity is unsuitable; the ideal radionuclide has a very short half-life and comparatively high radioactivity during that short time, resulting in a high scintillation count and the disappearance of the radionuclide by bodily excretion in a few hours. Several hundred suitable radionuclides are available.

The image produced by the scintillation camera can be used in several ways. The image can be photographed with a still camera or can be recorded on X-ray film, or the movements of the functioning organ can be stored in the computer memory for later call-up.

Information can be obtained quickly. If, for example, a patient arrives in an emergency room with severe abdominal pains and the gallbladder is suspect, it's necessary to know if there is acute blockage there. Nuclear imaging can supply the information within thirty to sixty minutes.

Imaging the Gallbladder—and Environs.

Gallstones and their complications are the most common indications for abdominal surgery and the fourth most common cause for surgical hospitalization in adults. In this country, more than 500,000 operations are performed yearly for gallbladder disease.

For years, evaluation of suspected cholecystitis (gallbladder inflammation, most often caused by gallstones) has depended on X-ray studies made after the patient swallowed or was injected with a contrast material (dye) that would outline the gallbladder and its ducts on the radiograph. More recently, ultrasound and, to a limited extent, CAT scans have had some diagnostic value.

Nuclear imaging has been reported to be more accurate and reliable than the other methods. In one study, for example, the imaging procedure was used by Dr. Leonard M. Freeman and co-workers at Montefiore Hospital and Albert Einstein College of Medicine, Bronx, New York, to study ninety patients with suspected cholecystitis. In thirty-eight of the ninety, imaging indicated actual cholecystitis, and all 38 were found on surgery to have the problem.

Imaging provides information not obtainable from oral and intravenous X-ray procedures. It can detect liver lesions during the first fifteen minutes the radionuclide is passing through that organ. Liver ducts can be visualized, especially if they are partially obstructed, and common-bile-duct obstruction can be determined. Moreover, because both the small and large intestines are clearly visualized, abnormal space-occupying masses in the abdomen may be inferred by detection of intestinal displacement.

In the course of imaging their ninety patients with suspected gallbladder disease, the Montefiore physicians discovered other abnormalities in fifteen patients. These included abnormal fluid collection in the abdomen, liver masses, mass lesions in the head of the pancreas, mass lesions displacing the bowel, and obstruction of the urethra (the channel carrying urine from the bladder).

Imaging the Heart.

Coronary artery disease is the most common serious health problem in the U.S., responsible for more than a million heart attacks yearly. Recent medical and surgical advances in managing the disease have made it imperative to diagnose it early and assess its extent accurately.

Recently developed nuclear imaging techniques can accurately measure the effectiveness of heart performance, show graphically the distribution of blood flow to the heart at rest and during exercise, and pinpoint regions of damage to the heart from heart attacks.

Various radionuclides can be used, depending upon what the imaging seeks to determine. In a test called a "ventriculogram," technetium is employed. It provides an image of the ventricle pumping blood from the heart as a means of determining heart-function efficiency. If there has been damage to the heart muscle, the image will reveal failure of the muscle to contract normally.

A technetium isotope may be used for a scan known as "infarction imaging." An infarction is a localized area of heart damage. Such an area attracts large amounts of the isotope, producing a "hot spot" visible via the scintillation camera. Its appearance indicates that a heart attack has occurred—and that it has occurred within the past five days, the maximum time during which a damaged area will attract the isotope. Thus, a recent heart attack can be distinguished from an old one.

For myocardial (heart muscle) imaging, a thallium isotope is used. Thallium tends to concentrate in live tissue, so any area of heart muscle in which it does not concentrate is likely to be damaged. This test is useful in determining the degree of damage caused by a heart attack.

Nuclear imaging can help in the diagnosis of suspected coronary artery disease by revealing the flow of blood through the heart muscle, and it can help establish whether or not a coronary artery lesion seen with angiography is significant (see ANGIOGRAPHY).

Because the imaging is noninvasive—requiring only the intravenous administration of small amounts of radionuclides—studies can be carried out sequentially to determine the effects of medical or surgical management. Its use before and after drug treatment can establish whether or not a particular drug and the particular dose of the drug are appropriate for the individual patient.

Cancer.

Nuclear imaging can sometimes be useful for cancer detection. A common site to which cancer often spreads is the skeletal system. A complete skeletal scan requires less than an hour. It is a highly sensitive procedure for detecting malignancy in bone and is usually able to do so several months before bone cancer can be seen on X-ray.

Efforts are being made to develop imaging techniques for early diagnosis of other cancers, including cancer of the lung.

Nuclear Magnetic Resonance (NMR)

Among major medical advances in recent years are CAT scans, which provide detailed images of structures inside the body, allowing early and more accurate diagnoses, sometimes revealing conditions that might otherwise go undetected (see CAT SCANS).

As valuable as that diagnostic tool is, however, it may be rivaled in coming years—and even surpassed, in the view of some physicians —by a technology called "nuclear magnetic resonance," or "NMR." Unlike CAT scans, which use radiation that may be at least theoretically of some risk, NMR employs a combination of magnetic fields and radio waves that is considered free of risk. NMR images of body organs are almost as detailed as CAT scans, and NMR works better than CAT for certain parts of the body, such as brain areas covered by thick sections of bone. NMR holds promise of being able to uncover some tumors too small to be picked up by CAT, and of being able to indicate as well whether a tumor is malignant. The newer technique can produce a map revealing not only basic anatomic structures (as CAT does) but also how various organs are functioning, even allowing chemical processes within individual cells to be seen.

The Basic Tool.

NMR works by focusing on the nuclei in the atoms of a single element (such as hydrogen, phosphorus, carbon, or potassium, among others) in biological tissue, and by detecting whether or not these nuclei behave normally in response to external magnetic forces.

These nuclei, as some researchers have suggested, can be thought of as microscopic versions of the toy tops spun by children. The nuclei tend to spin and occasionally wobble as tops do, and it is this wobbling that is detected by NMR and relayed to a computer for analysis. The images that are reconstructed resemble a cross-sectional view through, for example, an organ. Possibly even more important, the reconstruction sometimes can display a kind of biochemical blueprint of cellular activity.

The basic tool of NMR is a huge, doughnut-shaped electromagnet large enough to enclose either a patient's entire body or a smaller area under study. The magnet is very powerful, capable of producing a magnetic field as much as 3,000 to 5,000 times greater than the earth's —powerful enough to stop any wristwatch coming within yards of it and of creeping into the wallets of people walking by and erasing the magnetic strips on the backs of credit cards and bank cards.

Ninety percent of body tissue is made up of water, and within each molecule of water are hydrogen atoms. The nuclei of hydrogen atoms act like tiny magnets, but usually these natural "magnets" are pointed in random directions. When the NMR electromagnet is turned on, however, the millions of tiny magnetic axes in the patient's body line themselves up with the field, much as a steel needle points toward the pole of a nearby magnet. When weak radio waves of a certain wavelength are aimed at the body, the hydrogen nuclei in the body "flip" —that is, align themselves against the magnetic field. When the radio waves are turned off, the nuclei flip back to their original position, sending out radio waves that are detected by a receiver and used to create a computer-generated image that gives both structural and functional information.

The safety of NMR appears to be outstanding. No injections are given; and even at much higher magnetic-field strengths, there are no measurable effects on tissues. Workers in high-energy physics have been exposed to more-powerful magnets for many years without ill effects. Probably the most difficult part for the patient is having to remain motionless within the magnet while the procedure takes place—a period of three to twenty-five minutes, depending on the image desired. While the magnet is operating, the patient hears a loud thumping noise.

Uses.

The applications of NMR are potentially vast and only beginning to be explored.

For example, conventional X-rays are fine for orthopedic applications when bones need to be visualized, but of little use in showing the soft tissue around bones. NMR, on the other hand, ignores bones because they contain little hydrogen. It can therefore focus on such areas as the interior of the spine and the base of the skull.

Because flowing liquids produce a very weak NMR signal, the insides of blood vessels can be studied as if they were empty. NMR is sensitive to fatty compounds, such as the myelin sheath that surrounds nerves, and is thus proving useful for early diagnosis of diseases such as multiple sclerosis in which the myelin degenerates. It is also expected to allow physicians to pinpoint tiny fat deposits on blood-vessel walls before they become the focus for circulation-impeding atherosclerosis.

The technique is being used to measure blood-flow rates from specific locations in the brain to identify patients at risk for developing a stroke. In clinical trials on patients with decreased flow, NMR findings not only correlated with those from other techniques but appeared to provide superior information. "Preliminary reviews of these data suggest that it will be a valuable method to predict an impending stroke," says Dr. Joseph F. Cusick, professor of neurosurgery at the Medical College of Wisconsin.

NMR may be used to detect abnormally functioning cells within the pituitary gland and elsewhere in the brain. Antidepressant and other drugs may be labeled with NMR-sensitive compounds and traced to their sites of action within the brain, making a significant contribution to psychiatric treatment. In fact, at the Department of Psychiatry of the New York Hospital-Cornell Medical Center, patients with schizophrenia, affective disorders, dementia, and Tourette's disease have been scanned, and studies of autism and alcoholism are planned. "Although these studies are in their early stages," reports Dr. Richard Brown of Cornell, "NMR is expected to make a significant contribution to the theory and practice of psychiatry."

NMR also shows promise as a sensitive diagnostic tool for cancer, able to detect some brain tumors, for example, that do not show up on X-rays. In one recently reported case, a thirty-seven-year-old Wisconsin man suffered dizzy spells that became increasingly worse. Despite six months of testing with, among others, several sets of X-rays and electroencephalogram (brain-wave) studies, the diagnosis was not definitive. It seemed likely that a deadly type of cancer was invading the brain and pressing against the brainstem, but no growth could be seen on X-rays. When finally NMR scanning was tried, it revealed a tumor in the lower part of the brain, a tumor as big as the core of a golf ball. Surgical removal was successful.

Some physicians expect that NMR may do more than detect tumors, including those missed by other techniques; it may also provide information about whether the tumor is thriving or dying.

Another possible use may be in determining how donor organs from cadavers function after transplantation. Work at Oxford University in England, for example, indicates that NMR can reveal whether cellular activity is still continuing in a donor kidney; if it is, the outlook for successful transplantation is promising.

Costs and Benefits.

NMR is expensive. In addition to the cost of the machine itself—which may run $1.5 million or more—there is the cost of the special room needed to house it because of the magnetic fields, and this latter cost may run to a million or more. As a result, an NMR scan may cost the patient about $500.

Will NMR simply add to spiraling medical costs? Not if it lives up to promise and goes well beyond merely confirming what other diagnostic procedures show. If one Harvard Medical School expert is right, "NMR isn't just a better mousetrap. We'll diagnose disease earlier and monitor therapy better. With CAT scans we mapped the interstates of the body; with NMR we'll see the back alleys."

Pacemakers

The human heart is equipped with its own natural pacemaker. It's an area of special tissue called the "sinus node," which gets signals from centers in the brain and spinal cord that are sensitive to the body's varying needs under different circumstances. It also reacts to hormones released by the adrenal and thyroid glands. In response, the pacemaker produces electrical impulses that travel through conduction pathways in the heart and cause the heart muscle to contract and pump blood throughout the body.

Occasionally, the natural pacemaker becomes diseased and the electrical impulses are sent out too irregularly, too slowly, or too quickly. Or the impulses may be blocked along conduction pathways, resulting in an erratic heartbeat. Medications can usually overcome such disturbances and avoid the fatigue, dizziness, fainting spells, or other symptoms they may produce. When medications fail, an artificial, electronic pacemaker often can be used to restore proper heartbeat.

How It Works.

Much like the heart's natural pacemaker, an artificial pacemaker starts the contraction or pumping action of the heart by sending a tiny electrical signal into the heart muscle by means of a small insulated wire called an "electrode." The strength of the signal is so slight that it usually cannot be felt.

If a pacemaker is needed only temporarily, an external device is used: The pacemaker itself remains outside the body, and wires from it are moved up, in a relatively simple procedure under a local anesthetic, through a vein and into a heart chamber. When the pacemaker is then turned on, it substitutes for the natural pacemaker and maintains regular heart action until the heart's rhythm becomes normal again on its own, at which point the wires can be withdrawn almost painlessly. This may occur in a matter of a few days or a week or two.

When the heart's pacemaking system is damaged beyond healing, a permanent pacemaker can be inserted under the skin under local anesthesia in a procedure that takes about an hour or less.

Pacemakers today are generally reliable and remarkably effective. They can permit virtually normal living—work, golf, swimming, dancing, and other activities enjoyed before trouble developed with the natural pacemaker and conduction system.

Improvements.

Although the fact that electricity can influence the heart was known to physicians since the eighteenth century, it was not until the last century that they used electrical shocks to resuscitate victims of heart stoppage.

In 1933, the first device, called an "artificial pacemaker," was patented, but it was another twenty years before pacemakers began to be used extensively in hospitals. The first wearable, battery-operated external pacemaker was developed in 1958. Two years later, a totally implantable pacing system—electrodes, pulse generator, and power source—was developed.

In the early 1960s the first major pacing improvements were in leads, the wires connecting the pacemaker to the heart. The earliest stainless-steel leads, subjected to the constant flexing of the beating heart, fatigued and broke. To solve the problem, a spring-coil lead that would flex without fatigue was developed.

The new, flexible leads did something more: They transformed pacemaker implantation. An early implant was an operation of almost last resort. Surgeons had to open the patient's chest, expose the heart, and suture the lead into the heart muscle—a major ordeal. The new, flexible leads could eliminate all that. A lead could be slipped into a vein and guided gently into the heart without opening the chest; then the pacemaker could be sewn into a pocket under the skin in either the shoulder or the abdomen. The whole procedure could be carried out under local instead of general anesthesia and completed in less than an hour. Often the patient was out of bed the same day, usually resuming normal activities within two weeks.

The first pacemakers were "fixed-rate"—they gave off a continuous signal at a preset rate selected for the patient by his or her physician. Later pacemakers—which began to appear late in the 1960s and are now much more commonly used—are of the "demand" type. They have a special sensing circuit that monitors the electrical activity of the heart. As long as the heart rate (the number of beats per minute) remains at a proper level, the demand pacemaker remains inactive. If the patient's heart rate varies significantly from that level, the demand unit immediately begins sending impulses to regulate the beat.

There have been other improvements as well. Advances in microelectronics and battery technology allowed manufacturers to decrease the size of pacemakers dramatically, develop long-lasting power sources, and introduce pacemakers the physician can adjust and monitor externally. Since the invention of the first wearable pacemaker, the size has been reduced from that of a bedside clock to that of a pocket watch. Current pacemakers enable patients to consult with their physicians or follow-up services by transmitting their heart signals over the telephone. And physicians can use radio-frequency programming to fine-tune each patient's unit to meet his or her changing needs.

A pacemaker system has three basic components, two of which are implantable.

The pacemaker, or pulse generator, resting under the skin in the shoulder or abdomen, is protected from accidental bumping and moisture by a polished, hermetically sealed titanium metal case. Titanium is compatible with the body, resistant to corrosion, strong, yet lightweight.

Within the case are a power source—commonly a sealed lithium-iodine battery that supplies energy for up to a decade—and microcircuitry to process information and transform battery energy into electrical stimulation. Microcircuitry is a major reason for the dramatic decrease in weight as well as size of pacemakers. Early units weighed as much as 226 grams; today's smallest weigh only 45 grams, less than 2 ounces.

On top of the metal container is a flexible plastic connector that links the pulse generator to the second implantable component—the pacing leads, small-diameter coiled wire strands insulated with urethane, flexible, and corrosion-resistant. One end of a lead connects to the pulse generator; the other is a platinum electrode that touches the heart muscle.

The third component of the pacing system, which is not implanted, is the programmer. Similar to a small computer, it is used by the physician to externally adjust and monitor the pacemaker to suit an individual patient's needs. Signals travel to and from the pacemaker on radio-frequency waves.

Correcting Rapid Heartbeats, Too.

Until now, slowing an abnormally rapid heartbeat has been beyond the capabilities of pacemakers. The units have been effective for counteracting abnormally slow heart rhythms called "bradycardias."

Correcting an abnormally rapid heartbeat—tachycardia—poses an entirely different problem. The heart is *supposed* to beat rapidly at times. During exercise, the heart rate may shoot up to 150 or more beats a minute from its normal 60 to 100 beats to meet increased body needs for oxygen-carrying blood. For a pacemaker to stop this normal response of the heart would be dangerous. Now, however, newer pacemakers being developed can distinguish between a normally rapid heartbeat and an abnormal tachycardia. In fact, one that has been tested at the University of Chicago Medical Center can distinguish between the three different types of tachycardia and respond by delivering electrical signals to the proper sites in the heart.

The most serious type of fast beat, ventricular tachycardia, usually occurs in patients with a history of heart attacks or heart disease. It is the most common cause of sudden death—when a patient collapses and dies quickly.

Another type, known as "supraventricular tachycardia," usually occurs in patients without a history of heart disease. Unlike ventricular tachycardias, the supraventricular are not usually fatal, but the patient may feel dizzy or have to sit down to relieve the uncomfortable symptoms.

Sinus tachycardia, the third type, is the normal and healthy reaction to stress put on the heart from physical exercise or tension. This type requires no treatment.

To control the other two types, a microprocessor programmed with specific heart rates is contained within the pacemaker. When the heartbeat rises above one of these fixed values, the device determines the type of tachycardia, sensing it in just a few beats, and begins delivering the right amount of electrical signals. As the pacemaker starts working, it causes waves in the heart, which collide with the wavefront from the tachycardia. This collision causes the waves to cancel each other out, and the normal heartbeat resumes. If the pacemaker detects a supraventricular tachycardia, signals are sent to the atrium, an upper heart chamber. For a ventricular tachycardia, signals go to the ventricles, the heart's pumping chambers, where they are required.

Some tachycardias can be treated with medication, but others cannot. In addition, some patients do not respond well to medication. Common complaints are unpleasant side effects and the inconvenience of taking drugs every three to four hours. The new tachycardia pacemakers are expected to help many such patients.

Nuclear-Powered Pacemaking.

Not long ago, a vivacious twenty-one-year-old woman had a nuclear-powered pacemaker implanted at the Ochsner Clinic in New Orleans. Three weeks later she got married, hopeful that the pacemaker gave her the prospect of a long future.

Her pacemaker differs from others in that one-quarter gram of radioactive isotope plutonium 238 furnishes the power to a long-life battery that energizes the pacemaking. The projected life of this kind of pacemaker, according to Dr. John Ochsner, is greater than seventy years—a decided advantage for a young woman who has congenital heart blockage and will have to wear a pacemaker the rest of her life.

In the 1960s, the nuclear-powered pacemaker was proposed as a technological development within easy reach that could solve the major problem of then-conventional pacemakers: Their batteries had to be replaced as often as every eighteen to twenty-four months—hence tens of thousands of pacemaker patients faced additional surgery, with all the attendant expense and pain. A heart pacer powered by a pellet of plutonium, an effective power source good for many decades, would eliminate the battery problem, proponents said, ānd emit less radiation than the luminous dial of a wristwatch.

The Atomic Energy Commission, the National Institutes of Health, and several U.S. companies were soon collaborating on development of the nuclear pacer. Similar programs were under way in France and other countries. France won the "race" on April 27, 1970, when the first nuclear pacemaker was implanted in a human by a French surgeon.

In 1973, the U.S. began to catch up. On April 9 and 10, 1973, physicians at Beth Israel Hospital in Newark, New Jersey, placed the U.S.-developed device in fifteen patients. Over the next decade, however, the Beth Israel team implanted only 151 nuclear-powered pacers

—and in all, only 3,000 to 3,500 of the devices have been used around the world, according to the American Heart Association. Publicity about the danger of radiation, the paper work needed to meet governmental requirements, and rapid advances in battery-powered units are usually offered as reasons why the new technology was shelved. But at a ten-year anniversary celebration in April 1983, nine of the original fifteen patients (twelve are still living) came back to Beth Israel, and one remarked in a newspaper interview, "It is a fantastic feeling to be able to go ten years without an operation. The pacemaker has given me a new lease on life."

According to Dr. Victor Parsonnet, director of surgery at Beth Israel, 20 percent of Americans who need pacemakers are under age sixty and could benefit from the nuclear device. Odds are that they will outlive the new lithium battery units, but they are not being given a choice. "The high reliability of the nuclear unit," he observes, "leads one to wonder whether the nuclear pulse generator should be relegated to the shelf forever."

Controversy.

As of 1983, about 2 million pacemakers had been implanted worldwide and about 473,000 pacemaker patients were living in the U.S. In this country now, about 120,000 units are implanted each year, 100,000 of them first-time implants. The average pacemaker patient is about sixty-nine years old, but the units have also been implanted in tiny infants with heart problems that might otherwise have led to death.

Having a pacemaker implanted is expensive. "It's difficult to get out of the hospital for less than $12,000," according to Dr. Michael Bilitch, director of the Pacemaker Center at the University of Southern California-Los Angeles School of Medicine, and a consultant to the 1982 Senate committee that investigated pacemakers. Barring complications, patients are usually hospitalized from three to five days. Most recipients are over sixty-five and Medicare picks up most of the cost.

Complaints about the high cost of pacemaker implantation have led to a series of investigations into pacemaker use and allegations of fraud and kickbacks in the health-care industry.

The first group to investigate, the Maryland-based Public Citizens Health Research Group, did so in response to an eighty-nine-year-old pacemaker recipient who complained about the expense of the procedure and her need for reimplantation. The private consumer group concluded that 25 to 35 percent of the pacemaker implants in Maryland were unnecessary.

The Maryland group's conclusions, sent to the U.S. Senate, sparked an investigation by the Special Committee on Aging. The committee concluded there may be as much as $500 million worth of waste, fraud, and abuse in the pacemaker area each year in the U.S.

Another group, the Maryland Society of Cardiology, disputes the findings of the consumer group's study. The society's investigators reviewed the Maryland group's study and concluded that only about 1.7 percent of the 2,182 pacemaker placements were unnecessary, not the 25 to 35 percent claimed.

Dr. Bilitch notes several flaws in the consumer group's study, including reliance on only the front sheet of hospital discharge papers for information. The front sheet is subject to coding error and contains insufficient information to draw conclusions about medical need for pacemaker placement. Bilitch estimates that less than 5 percent of all pacemakers placed are medically unnecessary.

His suggestion to anyone who may be a candidate for a pacemaker is to find out exactly why the physician believes a pacemaker is necessary. "If a physician can't explain why, the patient should wonder about that—and perhaps find another doctor."

Percutaneous Stone Extraction
A new way of getting at kidney stones

It is one of the most agonizing of human experiences—the passage of a kidney stone. Each year more than 300,000 Americans require stone removal, and the classical treatment has been major surgery, with one to two weeks of hospitalization and prolonged convalescence.

Now promising, less-invasive therapy for many kidney-stone patients is becoming available. It requires no long and deep incision, allows kidney stones to be removed through a tiny opening in the skin of the back, and minimizes pain and the length of time needed for recovery.

The Attack.

A kidney stone is a hard mass that builds up gradually when various salt or mineral crystals are deposited on a kidney's inner surface, often at the site of origin of the tube that carries urine down to the bladder. As long as a stone does not break loose, it may cause only bleeding from local damage to the lining surface. The bleeding is usually harmless but leads to X-ray studies that disclose the stone.

Once a stone gets loose, however, it may block off urine drainage and produce an attack of very severe pain.

Each kidney is connected to the bladder by a ureter, a thin tube about a foot long and a quarter-inch in inside diameter. Strong muscles in the ureter wall push urine into the bladder even when you are lying down, but stones are often too big to get through readily. The ureter

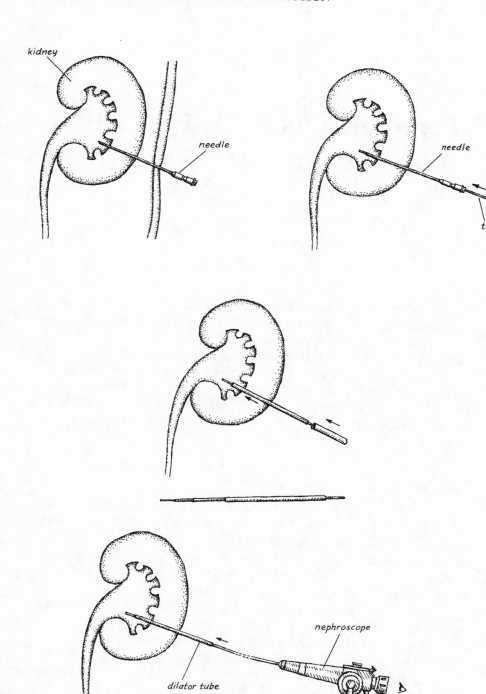

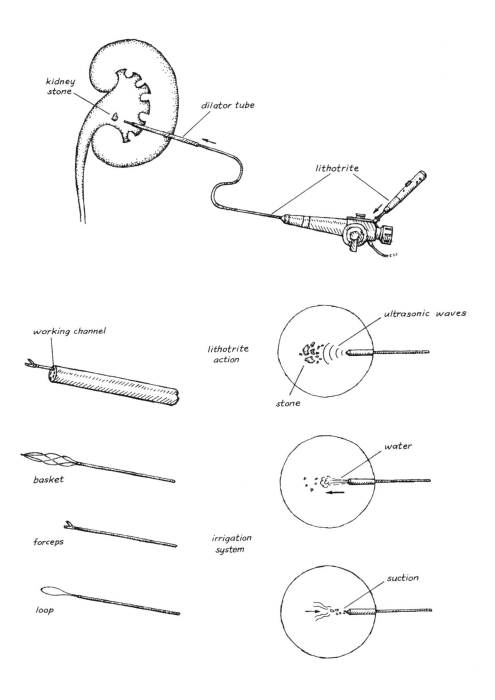

kidney stone

dilator tube

lithotrite

working channel

lithotrite action

ultrasonic waves

stone

basket

forceps

irrigation system

water

loop

suction

squeezes and squeezes in efforts to push a stone along—and until the stone gets out, the pain is extreme.

Baskets and Open Surgery.

If a stone fails to pass spontaneously, a hollow tubular instrument called a "cystoscope" may be inserted through the urethra (the canal extending from the bladder to the outside of the body) and moved up into the bladder. Through it, a thinner tube is threaded up to the stone. At the end of the tube is a basketlike device that is used to try to extract the stone. Sometimes, instead, stones that are stuck in the bladder can be crushed by a tiny instrument inserted with a catheter (tube).

Often, however, a kidney stone must be removed by surgery. The traditional method involves making a five- to 6-inch incision through the layers of skin and underlying muscles to expose the kidney. Then, after an incision is made in the kidney's collecting system, the stone must be found and removed. The stone may move around inside the kidney, making it difficult to find and remove.

The operation is major surgery. Patients tolerate the procedure itself well, but the postsurgical course is hardly without discomfort, the hospital stay may be as long as two weeks, and convalescence can be prolonged. There is some possibility, too, that the scar left by the operation may become a focus for formation of another stone.

The Percutaneous Approach.

With techniques largely devised and refined in the 1980s, many stones now are being removed through an entirely new approach.

While the patient is under local or general anesthesia, a long needle is inserted through the skin and underlying structures into the kidney, and the needle's path is gradually dilated with progressively enlarging tubes. Through the last tube, a fiberoptic telescope called a "nephroscope" is inserted, allowing the physician to see a stone. The working channel within the nephroscope can admit loops, baskets, or forceps to extract a smaller stone.

If a stone is too large to fit through the tube, the physician now can break it up. A hollow, rodlike device, called a "lithotrite," is passed into the kidney through the nephroscope. The lithotrite contains a sonotrode, which transforms electrical impulses fed to it from an external generator into ultrasonic vibrations. Also in the lithotrite is an irrigation system to flush stone fragments out of the kidney as they break loose. When absorption of the ultrasonic waves causes the stone to loosen and disintegrate, the doctor chips away until fragments measure only one to two millimeters in diameter and can be flushed out.

All this hardware enters the patient through an incision that need be only wide enough to accommodate a tube about six millimeters (approximately one-quarter inch) in diameter. The entire process normally takes less than an hour.

Stones that cannot be removed by this method can usually be identified in advance. Moreover, if the procedure should fail, the surgeon can proceed with conventional surgery while the patient is still in the operating room.

Recovery from percutaneous stone removal is remarkably quick because there is virtually no trauma to the system. Indeed, many patients are up and around, pain-free, the next morning, out of the hospital in six days—often as little as two days— and usually, are able to return to work soon after. At one hospital, when a member of the kidney-stone-removal team developed a stone himself recently, it was removed percutaneously and he was back at work treating patients in only four days.

Success rates are high. For example, about 95 percent of the first 160 percutaneous procedures done at the Mayo Clinic have been successful. According to Dr. Joseph Segura of Mayo, "We can remove large stones percutaneously, but the very largest stones and those that are located in positions that we can't reach must be removed by standard open surgical methods. However, most stones that can't be reached percutaneously are not symptomatic and need not be removed. We can get at most symptomatic stones."

At Presbyterian Hospital in New York City, Dr. Carl Olsson, director of urology, estimates that 75 percent of the surgery for kidney stones will no longer be necessary, with cost and disability both sharply reduced.

Other Advances.

A procedure called "coagulum pyelolithotomy" can sometimes be used as a relatively simple, rapid means of removing multiple kidney stones. It involves the injection into the kidney of a liquid containing calcium chloride, cryoprecipitate, thrombin, and indigo carmine. It is allowed to form a jellylike clot. Within minutes the stones are trapped inside the clot, which the surgeon then extracts with forceps.

Still another development—esoteric but potentially of major significance—is a technique called "extracorporeal shock wave litho-tripsy," which applies shock waves from outside the body to blast kidney stones. Developed at Munich University's Urological Clinic in West Germany by Dr. Christian Chaussy, the procedure involves producing high-energy acoustic shock waves by an underwater high-voltage condenser spark discharge that causes an explosive evaporation of water surrounding the condenser. This action leads to generation of shock waves through the surrounding fluid.

Before treatment, the patient is anesthetized and positioned in a water bath so that the kidney stone is precisely targeted to receive the highest energy of the shock wave. The blast, which does no harm to other areas, penetrates the stone and shatters it as the waves bounce back from the surrounding soft tissue of the body and collide with oncoming waves. After a few days, the stone fragments, which may be as fine as sand, pass out of the body on their own, although there may be some cramps while the fragments are being excreted.

Of the first 351 patients treated in Munich, only two have required subsequent surgery to remove seemingly shatterproof stones.

Studies are now under way with shock-wave therapy at several major U.S. medical centers. Because of the expense of the equipment —close to $1.5 million—not every local hospital is going to have it, but it should be available at regional medical centers before long. According to some estimates, there will be a saving on the order of $2,000 per patient because of shortened hospital stays.

PET Scans
Scanning the mind
and living processes

Imagine a technique that would allow physicians and scientists to look —without surgery—directly into the brain or the heart and observe the biochemical reactions taking place. Used on the brain, it would allow monitoring of the patterns of chemical activity that take place there during speaking, hearing, and thinking. It would allow the observation and evaluation of changes in brain chemistry before, during, and after a stroke. It would show the response of a brain tumor to drug treatment. The process of formation of brain lesions in multiple sclerosis and the biochemical abnormalities in disorders such as Parkinson's disease, Alzheimer's disease (dementia), and schizophrenia would be seen. Understanding of the brain's organization and of many specific disturbances would be tremendously increased.

Applied to the heart, such a technique would immediately show the scope of damage (measured in cells killed) wrought by a heart attack. At the same time, it would reveal the precise region affected, critical information in revitalizing traumatized tissue.

Such a technique exists. Called PET—for "positron emission tomography"—it is being used as a research tool in more than a dozen medical centers around the country. It is not yet a diagnostic technique at this stage of its development, because it is as yet too expensive and too complicated. But its development has been rapid in just the last few years; it is allowing extraordinary things to be done in research, things never possible before, and its use for patients may soon become commonplace.

The Technique.

PET scanning differs significantly from the CAT (computerized axial tomography) scanning now well known in diagnostic medicine. Scanning by CAT is limited to anatomy. CAT shows an organ's shape and form—its structure—but not how it is functioning. PET provides metabolic portraits, revealing the rate at which abnormal and healthy tissues consume biochemicals. It offers a functional perspective of biochemistry occurring within living tissue.

A PET scan begins with radioactive versions (isotopes) of natural body substances like oxygen or glucose (blood sugar). A cyclotron machine makes the isotopes by accelerating charged particles in circles and then smashing them into targets. The radioactivity dissipates within minutes, so the cyclotron has to be built next door to the PET scanner.

The patient inhales or is injected with a very small amount of the radioactive material, and is then positioned within the scanning device. The radioactive material—which has been absorbed by brain or body cells—emits positrons (positively charged particles). These immediately collide with negatively charged electrons present in the cells. The collisions produce gamma rays, which are detected by the scanner's 288 highly sensitive crystals surrounding the patient.

A computer collects and translates the gamma rays into images, which appear as horizontal "slices" of the tissue being scanned. By comparing a series of slices taken of the brain, for example, at regular intervals, physicians can detect metabolic or chemical changes in the brain. Seven such slices are imaged simultaneously, and the images can reveal how an isotope is taken up by the tissues: Dark patches indicate areas of high radioactivity where the isotope is concentrated; light patches indicate areas where the substance is not taken into the cells. For example, when a stroke patient inhales radioactive oxygen, large light-colored areas on the PET images show parts of the brain where the radioactive oxygen is not being used, where the tissue is dead.

It is possible, too, to calculate the local metabolic rate for glucose in any region of the brain. Using this technique, the functional nerve pathways can be measured, because alterations in functional activity change the metabolic rate of the involved brain regions and these can be detected. In studies with volunteers who were subjected to three different types of stimuli—visual, tactile, and auditory—the precise areas of the brain affected by the stimuli were revealed by changes in the local cerebral metabolic rates. With auditory stimuli to the ear, for example, the local metabolic rate increased in the right temporal lobe of the brain, the part that controls hearing.

Answering Old Questions.

Although the origins of PET scanning can be traced back to the 1950s, the first results were of little value. Researchers were getting no more than pictures of radioactive tracers in the brain. The pictures became better and better over the years, into the 1970s, but by itself PET scanning wasn't anything significant—just an instrument. It needed something worth measuring. This was finally provided by radioactively labeling glucose and other natural body substances—a development for which the Albert Lasker Medical Research Award was bestowed in 1981 upon Dr. Louis Sokoloff, chief of the Laboratory of Cerebral Metabolism at the National Institute of Mental Health.

Thus, it is just in the last few years that PET studies have begun to provide answers to many old questions.

At UCLA School of Medicine, investigators have studied the brains of normal people to learn how the brain processes basic information. By measuring the use of glucose and oxygen, they have determined that certain brain areas become active during passive activity, such as listening to a story, and additional areas become active when the listener tries to remember the story. Such research may help identify the brain area responsible for memory.

At the University of Pennsylvania School of Medicine, PET has shown differences in regional brain metabolism while subjects were engaged in verbal analysis and spatial analysis, with each task producing a different degree of metabolic activity in various brain regions. UP investigators believe such information can lead eventually to complete understanding of functioning in the normal brain.

As the normal brain becomes better understood, abnormalities can be better studied. One very important neuropsychiatric disorder already being studied with PET is schizophrenia. Investigators have found significantly lower metabolism of glucose in the left frontal cerebral cortex area of the brain in newly diagnosed schizophrenics—a phenomenon that did not change with administration of drugs even though the drugs relieved symptoms. Investigators believe that the metabolic abnormality may be a marker for schizophrenia—a means of diagnosing a disease that otherwise can often be difficult to diagnose accurately.

Alzheimer's disease is also being examined with PET. At UCLA, studies indicate that the ratio of glucose metabolized in one brain area, the cerebral cortex, to that metabolized in another area, the caudate-putamen region, differs in Alzheimer's disease from the ratio in other types of dementia. This finding may lead to faster differentiation of Alzheimer's from other, treatable forms of dementia.

At the National Institutes of Health, investigators have found a strong correlation between the malignancy of central-nervous-system tumors and the rate of glucose metabolism. They believe that with PET they can now establish exactly how malignant a tumor is and, moreover, recognize very early transformation of a tumor from benign to malignant.

With a recently installed PET scanner, University of Chicago researchers are undertaking, among many projects, comparisons of states of sleep in normal patients and those with specific sleep disturbances such as narcolepsy. Neurological disorders such as Huntington's chorea, Parkinson's disease, and amyotrophic lateral sclerosis (Lou Gehrig's disease) will also be studied in states of sleep and wakefulness. The involuntary movements associated with these disorders often stop during sleep. The hope is that further insights into the disease process through PET scanning may suggest effective medical therapies for these severe, frequently deadly disorders.

Elsewhere, investigators are finding evidence that PET may be useful in the treatment of epilepsy. It detects glucose-activity changes in parts of the brain involved in seizures. By pinpointing the affected area, it can help surgeons locate and destroy seizure-inducing cells.

PET scanners are being used to study stroke—trying, among other things, to gauge how much recovery the patient can expect. At UCLA, investigators are placing the scanner over patients' hearts to monitor blood flow.

PET has much promise for cancer. It could, for example, show how much oxygen a tumor uses. This is important because animal studies indicate that tumor cells using more oxygen are more vulnerable to radiation therapy—thus a PET scan showing a tumor's oxygen consumption might be used to predict whether radiation therapy will benefit a patient.

PET could also help identify tumor types without taking tissue samples. It's known that different types of brain tumors, for example, use certain amino acids for growth. By establishing which amino acids a tumor accumulates, PET could indicate the tissue type of the tumor without biopsy, helping the physician to determine the most effective treatment. (Compare CAT SCANS.)

Photoradiation Therapy
Light as cure

Late in the nineteenth century, Niels Finsen, a Danish physician, suffering from anemia and great fatigue, began to wonder: He lived in a house facing north; might he be helped if he received more sunlight?

Finsen himself wasn't helped, but when he died in 1904, it was one year after receiving the Nobel Prize in medicine for his work using light to cure lupus vulgaris (a then-common tubercular skin infection) and to greatly reduce the scarring left by smallpox.

Only very recently has photoradiation therapy begun to be extended to present-day problems—with promising results.

Neonatal Jaundice.

In the pediatric wards of many hospitals today, a common sight is babies lying naked in bassinets, their eyes shielded by bandages, while being bathed in a bright blue glow from fluorescent bulbs.

The infants are receiving phototherapy for a common and potentially deadly problem called "neonatal jaundice," a form of hyper-bilirubinemia in which abnormally high levels of bilirubin (a red bile pigment) occur in blood. Bilirubin is released when old red blood cells are broken down to be discarded in order to make room for fresh new red cells. In adults, the liver readily gets rid of bilirubin along with the old cells, but in newborns—especially prematures—the liver is often not yet up to the job. As a result, the bilirubin buildup may reach dangerously high levels, causing damage to the nervous system and sometimes even death.

Happily, in the last twenty years, it has become apparent that the cure for the problem is simple: light. Light as therapy for hyper-bilirubinemia is the result of an accidental discovery in England in the mid-1950s by an observant young physician. It was the custom of the nurse in charge of the small premature unit in the Rochford, England, hospital to take her little patients out into the sun and let them bask nude whenever weather permitted. One day, young Dr. R. H. Dobbs noticed a little patch of yellow on the abdomen of one baby while the rest of the infant's skin was relatively nonyellow. Investigating further, Dobbs determined that the yellow patch was where a blanket had fallen across the infant's stomach. Elsewhere, the sun apparently had greatly modified the jaundice.

Actually, only very recently has the mechanism become clear. Normally, when bilirubin reaches the liver, a chemical there hooks on to it and tows it into the bile for elimination. But in newborns' livers, the necessary chemical is deficient and bilirubin accumulates. As the accumulation builds up, bilirubin starts to circulate near the skin surface. There, light can filter through to it—and as blue light impacts on bilirubin, it changes the shape of the bilirubin molecule in such a way that it is able to be excreted in the bile.

Combating Tumors.

A novel photoradiation technique is extending the lives of some cancer patients for whom conventional treatment has failed.

In the human body, certain chemicals called "porphyrins" play a vital role: They combine with iron to form the oxygen-transporting part of the blood's hemoglobin. But in some conditions, known as the "porphyria diseases," the porphyrins are far from beneficent. Not properly handled by the body, their levels build up abnormally, and when activated by light, they have a destructive effect on tissues.

At one of the country's major cancer centers, Roswell Park Memorial Institute in Buffalo, a team led by Dr. Harold O. Douglass, Jr., has been putting this destructive effect to use. The investigators have teamed red laser light with a porphyrin derivative called "HpD," and although optimum doses of HpD and light are still being sought, photoradiation therapy is proving of great value.

Originally, photoradiation therapy with HpD was limited to skin or subskin tumors. Now the experimental technique is being used for cancers in less accessible sites, including the esophagus, stomach, bladder, and air passages. In a study with more than 100 patients receiving intravenous injections of HpD and exposed to red light, the Buffalo team has found the technique most promising for cancer obstructing the esophagus or stomach and beyond surgical help. Often, photoradiation reduces the size of an inoperable tumor enough to make surgical treatment possible.

HpD given by vein disappears from cancerous tissue more slowly than from other tissue. Taking advantage of that delayed clearance, the Buffalo workers wait seventy-two to ninety-six hours after administering HpD before delivering the laser light to the tumor.

At a recent international cancer congress in Seattle, Dr. Yoshihiro Hayta of Tokyo Medical College reported on experience in Japan with 126 patients with cancers of various organs. Photoradiation proved helpful for early cancers and improved patients with advanced disease. In fourteen breast-cancer patients with a total of eighty-eight metastatic skin lesions, photoradiation led to complete remission in 36 percent, significant remission in 40 percent, and partial remission in 19 percent.

The technique also has diagnostic potential. One case cited at the international congress was that of a patient who, after six months of conventional treatment for malignant melanoma of the eye, appeared to be free of tumor, but in whom photoradiation detected remaining malignant cells missed by other diagnostic methods. German investigators reported using HpD's affinity for malignant tumors to find tiny areas of bladder cancer undetectable with other methods.

The technique is not without possible complications. Among patients treated in Buffalo, one developed a fistula (an abnormal passage) between the esophagus and the trachea (windpipe). However, investigators are optimistic that better understanding of how to control the extent of tumor destruction may make photoradiation more effective and extend its usefulness to pancreatic and other cancers.

PUVA.

For thousands of years, the Egyptians have used the seeds of a weed to treat vitiligo, a condition in which patches of skin lose their pigmentation and become white. When stimulated by sunlight, the oil of the seeds restores the natural color in the vitiligo patches.

The active ingredient in the oil has proved to be a psoralen compound. And recently, a treatment called PUVA—for psoralen plus a type of ultraviolet light known as "UV-A"—has come into use for psoriasis.

Psoriasis is a skin disease in which rapid multiplication of underlying skin cells leads to replacement of the normal outer skin layer, producing a rough, red, scaly surface. PUVA therapy—in which a psoralen pill is taken and the skin is exposed to UV-A—decreases the cell multiplication and often clears the skin.

But PUVA therapy is not without risk. The combination of psoralen and ultraviolet light has been found to trigger skin cancers in animals and increase risk for such malignancies in human patients. Such cancers are generally curable, and for many patients the benefits of PUVA therapy may outweigh the risks.

Prostaglandins

Found in almost every tissue of the body and misnamed before their omnipresence was known, prostaglandins are a family of remarkably versatile substances—hormones with a dazzling variety of effects. They are protective—but when out of balance, destructive. Slowly but surely, however, they are becoming increasingly manipulatable for the treatment of discomforts and disorders.

The first of the family was discovered in 1935 by Ulf von Euler, a Swedish investigator. Because he found it in semen, suggesting that it was produced in the prostate, von Euler named it prostaglandin.

In the years since, it has turned out that there are at least a dozen prostaglandins. They are produced in many tissues of the body from polyunsaturated fatty acids, nutrients found in meats and vegetable oil.

PGs often work in antagonistic pairs. While one, for example, lowers blood pressure, another raises it. One dilates bronchial tubes while a second constricts them. One promotes inflammation; another inhibits that process. A type called "thromboxanes" helps blood to clot; while another, prostacyclin, inhibits clotting.

At the same time that PGs are coming into use in medical therapy, so are compounds that block PG formation. For a long time, no one knew precisely how that most common of all drugs, aspirin, acts; now it is known that it works by blocking the production of certain PGs.

PGs in Reproduction.

We have unknowingly used PGs for years in the form of intrauterine contraceptive devices. How IUDs work was, for a long time, a mystery, but it now appears that they irritate the uterus, causing prostaglandin-induced uterine contractions that keep embryonic cells from becoming implanted.

Similarly, abortions during the second trimester, once accomplished with saline injections or surgical procedures, now can be carried out with suppositories containing prostaglandins, which cause pregnancy-ending contractions.

The millions of women who have had to endure menstrual pain may be helped now by studies revealing that the pelvic cramps, headaches, backaches, nausea, and diarrhea suffered by these women result from the action of PGs. Researchers have found levels of PGs four to five times higher in women with chronic menstrual difficulties than in those who don't have the difficulties. Now drugs that act against the causative PGs—among them drugs used for arthritis, such as ibuprofen, naproxen sodium, and mefenamic acid—are providing relief.

For newborns with congenital malformations of the heart and great vessels, a synthetic prostaglandin is now helping to prevent cyanosis (blueness) until the babies are strong enough for corrective surgery.

Heart Attacks and Strokes.

PGs play a role in the constriction and blockage of blood vessels involved in heart attacks and strokes. One PG, prostacyclin, made by cells lining blood vessels, relaxes muscles around vessels, allowing them to open wider and thus making it easier for blood to move through.

Another PG, thromboxane, is made by small bodies in blood called "platelets." Platelets have the essential job of clumping together at the site of damage to a blood-vessel wall, forming a plug on which a clot can form, thus preventing potentially fatal hemorrhaging.

Thromboxane and prostacyclin are happily antagonistic when in balance. Thromboxane promotes platelet clumping and constricts blood vessels, while prostacyclin not only widens vessels but also suppresses platelet clumping. Trouble comes when the balance is disturbed, when much more thromboxane is produced than prostacyclin, causing needless clot formation and blood-vessel constriction, both important elements in heart attacks and strokes.

Now trials are under way to determine how effective aspirin and other drugs that affect PGs can be in avoiding heart attacks and strokes. There is evidence that a low daily dose of aspirin—about half a tablet —can stop platelet production of thromboxane while allowing blood-vessel walls to go on producing prostacyclin.

Peripheral Vascular Disease.

Impaired blood circulation in the extremities—peripheral vascular disease—is a common problem for which PG therapy is being studied.

In one study at the University of California-Davis, the prostaglandin PGE_1 was given by vein to a dozen patients with leg ulcers that had failed to heal and couldn't be operated on, or already had been operated on without effect. In half the patients, ulcers healed in a month or two. Nobody is certain of the full mechanism of the drug, but it is known to dilate blood vessels and inhibit platelet aggregation, and in doing so may improve circulation to the skin.

Early reports from the Copernicus Academy of Medicine in Krakow, Poland, tell of a study using prostacyclin for 100 patients, some with leg ulcers, others with leg pain at rest or after brief walking. About 35 percent have shown improvement.

The Krakow investigators believe there is a possibility that atherosclerosis—the disease that leads to artery deposits and clogging —may be a disease of prostacyclin deficiency. In studies with rabbits having atherosclerosis, they have found that prostacyclin production is much lower than in healthy rabbits. Studies at the University of Vienna, too, show blood vessels from atherosclerotic patients to be deficient in ability to produce prostacyclin.

Other Possible Uses.

When anginal chest pain, resulting from impaired blood circulation to the heart muscle, occurs not just with exertion but at rest, it can be a prelude to heart attack.

Early trials with prostaglandins—both in Krakow and at the University of California-Los Angeles—indicate that some patients respond with pain relief, in some cases only temporary but in others long-lasting.

Now under way, too, are trials with PGs and various PG derivatives that inhibit stomach-acid secretion and may be of value for healing peptic ulcers.

Possible uses of PGs are being explored for many other problems

—blood-pressure regulation, migraine, asthma, cancer spread, mental depression, and even schizophrenia.

Understanding of PG functioning in the body is still in relative infancy—for several reasons. The compounds not only are many and produced in many tissues, but also have fleeting lives, and their interactions with tissues and with one another are not easy to determine. There may also be other PGs or PG-like substances yet to be found.

But research is speeding up, its importance underscored by the award of the 1982 Nobel Prize for medicine to three major figures in PG research—John Vane of the Wellcome Foundation in England, and Sune Bergstrom and Bengt Samuelsson of the distinguished Karolinska Institute in Sweden.

Radiation Therapy (Radiotherapy)
New, more effective treatments for cancer

There was a time not long ago when a woman with breast cancer had little choice. Radical surgery was considered her best hope.

Now choices are more varied. Currently, breast-cancer patients may receive various combinations of surgery, chemotherapy, and radiation treatments. Especially promising is a combination of minor surgery and radiation therapy being used in more and more medical centers and in a long-term study at the University of Arizona Health Sciences Center.

Since the study began in 1972, seventy-eight patients have undergone a surgical procedure called "lumpectomy," which removes only the tumor while leaving the breast intact. The patients then receive a five-week course of external radiation of the breast and nearby lymph nodes. Treatment concludes with an intensive final radiation assault on the site of the tumor. The patients return for follow-up physical examinations or bone scans every three months for the first two years, then every six months.

"Of the 78 women," according to Dr. Robert S. Heusinkveld, professor and chief of radiation oncology, "only one has suffered recurrence of cancer in the breast itself, and this patient originally had advanced disease."

Results have been most dramatic for patients with limited early cancer. Some patients have had cancer recur elsewhere in the body, but there have been no recurrences in the chest areas treated by radiation.

Almost any treatment for cancer will have its side effects, and radiotherapy does. But recent advances allow the maximum potential for cure with a minimum of such side effects as nausea, vomiting, skin reactions, and scarring. Where once radiotherapy was relatively crude —the radiation dose distributed unevenly, with a large burden placed on healthy tissue—now almost any desired dose can be attained and distributed to almost any part of the body with sharp limits against harming healthy tissue.

With refinements in technique—and some remarkable new forms of radiation—survival rates for victims of some of the most important cancers are increasing, and the quality of survival as well is improving, with many more patients left whole.

Breast cancer is only one—a very important one—of the malignancies responding. In any year, it strikes more than 100,000 women, accounting for more than one-fourth of all feminine malignancies. Fortunately, in the last decade there has been a major shift toward earlier and earlier detection of breast cancer. Currently about 67 percent of the malignancies are being found in the very earliest stages, making lumpectomy and radiation treatment, in the opinion of many experts, as viable now as radical surgery. Reports from many centers indicate that with radiation therapy the five-year survival rates—usually looked upon as cure rates—are now ranging up to 92 percent for Stage I breast cancer (tumor up to two centimeters, or four-fifths of an inch, with underarm lymph nodes negative for malignancy) and to 80 percent even for Stage II disease (tumor two to five centimeters, or up to two inches, with nodes positive for cancer).

Prostate Cancer.

Cancer of the prostate among men is second only to lung cancer in frequency, with 60,000 new cases each year. Here, too, radiation is producing excellent results.

With the use of supervoltage radiation, 100 percent five-year survivals are being reported for the very earliest stage of prostate cancer; 80 to 90 percent for a later stage in which the tumor is still confined to the prostate, and 60 to 70 percent when the tumor is more advanced but still not spread through the body.

Happily, too, radiotherapy can be used in many cases that cannot be treated by surgery because of the stage of the malignancy or the condition of the patient. It is also reported to allow six times as many patients to retain sexual function as does surgery.

Hodgkin's Disease.

This cancer of the lymph system, once 75 percent fatal, is responding well to radiotherapy, with 80 percent of patients now surviving five years or more.

Vocal-Cord Cancer.

Radiation for early vocal-cord cancer can be highly effective—both life-saving and voice-sparing. For example, in 177 patients treated at Washington University School of Medicine in St. Louis, the survival rate at an average follow-up of ten years is 95 percent and voice has been preserved in 90 percent of the patients. Voice quality in 77 percent is rated as good (entirely normal or with only intermittent hoarseness), fair in most others (persistent minimal or moderate hoarseness). Even when radiation fails to eliminate malignancy entirely, surgery often can preserve the voice when only part of the larynx needs to be removed.

Eye Cancer.

Retinoblastoma, a tumor of the retina of the eye, is responsive to radiotherapy. An 85 percent five-year cure rate, with preservation of eye and vision, has been reported.

A special form of radiotherapy can also save the eyes of most patients with choroidal melanoma, a malignant tumor of the pigmented layer behind the retina of the eye, for which treatment in the past has usually been eye removal.

For 110 patients, Dr. Devon Char and other physicians at the University of California-San Francisco and Lawrence Berkeley Laboratory have used a beam of ionized helium atoms. Concentrating on the tumor without affecting surrounding tissue, the radiation has stabilized or shrunk 90 percent of the tumors, with eyesight of 20/100 or better preserved in more than two-thirds. No patient has developed new metastatic tumors spreading from the original—in contrast to 50 percent metastatic rates after other types of treatment, including eye removal.

Head and Neck Tumors.

Radiation is proving helpful for head and neck malignancies, including cancers of the base of the tongue, floor of the mouth, and tonsils.

Recently, Johns Hopkins studies have shown that doubling the usual dose of 200 rads a day to 400 not only is safe, it reduces the usual six-week treatment period by nearly a month and doubles the survival rate.

Liver Cancer.

Experimental work holds out some hope that liver cancer, which has been virtually 100 percent fatal, may be made amenable to radiotherapy.

One effort, at Georgia Institute of Technology, uses tiny spheres of resin—microspheres—which are made radioactive and then injected into the liver artery. The spheres can deliver large doses, as much as 5,000 rads, to the cancer with no serious harm to normal tissues of the liver or other organs. Of the first twenty-five patients treated, seventeen are reported to have shown a decrease in tumor size, with seven still alive and showing evidence of continued improvement.

Another effort, at Johns Hopkins, is called "radioimmunoglobulin therapy." It delivers radiation through the bloodstream using radio-isotopes piggybacked to cancer antibodies. The antibodies are made by injecting proteins from cancers into rabbits. The rabbit antibodies, after being treated with radioactive iodine, are injected into the human patient. Attracted to the tumor, they carry with them the radioactive iodine, which can then concentrate at the tumor site. Although there have been no cures, tumors in many patients have been reduced markedly in size and kept under control for many months. More recently, adding to the hope of eventual curative therapy, the potency of the injected material has been increased fifteen times.

The same treatment is now under study for inoperable lung cancer, for neuroblastoma (a nervous-system cancer in children), and for multiple myeloma (a bone marrow cancer).

Intraoperative Radiation.

A new treatment for patients with abdominal and pelvic cancers (colorectal and pancreatic tumors are the most common) is showing promise in studies at Massachusetts General Hospital, the Mayo Clinic, Howard University, and the National Cancer Institute. It involves opening up a patient in surgery and delivering an intense burst of radiation directly to the tumor.

The standard treatment is to surgically remove as much of the tumor as possible and irradiate the site with external X-rays. But because healthy organs such as the stomach and small intestine are commonly in the way, radiation has to be limited to dosages that have only marginal tumor-killing power.

The new treatment—best suited for patients whose tumors have not spread beyond their point of origin—starts with preoperative external radiation given in small doses over five and a half weeks to shrink the tumor. After an interval of three to five weeks to allow any reaction to subside, the patient is operated on and as much of the tumor as possible is removed. With just a temporary closure, the patient is then draped and wheeled to the radiation-therapy suite. There, the incision is opened again, normal tissues are moved aside or shielded, and a plastic cone is positioned over the area to be irradiated. The cone is attached to a linear accelerator, which delivers the radiation dose, and the incision is then closed. The entire procedure takes about two and a half hours.

Patients with colorectal cancer receiving intraoperative radiation at Massachusetts General Hospital have shown a three-year survival rate of 68 percent, as against 45 percent for comparable patients receiving conventional radiation and surgery.

Arthritis.

The possibility that radiation therapy may be helpful for at least some patients with intractable rheumatoid arthritis is being explored in preliminary studies.

In one study at Stanford University, radiation was used to treat eleven patients with rheumatoid arthritis and multiple, disabling joint involvement not adequately controlled with the usual anti-inflammatory drugs, gold compounds, or penicillamine. Each patient received a total dose of 2,000 rads to the lymph nodes and thymus gland. Follow-up evaluations of up to twenty-eight months have shown that nine of the eleven patients experienced substantial improvement in disease activity as demonstrated by declines in joint tenderness, swelling, morning stiffness, and difficulty in working, bathing, doing housework. The height of improvement was reached about six months after irradiation and remained at that level.

Much more research is needed—and is being carried on—to determine just how practical, valuable, safe, and long-lasting such treatment may be.

Radiology, Interventional

In Baltimore, an automobile-accident victim is brought into a hospital in danger of bleeding to death from a massive gastrointestinal hemorrhage. Guided by X-ray imaging, a radiologist inserts a flexible catheter (tube) into a vessel in the groin, carefully threads it upward until he can see it has reached the hemorrhage site, then infuses through it a drug that contracts the bleeding vessels and stops the hemorrhaging.

In New York, an elderly woman suffers excruciating headaches and convulsions. The cause: a rapidly growing brain tumor so positioned that any attempt to remove it by surgery would be extremely hazardous. Pushing up a catheter, a radiologist guides it to the right spot near the tumor, then introduces plastic pellets to block the blood supply to the growth. As the blood-starved tumor shrinks, the patient's symptoms are relieved.

Radiology in very recent years has come far. From a medical discipline with a limited but vital function—aiding diagnosis—it has become interventional. Using not only the tools ordinarily employed for diagnosis but special new devices as well, it has moved into therapy, repairing a growing variety of abnormalities, averting surgery, sometimes achieving results beyond the reach of surgery.

The valuable new direction may well have stemmed from a happy observation made some years ago when a radiologist was using a barium enema to try to determine the reason for a child's severe vomiting and crampy pain. He found that the youngster had a condition called "intussusception," in which one part of the intestine telescopes into another, causing obstruction. But even as he made the diagnosis by following the course of the barium with a fluoroscope, the radiologist could observe that the pressure of the barium pushed the bowel back into normal position. The diagnostic procedure had turned into a therapeutic weapon.

Interventional radiology as practiced now, however, had to wait for a whole series of essential developments: image intensification along with greatly reduced radiation dosages; TV equipment hooked up with intensification to permit motion studies; special catheters and other tools; and contrast substances (dyes) that when injected into blood vessels otherwise not visible on X-ray or fluoroscopy could make the vessels stand out.

Then, less than twenty years ago, came the pioneering work of two radiologists at the University of Oregon Medical School Hospital, Drs. Charles T. Dotter and Melvin Judkins, in saving a frail, eighty-three-year-old woman from leg amputation by opening up her blocked leg artery with catheters. That feat (see BALLOON THERAPY) was to lead years later—after evidence of its value accumulated from many trials —to the use of radiological techniques employing balloon-tipped and other catheters to open blocked arteries in many parts of the body— the legs, arms, kidneys, and heart. And the scope of interventional radiology keeps broadening.

Constricting and Blocking.

Internal hemorrhaging from any of many different organs within the body can be a serious threat to life. Here, interventional radiology has been achieving notable successes.

With a catheter moved close to a bleeding site, a dye injection can pinpoint the source exactly. There are then many options for suitable treatment.

A drug, vasopressin, can be infused through the catheter to constrict the bleeding vessels. If that should fail, a clot of the patient's own blood or bits of a spongelike material, Gelfoam, can be moved in to plug the bleeding point. A special kind of glue can also be infused through a catheter; it solidifies and forms a plug only on contact with blood at the bleeding site.

In some studies, such measures have been successful for 80 percent of patients with stomach bleeding, nearly 60 percent of those with duodenal-ulcer hemorrhages, and up to 95 percent of those with bleeding from varices (enlarged, tortuous veins or arteries) in the esophagus and stomach (see ENDOSCOPY).

At The Johns Hopkins Medical Institutions in Baltimore, a recent head-injury patient was found to have a rapid leak of blood from a damaged brain vessel. Pressure was building up, threatening blindness. The problem was quickly solved when a radiologist threaded a catheter through the carotid artery in the patient's neck up to the hemorrhage site, inflated a balloon at the end of the catheter, and left it there to stop the bleeding and the buildup of pressure.

In some (fortunately relatively few) patients with diverticular disease—in which there are abnormal outpouchings of the colon—bleeding is so severe that emergency removal of the colon, with a high morbidity and death rate, has often been needed. In as many as 90 percent of such patients now, interventional radiology techniques can arrest the hemorrhage without the risky surgery.

Another bright area for interventional radiology lies in plugging blood vessels leading to benign tumors and to abnormal masses of blood vessels known as "arteriovenous malformations." In many cases, blocking such vessels with silicone plugs is allowing surgeons to remove tumors and malformations in the brain or spinal cord more safely, without risk of hemorrhage. And in some cases, as in that of the woman mentioned earlier, plugging alone has provided so much relief that surgery has not been required.

Other Uses.

Abscesses within the abdomen can sometimes be life-threatening: The death rate, even with surgical drainage, has been about 30 percent. In a study at one hospital, with catheters introduced through the skin, abscesses could be drained completely in thirty-two of forty-two patients, avoiding surgery.

Catheterization is being used by radiologists to help patients with jaundice resulting from obstruction of bile flow. In some cases, the problem lies with narrowing of the bile duct; these can be treated by balloon widening of the duct (see BALLOON THERAPY). In other cases, the duct is blocked by gallstones, some of which can be removed with a tiny basket (see PERCUTANEOUS STONE EXTRACTION); others, too large for that kind of removal, have been successfully removed with other catheterization procedures (see ENDOSCOPY).

Patients with ureters obstructed so that urine could not flow from kidney to bladder used to require surgical diversion of urine into a segment of the intestine, a messy procedure. Now, via a small incision, a catheter can be anchored in the kidney and fastened at the lower end in the bladder, bypassing the obstruction.

Balloon widening has been used successfully to overcome urinary-tract narrowings, establishing satisfactory voiding without surgery.

In some cases, catheterization is replacing surgery in the necessary destruction of internal organs. For example, in some patients with breast or prostate cancer, secretions from the adrenal glands atop the kidneys act to stimulate malignancy, and surgical removal of the adrenals has been used. With catheters moved up to the blood vessels supplying the adrenals, the glands can be destroyed either with drugs or with tiny, locally acting radioactive microspheres.

Catheters are being used to place anticancer drugs directly in the liver and other internal sites, where they may have a chance to be more effective.

Also through catheters moved to blood vessels feeding a cancer site, microspheres containing sources of short-range radiation can be placed so tumor doses far in excess of those possible with conventional radiation therapy can be used without danger to surrounding normal tissue. The technique is being used mainly as an adjunct to surgery and conventional radiation, but it also holds promise as a definitive treatment in itself—as in the following case.

The patient, a woman, had a tumor of the parathyroid glands (situated near the thyroid gland in the neck) that was causing life-threatening blood disturbances. She had undergone three unsuccessful surgical explorations to search for the tumor. First, with catheters, radiologists sampled the level of parathyroid hormone in various vessels near the glands in order to track down the area of excess hormone production. Then, with a dye injection, they found the tiny tumor and its blood supply. Finally, with a catheter placed directly in the tumor's blood supply, they injected radioactive microspheres that destroyed the growth. The patient is now well.

Interventional radiology has come far in a short time and is likely to have many other applications yet to be found. Like any medical approach, it is valuable for selected patients, not all. In some cases, its techniques do not apply; in some, other methods may better serve the cause of healing.

For a growing number of patients, however, interventional radiology techniques can avert surgery and reduce hospital stays, costs, and time lost from work and family.

Sterilization Without Surgery
The silicone plug for tubal occlusion

A New York woman was one of the first 1,000 women in the country for whom a new experimental contraceptive procedure was employed. In a physician's office, without general anesthesia and without an incision or a recuperation period, she underwent a procedure called "bilateral tubal occlusion," in which silicone is inserted to form removable plugs to block the openings of the fallopian tubes. She was in and out of the office in twenty-two minutes.

Background.

In recent years, tubal ligation ("tying" the fallopian tubes) has become a common procedure. For many years, however, its use was hampered because major abdominal surgery and an extended hospital stay were required. When it was used at all, it was usually done following childbirth while a woman was still hospitalized.

In the late 1960s, tubal ligation was encouraged by the development of the laparoscope, an instrument that permitted direct visualization of pelvic organs without need for a wide incision. In the mid-1970s, another technique, minilaparotomy, was developed, also requiring only a very small incision. Both procedures—so-called Band-Aid techniques —revolutionized tubal sterilization by converting it from a major surgical procedure with a relatively long recovery to a fairly simple one that could be performed under local anesthesia on an outpatient basis, with the patient able to return home after a few hours in a recovery room.

Closing of the fallopian tubes in tubal ligation requires stitches, electrocoagulation (forming a clot with an electric current), clips, bands, or rings. With these methods, tubal sterilization has to be considered a permanent procedure, even though microsurgery sometimes can make the tubes useful again.

The Plug Technique.

In addition to eliminating general anesthesia and incision, the new silicone-plug approach to tubal sterilization may allow relatively simple reversal without surgery if pregnancy later is desired, although this possibility remains to be studied.

In the procedure, an instrument called a "hysteroscope" is passed through the vagina and cervix into the uterus after a local anesthetic is applied. Through the instrument, the physician can see the inside of the uterus and the openings to the fallopian tubes, which carry eggs from the ovaries to the uterus.

Within the hysteroscope is a catheter (tube) with a soft tip. Through the catheter, the physician can pump liquid silicone rubber into one of the tubes. Within four to six minutes, the silicone hardens into a plug that blocks the opening. The procedure is repeated in the other tube, and an X-ray is then taken to make certain of proper placement and plug formation.

Early results have been excellent. While some pregnancies did occur in the very earliest stages of testing (possibly because of malformation of the plugs), no serious adverse reactions or major complications have been reported. Among the first thousand patients, only two developed pain and one developed pain and fever.

Because the plugs do not adhere to tissue and are removable, the sterilization is believed to be reversible, but this has yet to be tested.

Surrogate Embryo Transfer
Added hope for infertile women

Thanks to the availability of *in vitro* fertilization and adoptive pregnancy (see ADOPTIVE PREGNANCY), the opportunity to have children has been opened for many couples previously unable to have them. However, certain types of female infertility are not amendable to these procedures—notably, infertility in women who have a competent uterus but lack ovaries, or have nonfunctioning ovaries that fail to respond to conventional treatments. For such women, a new technique —based on animal studies that have been called "brilliant" and "landmark"—could provide new potential for pregnancy.

The technique is called "surrogate embryo transfer with a synchronous regimen of estrogen and progesterone" (SET for short). Developed by Dr. Gary D. Hodgen at the Pregnancy Research Branch of the National Institute of Child Health and Human Development, Bethesda, Maryland, SET is expected to help many thousands of women.

What Dr. Hodgen set out to determine was whether it might be possible to transfer a fertilized egg from a donor to the uterus of a recipient without functioning ovaries—and by making up for the lacking ovarian hormones, allow the recipient to go through the entire process of pregnancy and childbirth. She could then be the biological, even though not the genetic, mother, and in most cases the sperm would have been contributed by her husband.

The Research.

In his experiments, Dr. Hodgen mated fertile female monkeys. After about four days, the fertilized eggs and early embryos were washed out of their reproductive tracts and implanted in the uteri of other female monkeys, who were sterile because their ovaries had been removed surgically a year or more before. The recipients had been treated with estrogen and then progesterone beforehand, and the treatment was timed to make the recipients' reproductive cycles match those of the donors, and to provide, as normal ovarian function would, a suitable environment for embryo attachment to the uterus and development there.

A total of eleven early embryos were transplanted. As expected in the normal course of events, within five to six weeks into pregnancy, each conceptus (the products of conception—embryo and membranes) began to contribute hormones to further development. In four of the eleven cases, pregnancy tests were positive, and all four progressed uneventfully, with the delivery of normal live offspring near term.

Significantly, too, in one successful case, the transfer was between two different kinds of monkeys—a cynomolgus monkey and a rhesus. This success across species lines suggests that there will be no incompatability problems when transfers are made between two unrelated women.

As Dr. Hodgen has reported, the work "demonstrates for the first time the biologic feasibility of simulating the essential hormone milieu of the fertile menstrual cycle to accommodate SET to females lacking intrinsic ovarian function."

The implications, of course, are that the usefulness of adoptive pregnancy can be extended. In that procedure, a healthy woman donor is artificially inseminated with a prospective father's sperm and the embryo is transferred to the uterus of a prospective mother who has functional ovaries but whose ova, for various reasons, cannot be used. Now the transfer may be made to a woman who does not have the normal ovarian function previously required to set the stage for and nourish the embryo. Apparently, only two hormones are needed to create the proper environment, and those can be administered.

Although many investigators believe that the technique, which worked in monkeys, can be expected to work in humans, the definitive answer can come only with human trials. Within a month after publication of Dr. Hodgen's report in the *Journal of the American Medical*

Association, Oct. 28, 1983, plans were being made to test the technique in infertile women at Harbor General Hospital-UCLA Medical Center in Torrance, California. Undoubtedly there will be other trials as well.

Tactual Vocoder
To help the deaf

There are currently about 400,000 American children whose hearing problems are so severe that they cannot learn to understand or speak intelligibly.

For many of them, some hope is held out by an experimental device designed to help such youngsters learn to "hear" with their skin. Now under test at the University of Miami School of Medicine, the device, called a "tactual vocoder," converts voice sounds into electrical impulses that produce a specific pattern of "tickles" on the skin. The child learns to differentiate the tickles as words somewhat as infants with normal hearing learn to understand the babbling noises around them. The vocoder is strapped to a belt around the waist and allows the deaf youngster to learn to associate sounds made from his own mouth with the tickle sensations.

Evaluation.

The idea of perceiving speech through tactile stimulation is not new; intermittent research has been going on for fifty years. Only in the past seven years, however, has there been a resurgence of interest, thanks to the development of microelectronics, which has made possible the present device.

Currently, the vocoder is plugged into a twenty-pound, briefcase-size box, which in turn is plugged into a wall socket. It's expected that within the next three years the device will be miniaturized and powered by battery.

In the meantime, the program at the University of Miami School of Medicine's Mailman Center for Child Development is one of several in the country involved in refining and testing the vocoder. Headed by psychologist Dr. D. Kimbrough Oller, the program is investigating the gains that can be made in the classroom when deaf children are taught communications skills using the device. Thirteen children, aged four to eight years, have been receiving one-on-one instruction using the vocoder for half-hour sessions six times a week. In a year's time, according to Kathy Vergara, teacher of the deaf, the children have made significant strides in speech development. "These were all children who previously had trouble using speech and who are now starting to talk."

The youngsters are able to hear sounds made by the teacher and also footsteps, airplanes flying overhead, and other background noise. A touching experience described by Ms. Vergera involved a five-year-old girl who one day discovered a new sound in her environment when she picked up a rubber dog that squeaked. No mention had been made of its squeaking. When the child discovered that she could "hear" it squeak, that she had discovered a sound, "her eyes," says Ms. Vergera, "got big and she told me, 'Be quiet, I want to hear.' "

The tactual vocoder is one of three major approaches to artificial hearing. A second is the cochlear implant, which permits electronic signals to be transmitted by electrodes implanted in the inner ear (see ARTIFICIAL BODY PARTS). The third uses autocuer glasses, which convert sounds into visual symbols that are transmitted by light-emitting diodes on eyeglass frames.

All three involve building a whole new means of communication, and each has advantages that may in the future help the more than 6 million Americans with substantial hearing problems in both ears.

Thymosins
For immune-system aberrations

She was the first patient to be treated. The little girl, at five years of age, weighed only twenty-six pounds. All her life her body had been racked by repeated attacks of severe infections. She had an immune-system deficiency—an inability to produce white blood cells known as "T-cells," a major defense against infectious agents.

Just five days after she was started on a newly discovered substance, the child, who had been considered a terminal case, was amazing her physicians at the University of California Medical Center in San Francisco. She was producing T-cells in quantity; her infections were decreasing; she was gaining weight. Today, half a dozen years later, she is alive, well, growing, attending school, living a normal life.

What saved her life was thymosin, a hormone-like substance produced by the thymus, a human gland that not very long ago was believed to be without function. That picture has changed completely. In less than twenty years, because of the discovery of thymus-produced thymosins, the thymus has come to be recognized as anything but useless—as, in fact, the source of immunity.

The potential use of thymosins—for many kinds of immunodeficiency disorders and for cancer patients, in whom the immune system is often compromised—is now a major area of continuing medical research.

The Fascinating Vestige.

The thymus is a small, pinkish-gray body nestled above the heart and below the breastbone. What makes it unusual and what led to its being regarded as a useless vestige of evolution, much like the appendix, is that it mysteriously begins to shrink at puberty. Even as other organs are still growing, the thymus declines.

Not until the early 1960s did clues to the true importance of the thymus begin to appear. At the Albert Einstein College of Medicine in New York City, the late Dr. Abraham White, a distinguished biochemist, had begun to suspect that the thymus was an endocrine gland, part of the same system of glands of internal secretion as the pituitary, thyroid, and adrenals. But this was regarded as questionable until a 1961 study found that if the thymus was removed from newborn mice, the consequences were severe and often fatal.

Then, in 1965, Dr. Allan L. Goldstein, then a young postdoctoral fellow working in White's laboratory (now professor and chairman of the Department of Biochemistry at the George Washington University School of Medicine and Health Sciences, Washington, D.C.), finally succeeded in obtaining from thymus glands a whole family of biologically active hormonelike molecules, which he called "thymosins."

The Two Immune Systems.

Man, of course, lives in a hostile environment containing many kinds of potentially deadly microorganisms, toxic chemicals, and ultraviolet and other radiations with potential for inducing cancer. The body defense that provides protection against what would otherwise be quick mortality is, it's now appreciated, made up of two immune systems.

One consists of white blood cells called "B-cells." Made in the bone marrow, these cells, upon detecting an alien organism in the body, begin to produce antibodies, highly specific materials that attack the enemy. There is, for example, a specific antibody to combat the pneumonia virus, another to fight the tuberculosis bacterium. All told, there may be more than a million different specific kinds of antibodies in the bloodstream.

The second system is made up of white blood cells called "T-cells." Also produced in the bone marrow, these cells become functional when they are activated by thymosins from the thymus gland.

Upon detecting an invading organism or a cancer cell, the T-cells, the most important of the white cells, produce a family of materials known as "lymphokines" and sometimes referred to now as "the natural drugs of the immune system." The well-known interferon is just one lymphokine. Others, not yet household words but likely to become so, are known by acronyms such as MIF and MAF. Interferon can kill organisms and cancer cells directly. MIF can muster other cells, macrophages, to literally engulf and destroy microorganisms and malignant cells.

Moreover, T-cells can act as "helpers" for B-cells in producing more-effective antibodies. And they serve another vital function as "suppressors," forms of T-cells that restrain and regulate B-cells and other T-cells, keeping them from attacking the body's own normal tissues.

It has become apparent that any disproportion in the numbers of various T-cells can impair health. When helper cells are too few, the immune system reacts sluggishly to threatening disease. Too few suppressor cells can lead to an attack by other T- and B-cells on body tissues, as in rheumatoid arthritis and other autoimmune diseases.

The Crucial Thymosins.

From the work of Dr. Goldstein and many others recently, it now appears that thymosins, the hormones of the thymus gland, are responsible not only for the development of T-cells but also for the balance of killer, helper, and suppressor cells.

In very recent work, too, evidence has been found that thymosins also may be a factor in regulating certain brain hormone systems—those such as luteinizing hormone-releasing hormone (LH-RH) and luteinizing hormone (LH), which regulate the reproductive system.

Observes Dr. Goldstein: "The discovery of a thymus-brain relationship may help us unravel the mystery of what causes human aging. One theory is that aging is related to inability of the brain to produce and control certain hormones. Our latest research results indicate that thymosin may be among the critical regulating factors of brain hormonal activity and thus may well be the key to determining the cause of senescence."

And Goldstein adds: "This is encouraging inasmuch as the immune system workings are accessible to clinical intervention. And the hormones of the thymus are likely candidates for providing a new generation of drugs."

The Testing in Humans.

Two types of thymosin preparations are currently in use, and almost certainly more will follow. The parent preparation, made from calf thymus, is called "thymosin fraction 5" and consists of a mixture of at least forty different components of the thymus, including its hormones. Working to extract, purify, and characterize the various components, Goldstein and his colleagues have isolated from the parent preparation a material called "thymosin alpha-1," the first biologically active component, and are searching for more.

At the University of California Medical Center in San Francisco, Drs. Diane W. Wara and Arthur J. Ammann have treated thirty-four immunodeficient patients with fraction 5, among them the five-year-old girl mentioned earlier. About half have responded favorably. (Immunodeficiency diseases have been thought to be uncommon, but in fact they may be far more common than long supposed. They may be the reason why some children fail to thrive, fail to grow, and die at an early age for what have been "unknown reasons.")

Trials in cancer patients have been showing promise. Not only is cancer itself prone to suppress the immune system; radiation and chemotherapy treatments can be suppressive, even if only temporarily. "Thymosin," believes Dr. Goldstein, "may well be able to reverse the suppression and in this way help patients, in effect, to help themselves."

In one trial in patients with advanced small-cell lung cancer beyond surgery, Drs. Paul Chretien and Martin Cohen at the National Cancer Institute found that thymosin used in conjunction with chemotherapy almost doubled average survival time, from 240 days to 450. In another trial, six of twenty-one patients receiving high doses of thymosin were free of all indications of cancer at the end of two years.

At the University of California Medical Center in San Francisco, when thymosin fraction 5 was given to nine patients with far advanced kidney cancer, seven responded favorably.

Many other trials are currently under way to determine thymosin's potential for correcting imbalances in patients who have undergone cancer chemotherapy.

Other Disorders.

The potential for usefulness of thymosins in other disorders is being explored at many medical centers.

RHEUMATOID ARTHRITIS.   Rheumatoid arthritis is one of a number of difficult problems called "autoimmune diseases." (Multiple sclerosis and systemic lupus erythematosus are among the others.) In all of them, the immune system is overly responsive, acting not just against harmful organisms and malignant cells but against the body's own normal tissues.

A first trial of thymosin fraction 5 in sixty patients with adult-onset rheumatoid arthritis has begun at George Washington University Medical Center in Washington, D.C., under the sponsorship of the National Institutes of Health. The sixty arthritis patients have been divided into two groups: one receiving thymosin injections twice weekly; the other receiving injections of placebo (an inert preparation) for scientific comparison (essential for determining true value). Hopefully, thymosin can increase levels of T-cells of the kind that regulate and slow excessive immune activity.

HIGH BLOOD PRESSURE.   That an immune-system malfunction may be involved in some forms of hypertension has been suggested recently by the work of Dr. Helen R. Strausser of Rutgers University, Newark, New Jersey. She and her colleagues have found that thymosin fraction 5 lowers the blood pressure of genetically hypertensive animals but has no effect on animals with normal blood pressure.

Dr. Strausser and her co-workers believe that thymosin increases the number of suppressor T-cells in hypertensive animals deficient in them. This increase could inhibit a series of events that might lead to an autoimmunelike disorder and damage to the blood-vessel system that could result in elevated pressure. There are now plans to test humans with hypertension to determine whether a similar T-cell deficiency is present.

INFECTIOUS DISEASES.   Continuing studies with fraction 5 and alpha-1 thymosins are showing that the materials are effective in protecting immunosuppressed animals from otherwise fatal viral, fungal, and bacterial infections. In China and Italy, trials with fractions 5 indicate that it is increasing the survival of patients with comatose hepatitis and helping patients with leprosy, Candida, and many serious fungal and viral diseases.

Still Other Possibilities.

Trials to explore other thymosin potentialities are almost certain to come. For example, hay fever and other allergies involve, at least in part, a sharp rise in immune substances in the blood. Theoretically, it is possible that some allergy patients would be helped by use of thymosins to increase suppressor T-cells and check excessive immune activity.

Brain studies have indicated that stress produces an undesirable effect on certain brain chemicals—among them, serotonin and dopamine. Further research has indicated that when these chemicals are affected, so are B- and T-cells, suggesting a possible use of thymosins in stress-induced and emotionally-aggravated disorders.

To be explored, too, is the possibility that thymosins might be of some value in diseases of the elderly since mounting evidence indicates an age-related decline in the working of the immune system.

There may be a role as well in some cases of infertility. One of the major causes of infertility in women is failure to ovulate because of deficiency of the hormone LRF. Most recently, Dr. Goldstein and his co-workers have isolated another thymosin—thymosin beta-4—and have found in animal studies that it stimulates the brain to secrete LRF, suggesting that it may be of value in restoring normal ovulation in women who fail to ovulate because of LRF deficiency.

Some enthusiasts believe that given much more research, the thymosins—those already known and others yet to be isolated and tested—may turn out to be as valuable for correcting many disorders related to immune-system malfunctioning as antibiotics are for many infectious diseases.

Tinnitus Masker

Tinnitus (persistent ear noise) afflicts millions. For an estimated 2.5 million Americans, according to a 1982 National Research Council report, the condition is severe, sometimes debilitating.

The noises—buzzing, hissing, roaring, crackling, or ringing—may occur in just one ear, or the same sounds may be heard in both ears, or different sounds may develop in each ear. The sounds may appear to come from different locations inside the head or in some cases from outside the head. They may become worse or better at different times of the day, may change in intensity or pitch, and may come and go at random.

Tinnitus has many possible causes. It may result from constant exposure to loud noise. A viral infection or a head injury may produce it. Excessive amounts of aspirin, alcohol, or tobacco may be aggravators. Emotional stress can be an influence. Sometimes there are readily correctable causes such as earwax, middle-ear infection, or high blood pressure, but in most cases the cause is unknown.

Masking.

When no correctable cause can be found, a new device called a "tinnitus masker" often offers relief. Developed by Dr. Jack Vernon of the Tinnitus Clinic of the University of Oregon in Portland, it is now being used in other tinnitus clinics in many areas of the country.

At such clinics, patients referred for tinnitus may first be examined by an ear, nose, and throat specialist to rule out a disease as a possible cause. A trained audiologist assesses hearing and, with special equipment and the patient's help, determines the pitch, loudness, and frequency of the tinnitus. Since each patient's tinnitus is different and few hear the same sounds, the patient selects a tone or band of noise that most resembles his tinnitus. When the sound is matched, the audiologist fits the patient with a tinnitus masker.

Although it resembles a hearing aid and is worn in or behind the ear, the masker does not amplify environmental sounds; instead, the electronic device produces its own sound, often described as resembling the hum of an air-conditioner. It may seem odd that anyone already suffering from hearing too much noise can benefit from listening to still another sound, but the masker's sound is apparently far more acceptable than the tinnitus. It overrides the inner noises and does not interfere with hearing since the volume can be controlled.

"Not all persons with tinnitus can be fitted with a masker," reports Dr. Steven E. Berman, associate professor and director of audiology at the Medical College of Pennsylvania in Philadelphia, "but those who can seem to prefer the sound of the masker to the ringing in the ears. Although the masker is not a cure for tinnitus, it does provide relief."

At the University of Oregon, Dr. Vernon has found that 81 percent of masker users have complete relief and many of the others experience at least partial relief. Interestingly, many find they have varying periods of extended relief after removing the device. Usually these periods last thirty to forty minutes before the tinnitus reappears. Some users, however, report several hours of continued relief without the masker, and a few have gone for several days before needing the device again.

Total Parenteral Nutrition (TPN)

And now Home Parenteral Nutrition (HPN) as well

Because of severe chronic intestinal inflammation, the eighteen-year-old Texas boy needed radical surgery to remove his entire inflamed, diseased colon. But he had lost sixty pounds, was almost literally "skin and bones," and had little chance of coming through the operation unless he could be fed.

In fact, the operation was never performed. When he was fed in the hospital totally by vein—in a way and to an extent once impossible—his bowel could rest even as he gained weight and his body was nourished. His overall improvement was so great that surgery was deferred to see what would happen. That was more than half a dozen years ago. He has been well ever since.

Total parenteral nutrition (complete feeding by vein) has been a boon for many: infants born with gastrointestinal-tract abnormalities, adults who develop severe gastrointestinal disease, cancer patients, burn and accident victims. And it's an even greater boon now that its use—until very recently limited to hospitalized patients—has been extended to the home, allowing many of the once deathly ill to lead active lives, keep house again, go back to work.

The Old—and Limited—Vein Feeding.

In the past, an estimated 30 percent of all deaths in hospitals involved malnutrition. Frustration over that unhappy state of affairs is what motivated a major pioneer of TPN, Dr. Stanley J. Dudrick, now chairman of the surgery department at the University of Texas Medical School in Houston.

As a young intern in the early 1960s, Dudrick was impressed by feats of surgery he witnessed but anguished to find patients dying of starvation not long after their operations. Although they were fed intravenously, too often that was inadequate because feeding by vein had severe limitations. A seriously ill patient might need as much as eight liters a day of intravenous solution with enough fats or carbohydrates to preserve body nitrogen required for tissue building. But in excess of three liters a day, the fluid could harm heart and lungs, and increasing the nutrient concentration so less solution might be needed was equally dangerous; the solution had to be dripped into a small vein in the arm or leg, where a very high concentration could lead not only to agonizing pain but even to vein inflammation and a deadly clot.

Finally, it occurred to Dudrick that he might be able to introduce a catheter (tube) through a smaller vein such as the subclavian, accessible under the collarbone, and maneuver it until it reached the superior vena cava, a very large vein that receives blood from many other veins and empties into the heart. Blood flow in the vena cava is so great that it could easily dilute a solution several thousand times, allowing for heavy nutrient concentrations.

The first patient was a baby with a potentially fatal bowel deformity, unable from birth to take anything by mouth. With Dudrick's new technique, which was to be called "TPN," the four-pound baby almost doubled her weight and gained two inches in little more than a month.

After a series of other infants with similar problems were treated successfully, TPN was tried in adult emergency cases. One, a middle-aged woman, was dying after dwindling to only forty-nine pounds after surgery. In two months, she gained thirty pounds, and a month later could go home, weighing 100 pounds and able to eat normally.

With TPN's further development, as much as 7,000 calories a day could be fed by vein—particularly important for severe burn patients. Such patients require up to 10,000 calories a day because of their huge requirements for tissue-rebuilding nutrients. But not even healthy people can take that much food, nor is the body able to assimilate it fast enough. Many burn patients died for lack of a way to meet their nutritional requirements. Today, however, such patients receive 3,000 calories a day by mouth or stomach tube and another 7,000 by TPN.

Cancer patients, too, have benefited. Although there was some concern at first that nutritional support might accelerate tumor growth, it turned out that cancer patients strengthened through TPN could tolerate two to three times the usual dosage of anticancer drugs.

Expanding Use.

Among those who have benefited most dramatically from TPN have been patients with such severe inflammatory bowel diseases as ulcerative colitis and Crohn's disease (regional ileitis). Studies at many centers have found that with the sustained bowel rest allowed by TPN, as many as half and more of these patients go into remission, avoiding surgery.

TPN is also being used for babies with severe chronic diarrheal disease (resulting from bowel inflammation, infection, or other disturbances), sustaining them until the bowel has a chance to regain normality.

Some women experiencing pernicious vomiting during pregnancy, unable to take food by mouth, are being sustained by TPN.

Among patients requiring surgery but in poor nutritional states, TPN before and after operation often means a significantly improved chance for better and faster healing and for freedom from postoperative complications.

TPN at Home.

TPN's adaptation for use at home has produced gratifying results in the experience of the Mayo Clinic, one of the first centers to adopt the procedure.

One Mayo patient on HPN is a woman with a very serious case of Crohn's disease, her small intestine unable to absorb nutrients from food. Three years before, she had spent twelve months hospitalized while doctors, first in Chicago, then at Mayo, fought her disease with drugs and surgery. After numerous operations, she was left with only one foot of her small intestine instead of the normal fifteen to twenty feet. She could no longer eat at all.

Another patient, a fourteen-year-old boy whose diseased intestine was unable to supply nutrients to his body, had stopped growing; his bones were those of an eight-year-old and he had not added any height in six years.

Today, on HPN, the woman, once near death, plays golf and bridge and is active in many civic and social affairs. The boy has grown more than ten inches and gained forty pounds in his first eighteen months on HPN.

These recoveries are reported to be typical of many treated with HPN at Mayo. Most have either extensive Crohn's disease or a severe short-bowel syndrome. About 75 percent of them, deathly ill before, are back at work, keeping house again, leading active lives.

In the Mayo program, each night a person on HPN hooks the implanted catheter to a special pump that delivers the nutrient solution while he or she sleeps. Not a common procedure, HPN is used as a last-resort kind of treatment in patients for whom all options for meeting nutritional needs by the usual oral means have been tried and have failed. Of some 500 patients a year with Crohn's disease, for example, who are seen at Mayo, only about 1 percent end up on HPN.

Part of the reason why HPN is not more widely recommended, according to a Mayo report, is its cost—about $20,000 to $30,000 a year for the solutions, in addition to the costs of surgically inserting the catheter and two weeks of hospitalization needed for training in the technique. While insurance usually pays 80 percent of these costs, that still leaves a substantial bill. As the Mayo report notes, however, the expenses would be even greater if the person were not on HPN. It costs three times as much to feed such a patient in the hospital.

HPN also requires commitment from patient and family in administering the treatments, maintaining equipment, and following prescribed sterile procedures to prevent infection.

Transplants

When surgeons at The Johns Hopkins Hospital in Baltimore transplanted a new heart into a twenty-two-year-old Springfield, Virginia, man in a four-hour operation that ended at 2:00 A.M., it was unusual only in that the operation inaugurated The Johns Hopkins Heart and Heart-Lung Transplant Service.

The patient in all likelihood would have died within a year without the surgery, because a viral infection had damaged his heart muscle, making its pumping action inefficient and depriving his body of oxygen. Once healthy and active, a college basketball player, he first developed symptoms—weakness and shortness of breath—six months before the operation. By the time he went to surgery, he had at best a 50 percent chance of surviving another six months without a transplant.

According to statistics, heart-transplant patients generally have an 80 percent chance of surviving one year and a 50 percent chance of surviving five years. But the young Virginia man and other recent transplant recipients probably face even better odds because of recent developments.

After years of disappointing failures, heart transplantation is burgeoning anew. After the first heart transplant was performed in 1967 by Dr. Christiaan Barnard, a South African surgeon, more than sixty teams around the world replaced failing hearts in about 150 people. Unfortunately, barely 20 percent of the patients survived after twelve months, and by the mid-1970s the operation was abandoned by nearly all of its early enthusiasts.

In 1982, however, U.S. surgeons performed 103 heart transplants, compared with just twenty-four in 1976. In the same period, liver transplants increased from fourteen to sixty-two, and there were more than 5,000 kidney grafts. Moreover, there were remarkable increases in survival rates, too. For example, whereas only 33 percent of patients receiving liver transplants between 1963 and 1979 survived for a year or longer, between 1980 and 1982 the survival rate shot up to 65 percent.

The reasons for the upsurge in organ-transplant survival rates include significantly improved surgical techniques, new discoveries about more effective handling of the organ-rejection problem, and the recent introduction of a revolutionary drug, cyclosporine (see CYCLO-SPORINE).

Overcoming the Technical Problems.

In 1950, a Chicago surgeon tried transplanting a cadaver kidney into a forty-nine-year-old housewife dying of kidney failure and uremia. Before long, the graft stopped functioning. Reoperating to see what had happened, the surgeon, horror-struck, found the new kidney replaced by shriveled dead tissue, the result of rejection.

Rejection, the major roadblock to organ-graft survival, came in for intensive study. White blood cells, part of the body's immune system, are meant to attack invading disease microorganisms, but they also can attack a transplant of foreign tissue. They do so in response to antigens, the protein molecules found on the surface of all cells. Genetically determined, antigens on the surface of cells of a graft are different from those of the recipient, and the recipient's body therefore orders a white-cell attack.

In identical twins, antigens are identical and transplant rejection is not a problem. Siblings have a 25 percent chance of sharing the critical antigens. In unrelated individuals, chances of a good match are only about 1 in 1,000.

To improve the odds, tissue-typing techniques were developed. In one procedure, for example, the white cells called "lymphocytes" that are involved in rejection are taken from both organ donor and potential recipient, placed on laboratory plates, and exposed to antibodies that attack different antigens. When an antibody destroys a set of lymphocytes, it indicates that the corresponding antigen is present on the cell. Analysis of the results of the lymphocyte-antibody tests can indicate how many antigens the donor and recipient share and don't share.

Tissue typing is helpful but no guaranty of success. Going further, surgeons employed drugs—among them, Imuran and prednisone—that could suppress a recipient's immune responses by killing lymphocytes. But except for a 70 percent success rate for kidney transplants from related donors, most patients receiving other organs died because of lack of lymphocytes to fight infections.

Then, late in the 1970s, came the drug cyclosporine. Unlike other drugs, it doesn't kill off the body's defenses against infection but affects only the particular part of the immune system involved in rejection. Recent reports have underscored its great value. At Stanford University Medical Center, heart-transplant patients receiving cyclosporine have an 80 percent survival rate at two years, compared to only 58 percent for those getting conventional immunosuppression treatment. At the University of Pittsburgh, the eighteen-month survival rate among patients receiving liver transplants since 1980 has been 65 percent, compared with only 28 percent among previous patients who had received conventional immunosuppression.

Much the same significant improvements in survival have been achieved among patients receiving kidney and other organ grafts.

Other Advances.

Still other major developments have been improving the odds in favor of transplant recipients.

Surgical techniques are being refined. Liver transplantation, for example, has become less hazardous because of a bypass procedure developed at the University of Pittsburgh. During the liver-transplant operation, it's necessary to temporarily block off a large vein that carries blood from the body to the heart, even though this blocking may endanger life. Now, during the operation, blood is temporarily routed from the blocked vein externally to the upper part of the body.

At Stanford University Medical Center, surgeons trying to help terminally ill lung patients have found that transplanting two lungs and the heart simultaneously is superior to single-lung transplant. With the combination procedure, blood vessels heal better and risk of infection is reduced. The first patient to receive the combination treatment is still alive. And of twenty-one other patients, twelve have survived. After receiving the heart-lung combination because of severe pulmonary hypertension, a thirty-three-year-old Texas schoolteacher was out of the hospital in a month. Today he swims, jogs, lifts weights.

Another advance has been the recent discovery that if potential kidney recipients receive a series of blood transfusions from an imperfectly matched potential donor relative before transplantation, they are much less likely to reject the foreign organs. Exactly how the transfusions act to help prevent rejection is not yet understood.

Happily, too, doctors have been finding that it is possible to use lower doses of conventional immunosuppressive drugs and still prevent rejection while also cutting the risk of grave infections that result from excessive inhibition of the immune system.

On the horizon are other advances that may even further improve the survival rates of transplants. One would eliminate altogether any need for suppressing the immune system. In animal studies, investigators at the University of Pennsylvania School of Medicine in Philadelphia have found that if a donor organ is stripped of immune cells called "macrophages" (by use of high-pressure oxygen or other means), it is better accepted by the recipient. If this works out well in human trials, then, as one of the investigators has put it, "transplants may be accepted with impunity."

Newer Organ and Tissue Transplants.

Along with kidneys, hearts, lungs, and livers, other organs and tissues are being transplanted with increasing frequency.

For some severe diabetics, pancreas-tissue transplants may eliminate need for insulin injections and possibly prevent some of the eye damage and circulatory complications of the disease. When first tried almost twenty years ago, the grafts were quickly abandoned because of high rejection rates. Recently, however, given the better methods of avoiding rejection, surgeons at the University of Minnesota have performed pancreas transplants in eighty patients, and twenty-four are completely off insulin. Since only a portion of the pancreas has to be transplanted for an adequate insulin supply, live donors as well as cadavers can be used.

A new cornea-transplant procedure, called "epikeratophakia," is reported to greatly improve the vision of patients unable to wear contact lenses or glasses after cataract removal. Pioneered at Louisiana State University School of Medicine, it is also helpful for children born with cataracts and for those with cloudy vision resulting from eye injury. The procedure involves suturing a piece of donated cornea tissue to the front of a patient's eye after the tissue is shaped and corrected, much like a plastic contact lens. Eventually, it becomes a living part of the eye.

Bone-marrow transplants have tremendous lifesaving potential for patients with leukemia (a cancer involving the marrow), severe forms of anemia, and other diseases. In the procedure, a donor's marrow is removed from the pelvic bone with a syringe and injected into the recipient's arm. If the marrow transplant is successful, the patient is again able to produce healthy blood cells.

At the University of Washington, about half of patients with acute lymphocytic leukemia, the most common childhood form of the disease, are alive after marrow transplantation, and 75 percent of patients with aplastic anemia, an often-fatal disease, are surviving.

The limiting factor with marrow transplants has been the need for close tissue match, which too often is not possible. If the match is not good, there is not only the danger that the recipient may reject the transplant but also danger that the transplant may reject the recipient, causing a potentially fatal condition called "graft versus host disease" (GVHD). In GVHD, the lymphocytes contained in the marrow turn against and attack the host.

Now an important new step has been taken toward broad use of marrow transplantation. It results from knowledge acquired in recent years that GVHD is produced mainly by one class of white blood cells —the T-cells. (For more about T-cells, see THYMOSINS.) In a new technique, a bone-marrow sample is mixed with lectin, a soybean substance, with which T-cells clump together. When the lectin-treated marrow is then placed on top of a thick substance such as albumin in a test tube, the T-cell-and-lectin aggregates sink to the bottom because they are heavy, leaving the remaining marrow cells on top almost entirely free of T-cells. In a second purification step, the marrow cells are mixed with sheep's red blood cells, which grab any remaining T-cells. Following this double purification procedure, the marrow can be transplanted with little or no risk of GVHD, researchers have found.

Recently, at Memorial Sloan-Kettering Cancer Center in New York where the technique was developed, it has been used successfully in eighteen of the first twenty-two attempts to help children born with severe combined immunodeficiency disease, a genetic defect in which the immune system produces no germ-fighting cells to combat even the most minor infection. The children in whom the new technique was tried had no perfectly suitable donors, and thus received their transplants from donors whose tissues were far from perfect matches. With conventional treatment, the mismatches would have been doomed to fail. Yet five months to two years after the transplants, the eighteen successfully treated children remain healthy, have normal immunity to infection, and are considered cured.

Until recently, transplants of intestinal tissue have been considered impossible. The intestine has a high bacterial content and, for a patient treated with immunosuppressive drugs in order to accept a graft, the risk of infection overwhelming the depressed immune system was far too great. But at the University of Toronto, making use of the new drug, cyclosporine, investigators have been able to perform intestinal grafts in animals with a 60 percent success rate. Some experts believe it will not be long before transplants of intestinal tissue become possible for humans.

Although transplantation of the entire brain is unlikely in this century, if ever, transplantation of portions of brain tissue is a whole new frontier. Based on animal studies to date, such transplantation to correct at least some forms of brain damage may become possible.

Recently, at Clark University in Worcester, Massachusetts, investigators set about trying to restore mental functioning in twenty-one rats with brains damaged by removal of large sections of the frontal cortex—an area that plays a major role in the learning of complex spatial relationships. Typically, rats with such severe brain damage take at least eighteen days to learn to get through a maze to a drink of water, while normal rats take only two and a half days.

When the investigators took pinhead-size lumps of frontal-cortex tissue from normal rat embryos and implanted one in each of the brain-damaged rats, maze learning was reduced to eight and a half days —still slower than normal, but an indication of some functional recovery. And, indeed, new connections were found to have grown between the transplanted tissue and the rest of the brain.

At St. Elizabeths Hospital in Washington, D.C., investigators have used brain-cell implants in rats with symptoms similar to those of human Parkinson's disease (shaking palsy). Parkinson's involves the slow degeneration of brain cells that secrete dopamine, a movement-coordinating chemical. By transplanting fetal cells able to produce dopamine, the St. Elizabeths researchers succeeded in relieving the Parkinson-like symptoms.

Because ethical questions about the use of tissue from human fetuses must be resolved, investigators are seeking alternatives to fetal tissue. For Parkinson's disease, some suggest that transplantation of dopamine-secreting cells taken from the patient's own adrenal gland atop the kidney may be useful. And in fact, in 1983, Dr. Lars Olson, a neurosurgeon at the Karolinska Institute in Sweden, did transplant adrenal cells into the brains of two Parkinson patients by means of a hollow needle. The first patient, a sixty-two-year-old man, showed only fleeting improvement, but a forty-six-year-old woman has shown improved facial movement, less rigidity of her arms and legs, and walks better. The procedure is still considered highly experimental.

Still other possibilities are being explored. One involves altering monkey fetal cells for use in humans. Ultimately, if researchers can identify what it is that gives fetal cells their regenerative ability, ways may be found to synthesize the substances or produce them in laboratory cell cultures.

In such work, believes Dr. Vernon Mark, director of neurosurgery at Boston City Hospital, lies "the best hope we have for those who have lost brain cells because of a stroke, an injury, or a degenerative disease."

Two Problems.

One problem with transplants is their cost. Following are some recent cost-range figures for various types: bone marrow, $60,000–$150,000; lung, $50,000–$150,000; heart-lung, $78,000–$92,000; heart, $57,000–$110,000; liver, $54,000–$238,000; pancreas, $18,000–$50,000; kidney, $25,000–$35,000.

Such costs may seem a little less extreme when compared, for example, to a cost of perhaps $80,000 to care for a person with end-stage heart disease who does not receive a transplant. Still, they place a huge burden on patients. Many insurers, looking upon many transplants as still experimental, refuse to pay for them.

Another major problem is organ availability. With transplant operations becoming more common and successful, there is an increasing need for organ donors. Although about 20,000 of those who die each year in traffic accidents, for example, could be potential donors, organs were obtained from only about 2,000 in 1982. At least 2,000 people in the U.S. would benefit from a heart transplant; according to some estimates, as many as 10,000 currently need kidney transplants; and about 100, mostly children, are in need of liver transplants. Yet each year, only about 100 patients receive new hearts and about 5,000 receive new kidneys. At the University of Pittsburgh alone, seventy-one patients have died in a two-year period while waiting for donor livers.

There are now about 110 organ-procurement agencies around the country trying to meet the demand for transplants, but many people have negative feelings about organ donation. Some fear that carrying a donor card may compromise their care if they should ever be in critical condition; others fear body mutilation; and some groups consider organ donation to be a violation of their religion.

Still, John Kiernan, organ-recovery coordinator at the Presbyterian Hospital in New York City, reports: "Very slowly, I'm seeing an improved public response to our requests that they consider organ donation. There also has been a noticeable increase in donor referrals by physicians." Kiernan notes that the success of a recovery program "depends on the generosity of the donor families during their grief and the caring professionalism of the doctors and nurses who are responsible for the medical management of the donor. Without these two elements, organ recovery is impossible."

Ultrasound
Seeing with sound

It helped when the abdominal swelling of a young mother-to-be became obviously too much to be attributed to her early pregnancy. Instead of invasive and potentially risky diagnostic procedures, physicians did a quick sound-wave scan. It showed the fetus alive and well—and revealed a benign muscle tumor of the uterus, an occasional pregnancy complication that sometimes may enlarge to the point where it disrupts normal delivery. The condition of both fetus and tumor was followed with subsequent scans. At thirty-eight weeks, a normal baby was delivered by cesarean section, the tumor was removed, and a healthy mother and child went home.

An ultrasonic scan located the site of a metallic object accidentally lodged in the eye of a little boy, permitting its quick removal.

A scan also solved the mystery of what had been wrong for three months in a man who had been a diagnostic puzzle to several doctors. It revealed a huge abdominal abscess, which, once found, could be treated.

Seeing within the body with high-frequency sound waves is a painless, relatively inexpensive technique with a wide range of usefulness. It is valuable for studying abnormalities affecting the liver, gallbladder, pancreas, kidneys, and larger blood vessels; for detecting retinal tumors; for observing the development of the unborn fetus (see FETAL MEDICINE), and for still more. It often obviates the need for CAT scanning and spares patients from exposure to the mild radiation of other diagnostic methods, and there is no evidence it has any negative effects on human health.

In one of its most recent applications, ultrasound is providing surgeons with what one of them calls "a window to the interior of the brain . . . an eye for the surgeon inside the patient's head."

Submarines and Fetuses.

First used to detect enemy submarines, ultrasound was originally tried many years ago in medicine when a professor of obstetrics in Glasgow, Scotland, considered the resemblance between a submarine in the ocean and a fetus in the uterus, both surrounded by fluid.

For a long time, however, the equipment was too primitive to be medically useful, and thus only very recently—as the result of a whole series of equipment advances—could ultrasound begin to live up to its original promise. Two pieces of equipment have been particularly important: One converts ultrasonic images from black and white to the range of grays that provide resolution and detail in a photograph; the second is a system for displaying moving images, allowing motion to be observed as if a TV camera were inside a patient.

For an ultrasonic examination, the patient can recline and an oil or gel is spread on the skin to facilitate sound-wave passage. A probelike instrument is then moved over the area of concern and the results are viewed on a TV-like screen and can be recorded on a photographic film or chart.

Use in Pregnancy.

Ultrasound, even as early as the fifth week, can help determine whether an ovum is blighted or a miscarriage threatens. It can reveal multiple pregnancy within the first three months, and if a pregnancy is difficult and there is concern about the welfare of the fetus, ultrasound can reveal heart activity at seven weeks, body activity at eight weeks, and limb movement at nine weeks. It can even depict the fetus sucking a thumb, and, by measuring fetus size, estimate expected delivery date within a few days.

Advances in ultrasound are enabling physicians to diagnose blocked kidneys in babies still in their mothers' wombs, and to perform corrective surgery within the first few weeks after birth. Forewarning of the problem alerts the physician to monitor the fetus closely and to recommend delivery at a major medical center so the extent of the problem can be evaluated as soon as the child is born.

Until as recently as 1982, pediatric cardiologists could not see their patients while they were still *in utero.* They knew that 1 in 500 babies would have some kind of congenital heart disease, but that was just a statistic; there was no way of knowing which baby would be that one.

Now, with sophisticated sound-wave techniques, they can see how well the fetal heart is functioning and how it has formed; can pick out details as small as one and a half millimeters (about the thickness of a quarter); and can monitor the blood flowing through a vessel as thin as a matchstick. If a heart problem that puts the baby at high risk is found, hazards can be reduced by modifying the care given the mother, and corrective action can be taken soon after birth.

Gynecology.

Ultrasound can reveal ovarian cysts and, in follow-up, can determine whether they have disappeared. It can also detect other growths of the uterus and ovaries. Along with showing up a pelvic abscess, ultrasound can indicate how well it responds to antibiotic treatment, and, if surgical drainage is required, can point to the best surgical route (vaginal or abdominal). Ultrasound can also locate a "missing" intrauterine contraceptive device so it can be retrieved.

The Brain.

Ultrasound imaging is proving useful in checking children with head wounds and in evaluating epilepsy. By determining the position of the brain's midline and showing any shift from normal position, it can point to a tumor or other problem.

In just the last few years, delicate brain surgery has become faster and more accurate because of ultrasound imaging. Unlike a CAT scanner, ultrasound equipment is portable and can be used in an operating room.

Brain tumors usually occur beneath the dura mater, an opaque, fibrous membrane covering the brain. During surgery, a portion of the skull is removed, exposing the dura mater. For ultrasound imaging, a saline solution is dripped onto the dura mater as a coupling agent and the scanner, covered with a sterile, transparent plastic bag, is placed directly on the dura mater to scan the brain. A tumor is easily seen on a video screen as a bright area in the brain. Once located, the tumor image is frozen on the screen, allowing a computer to calculate exact measurements of depth and diameter. With this information, the neurosurgeon can plan the best operative approach to the tumor, an angle that will be least disruptive to delicate brain tissue, avoiding the speech center and areas controlling movement.

Ultrasound is used to guide surgical instruments directly to the tumor and enables the surgeon to determine which part of the brain is attached to the growth and which blood vessels are supplying it. If the tumor can be removed, this information, obtained without surgically probing the brain, allows it to be removed rapidly and with minimal disruption of brain tissue. Once the tumor is removed, ultrasound can view the surrounding area to make certain the entire tumor is gone.

Ultrasound scanning has other uses in the neurosurgical operating room. It can be employed to locate and drain cysts and abscesses in the brain. Surgery for multiple cysts in the brain was not possible in the past because locating them took too long and required repeated exploration within the brain. With ultrasound, numerous cysts can be rapidly and precisely located.

Surgeons can also see abnormal ballooned areas on blood vessels —aneurysms—and locate bone fragments lodged in the brain from injuries. Soft tissue, not clearly visible in X-rays or fluoroscopy, can be viewed with ultrasound.

An unusual example of ultrasound's value involves a patient brought into an operating room at the University of Chicago Medical Center with a bullet lodged just beneath the cranium—or so it was supposed based on X-ray studies done immediately after the patient was brought in. But the patient had been moved from the emergency room to the radiology department and finally to neurosurgery, with frequent changes in position as he was examined. When ultrasound was used in the operating room to confirm the bullet's position, surgeons were surprised to find that, because of its weight and the changes that had been made in the patient's position, the bullet had moved on its own further into the brain tissue.

"Without ultrasound," remarks one of the neurosurgeons, Dr. George J. Dohrmann III, "we would not have known that the bullet had moved. We would have faced some difficult decisions, not to say surprises, if we had entered the skull without this knowledge and had been unable to find the bullet in the area where the X-rays indicated it originally was."

Other Uses.

Where once diagnosis of gallstones required a two-day X-ray test and twelve grams of diarrhea-causing pills, now ultrasound allows diagnosis in ten to fifteen minutes. Ultrasound is proving useful in diagnosing liver diseases, some spleen and pancreas disorders, and some kidney problems.

Recently a transrectal ultrasound probe has shown promise in evaluating prostate tumors. The sound-wave technique can also distinguish between cystic and solid breast masses.

A new lightweight ultrasound probe, about the size of an electric toothbrush, can be placed on the beating heart to help surgeons "see" inside blocked coronary arteries during bypass procedures. It allows better decision-making during the operation, giving the surgeon more information about where bypasses are best placed. It also allows seeing all vessels, including smaller ones that are not bypassed but may be candidates for new techniques such as balloon angioplasty (see BALLOON THERAPY).

Ultrasound has limitations—it is of no use for lungs or bones. But its uses are so many that at last count, in a single major medical center, 12,000 patients a year were benefiting from ultrasound examinations.

Uvulopalatopharyngoplasty (UPPP)

For sleep apnea and/or severe snoring

A new surgical procedure is designed to help two types of people: those with the potentially serious sleep disorder called "sleep apnea" and others with the problem of severe snoring.

Sleep apnea is a condition in which breathing stops frequently during sleep, with the cessations lasting twenty seconds or more. It may lead to several hundred awakenings during the night, producing a significant insomnia. The victim is unaware that he has these apneic episodes, but may be aware of insomnia or disturbed sleep, and most also complain of excessive daytime sleepiness. Characteristically, too, they are heavy snorers. Apnea may also lead to elevated blood pressure and in some cases to abnormal heart rhythms.

Apnea is easily detected with instrumentation in a sleep-disorders clinic. Often, a clue to it comes from a victim's bed partner, who reports that the apnea sufferer snores especially heavily and with snorting. The loud, heavy, snorting snore is the resumption of breathing after an apnea episode.

For severe apnea, a tracheostomy may be performed. An opening is made into the trachea (windpipe) through the skin to bypass upper airway structures that collapse and obstruct during sleep. The patient can close the opening during the day and so speak normally, and open it only at night for sleep.

For some apnea victims, tracheostomy may be avoided by a new surgical procedure, uvulopalatopharyngoplasty (UPPP). Some very heavy snorers who do not necessarily have apnea may also benefit.

The Operation.

UPPP involves removal of some tissue from the soft palate in the back of the mouth. The tonsils, if present, are removed, too, along with any excessive tissue on the sides and back wall of the throat. Also removed: the uvula, a small fleshy mass that is part of the soft palate and hangs down above the root of the tongue.

The procedure sounds complex but is relatively simple as surgical procedures go. Throat soreness afterwards keeps patients in the hospital and on intravenous feeding for one to five days. UPPP costs about the same as a tonsillectomy and is covered by some insurance companies.

Results.

At Stanford University Medical Center, Dr. F. Blair Simmons, professor of surgery, reports that UPPP succeeds for about half of patients with severe obstructive sleep apnea. About the same success rate is reported by Dr. Shiro Fujita of Henry Ford Hospital in Detroit. Among some fifty apnea patients treated with UPPP at Miami's Mount Sinai Medical Center, about a fourth have had the dramatic kind of success found with tracheostomy and half have improved enough to avoid tracheostomy.

Dr. Simmons at Stanford has been a pioneer in the use of UPPP for "simple" (without obvious apnea) but excessively loud snorers. He employs the procedure only when snoring is loud enough to be heard in an adjacent room and is not halted by a change of sleep position.

According to their spouses, nineteen of the first twenty "simple" snorers treated with UPPP have been silent sleepers for up to two years thus far since the operation.

Ventilator Therapy
(High-Frequency Jet)

For many who suffer diseases or injuries of the chest, the breath of life does not come easily. During recovery, they often endure weeks of labored breathing, dependent on ventilator machines that help inflate the lungs.

Replacing conventional machines, a new jet ventilator, tried at about two dozen medical centers in the United States, has been found to reduce pain, speed healing, and even help to lower medical bills, a rarity in an era when high technology often equals high cost.

The new machine can send 50 to 150 small, low-pressure pulses of air, oxygen, or anesthetic to the lungs each minute, whereas conventional respirators produce 10 to 20 larger, higher-pressure pulses. Because the pulses are smaller, the lungs move very little, and the tissues, remaining relatively undisturbed, heal more quickly. The reduced movement also cuts down on pain, allowing patients to rest more comfortably and thereby also contributing to recovery.

"We've seen dramatic results from jet ventilation respiratory therapy in patients who would have otherwise lingered for weeks," reports Dr. Gregg Love of the University of Missouri-Columbia School of Medicine. "One patient's lungs healed more quickly in a 48-hour period on the jet ventilator than they had in three weeks on a standard respirator."

In Surgery.

Similar machines capable of operating at even higher frequencies are being found to offer advantages in the operating room. One high-frequency ventilator delivers small breaths so fast—up to 600 a minute —that the lungs do not have to expand or contract. Remaining quiet, they provide a stable operative field, which is especially important in chest-trauma surgery and liver transplantation. A second major advantage is a significant reduction of the work load on the heart during surgery when there is no need for lung expansion and contraction.

According to a study with 300 patients reported to the American Society of Anesthesiologists by Dr. J. Marquez, Jr., and other researchers of the University Health Center in Pittsburgh, Pennsylvania, the high-frequency ventilator proved superior to conventional ventilation in maintaining good airway pressure, adequate lung gas exchange, and heart and blood-vessel stability. The study also found the new form of ventilation lifesaving in patients with head, neck, and facial injuries who require artificial means to support breathing.

The jet ventilators, which have been approved by the U.S. Food and Drug Administration, sell for half the price of conventional units, a savings that can be passed on to patients.

Vitrectomy, Open-Sky
Hope for RLF victims

Born prematurely at twenty-six weeks, the child weighed only twenty-two ounces. Sophisticated technology saved her life: In the neonatal unit of a midwestern hospital, she had to have mechanical help to breathe for fourteen and a half weeks, until her weak, underdeveloped lungs matured.

She survived her difficult neonatal period, but emerged from it blinded by retrolental fibroplasia (RLF), a disease that occurs in premature infants exposed to the high oxygen levels needed to save their lives. The child's doctors held out little hope: RLF, they indicated, was untreatable. Yet this baby now can see. She is one of a growing group of infants and young children with RLF who are being treated by two of the ophthalmologists associated with the Eye Research Institute in Boston—Dr. Tatsuo Hirose and Dr. Charles L. Schepens, president of the institute.

The treatment: open-sky vitrectomy, a special surgical procedure.

The Dilemma.

In 1941, Dr. Theodore L. Terry, a Harvard ophthalmologist, first described a disastrous new disease that blinded infants by leading to growth of fibrous tissues in front of the retina, causing complete retinal detachment. RLF was a serious problem into the early 1950s, and by 1953 an estimated 8,000 babies born prematurely had been blinded by the mysterious disease. Worldwide research led to the discovery that

RLF was related to the amount of incubator oxygen. Soon there-after, the oxygen concentration in incubators was reduced, and the disease disappeared almost as rapidly as it had appeared.

But that, unfortunately, was not the end of the story. Lowered oxygen levels in incubators, even as they reduced RLF incidence, in-creased the premature-infant death rate, and also the incidence of cere-bral palsy in surviving premature babies. Although it was clear enough that higher oxygen levels were needed in incubators if brain damage, respiratory problems, and death were to be prevented, it was almost impossible to determine a completely safe level of oxygen that would not result in RLF.

In the 1970s, RLF incidence began to rise again—and all the more so as improvements in intensive care for very-low-birth-weight babies increased the population of infants at risk for RLF. Thus, blindness is again a serious threat to prematures—and until recently it was believed there was no treatment.

The Surgery.

Open-sky subtotal vitrectomy was first performed in 1971 by Dr. Charles L. Schepens and his associates at the Eye Research Institute. During the surgery, the cornea (the clear, outermost layer of the eye) is opened and the lens is removed so that fibrous tissue tugging at the retina in the back of the eye can be excised. This is done with the aid of a surgical microscope and is followed by drainage of fluid behind the retina. The retina itself is returned to its normal position, flat against the back of the eye. If the retina fails to settle back properly, a separate operation may be used to implant a scleral buckle—a kind of plastic belt that can be tightened to change the shape of the eyeball and gently squeeze the back of the eye against the retina.

The very first operation performed in 1971 restored some vision to a young adult with RLF. Not long afterward, Drs. Hirose and Schepens began operating on infants.

The success of open-sky vitrectomy is still being evaluated. Al-though infants can see after a successful operation, with the aid of glasses and contact lenses, how well they will continue to see and for how long will become known only as the youngsters grow.

RLF still remains something of a mystery. There is no question but that it occurs in immature retainas exposed to high concentrations of oxygen. The oxygen constricts blood vessels in the retina, and as the infant is returned to a normal atmosphere, the retina overcompensates by producing too many new blood vessels, which lead to the formation of membranes within the vitreous fluid in the eye. The membranes pull at the retina, causing it to detach, and if it is detached for too long, permanent blindness occurs.

But some prematures exposed to high oxygen levels do not develop the disease, and RLF has been known to occur in full-term babies not exposed to high oxygen levels.

More information is needed about the disease, along with more research into its management. Surgery would be greatly facilitated by the development of instruments that can be used more easily in the very small eyes of infants. The perfection of diagnostic procedures that would allow evaluation of the retina and prediction of outcome before surgery is also needed.

Voice-Box Reconstruction
For some larynx-cancer patients

A new reconstructive surgical procedure may offer new hope for those patients with cancer of the larynx who are left voiceless and breathing through a hole in the neck.

Because only about 50 percent of patients with cancer of the larynx are able to learn esophageal speech, many efforts have been made to find ways to save the voice box. Now, for those who have as little as one-fourth of the box left after the growth has been removed, Dr. R. Brent Butcher II and his colleagues at the Ochsner Medical Institutions in New Orleans have developed a method of reconstructing the vocal apparatus, leaving the patient with what they report as "satisfactory vocal quality and the ability to breathe in a normal manner."

The new procedure involves taking a graft of cartilage and tissue from the nose to reconstruct the voice box by duplicating the part that has been removed. The cartilage taken from the nose is unnecessary for breathing and its removal leaves no disfigurement. Besides the fact that the surgery preserves vocal ability, the new cartilage serves as a splinting mechanism to hold the voice box open to facilitate normal breathing. In the first dozen patients to undergo the procedure, it has been possible to remove the breathing tube from the throat within two or three days.

X-Ray Fluorescence Spectrometer

To check on deficiencies and toxicities affecting health

A unique machine, nicknamed "Harry," is now providing a quick means of determining whether the health of an individual is being affected by mineral deficiencies or by contact with poisonous substances.

Formally known as an "X-ray fluorescence spectrometer" and located in the Environmental Health Sciences Center of the University of Rochester Medical Center, Rochester, New York, the machine can measure the content of a number of elements in a single human hair, and the levels of these elements found in the hair can then be related to those within the body. Moreover, by measuring changes in the amounts of chemicals preserved in various segments of a hair, the machine can date a patient's contact with a chemical, as in the case of mercury poisoning, and can monitor the progress of medical treatment and nutritional supplements.

The Technique.

The machine analyzes one-millimeter segments of hair, first irradiating the segments to excite the chemical elements in the hair, then measuring as many as sixteen of the elements simultaneously, with a computer printout delivering the results of each measurement within six seconds. It can accomplish in minutes what used to take many days by conventional methods.

By measuring a sequence of one-millimeter portions of a strand of hair and taking into account the standard growth rate of hair—one millimeter in three days—the machine allows dating of the initial contact with a chemical, or the onset of a deficiency, and also permits tracing the duration and any changes.

Multiple Uses.

"Harry" is expected to be an invaluable tool in hospital diagnostic centers and in environmental testing and forensic (crime) laboratories. It can be used for the accurate, noninvasive diagnosis of a wide range of health problems, such as deficiencies of calcium, iron, copper, zinc, and other essential trace elements. It can also be used to establish critical levels for mercury and other environmental contaminants. In one current study, investigators are measuring hair samples from Eskimos, Indian Ocean inhabitants, South Sea Islanders, and others who consume large quantities of fish, a major source of mercury exposure. In another study, researchers are using the machine to assess the effects on young children of a mercury compound used in Argentina as a fungicide for diapers.

The machine also has potential for use in forensic examinations, because it can produce a multielement profile without destroying the evidence, as occurs with conventional procedures that "ash" (incinerate) the sample. The spectrometer can pinpoint the time of a crime as well—for example, in the case of arsenic and certain other types of poisoning.

The capabilities of the machine are to be extended further by equipping it to test cells and other microscopic samples of body parts such as skin and blood.

Zona-Free Hamster Egg Test
For male reproductive capability

Although many tests have been used for years for infertility problems in women, until recently there has been no test for determining positively whether the man was the infertile partner. Such a test is now coming into use.

Called the "zona-free hamster egg test," the technique assesses a man's reproductive capability on the basis of how well his sperm react with eggs produced in the ovaries of hamsters.

The Need.

In medical efforts to establish the cause of a couple's infertility, the husband has usually been the most neglected partner. The wife may be given many different types of tests, involving virtually the entire reproductive system. The husband, on the other hand, may be judged just on the basis of a sperm count and motility (activity level of spermatozoa) check.

But a man can have a very low sperm count and motility level and still be fertile. There is no necessary correlation between the numbers and motility of sperm and their ability to penetrate an egg.

The Test.

Penetrating ability now can be assessed when a sample of sperm from the husband is placed with a specially prepared hamster egg and the reaction is checked under a microscope. The special preparation of the egg involves removing its zona (outer layer). The zona is impermeable to sperm from other species, but once it is removed, sperm from a fertile human male can usually penetrate the egg by releasing certain enzymes. These enzymes, however, are not released by most sperm in infertile men, so penetration of the egg by the infertile sperm is not possible.

Thus, the hamster egg can serve as a surrogate for the human ovum in assessing sperm's fertilizing capacity.

At the University of Nebraska Medical Center in Omaha, one of a growing number of centers in which the test is being employed, the technique has revealed that in about 20 percent of couples seeking help for infertility, the problem lies with the husband, allowing efforts to overcome infertility to be focused where they are needed.

Index

Index of Diseases and Disorders